W9-BNO-065

SAILING AROUND THE WORLD:

Volume 1,
Adventures of a second life

Howard & Judy Wang

Howard & Judy Wang

Copyright © 2017 Howard & Judy Wang
Wang Publishing Services, Santa Barbara, CA
All rights reserved.

Library of Congress Control Number: 2017916134
ISBN-10: 1977685927
ISBN-13: 978-1977685926

DEDICATION

We dedicate our story to pioneers, inventors, and explorers who took risks so that we may all journey. We are forever grateful to our parents and mentors for instilling in us an internal compass to navigate in sunshine and in storm.

Howard & Judy Wang

Contents

ACKNOWLEDGMENTS

We thank you, our friends and family, who encouraged and cheered us on during our journey. We are grateful for the complete file of our email preserved by Maureen Stonehouse, our daughter, and Susan Hill. We thank Bruce Thompson, the Forecaster, for his weather advice during Laelia's Atlantic crossing. Bruce also edited the early chapters of the manuscript and set the book on a favorable tack. We thank the late Don Anderson, Summer Passage, for his weather forecasts during our passages in Mexico and the Pacific Islands. If you enjoy this book, thank Alice Chaffee, our editor, who improved the flow and made the book more readable. The authors are fully responsible for any deficiencies within these pages. We also thank Maureen, our daughter, for building the website, <SailBoatLaelia.com>, to show the color photographs.

Howard & Judy Wang

A Note to Readers

Our sailing adventure around the world took us to forty-two countries in eight years. This book, in two volumes, is about a different way of life, discovering faraway lands, and meeting uncommon people. One day at a time, we learned as we went and did the seemingly impossible. Volume 1 begins with an account of how we almost met our doom, and tells how two novices managed to sail from California to Sydney, Australia. Volume 2 describes our arduous journey home by way of the pirate alley, the Suez and Panama Canals, and bashing upwind along the Pacific Coast.

There is a website, <SailBoatLaelia.com>, to show photos we took along the way, a glossary, and a page on Frequently Asked Questions. All maps are north up. The book is in American English, but local spellings are used for place names.

We wish you an adventurous journey, with fascinating discoveries, in the comfort of your armchair. Sit back, relax, and join us on this journey.

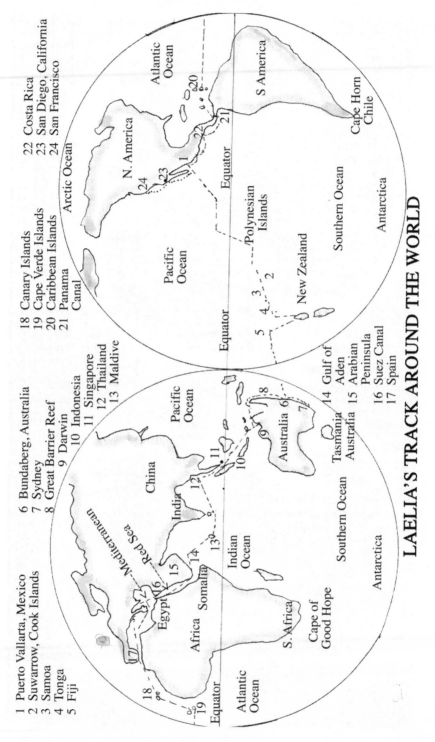

LAELIA'S TRACK AROUND THE WORLD

1 Puerto Vallarta, Mexico
2 Suwarrow, Cook Islands
3 Samoa
4 Tonga
5 Fiji

6 Bundaberg, Australia
7 Sydney
8 Great Barrier Reef
9 Darwin
10 Indonesia
11 Singapore
12 Thailand
13 Maldive

14 Gulf of Aden
15 Arabian Peninsula
16 Suez Canal
17 Spain

18 Canary Islands
19 Cape Verde Islands
20 Caribbean Islands
21 Panama Canal

22 Costa Rica
23 San Diego, California
24 San Francisco

1. A Thin Line from Tragedy

Cabo San Lucas, Mexico (22 52.855 N, 109 54.652 W), 04 to 11 November 2004. Lover's Beach (Playa de Amor, 22 52.610 N, 109 53.804 W), 10 November 2004.

Lover's Beach (Playa de Amor), touted to be the most romantic seashore on the Pacific Coast, is a must-see in Cabo San Lucas. It was a promising morning with bright sunshine and a clear blue sky. I would never have thought that this could be my last day on earth.

My wife, Judy, and I drove the dinghy to the famous beach on the point of land facing the Sea of Cortez. The beach was in the shadow of a large rocky outcrop.

"This is not so romantic; it's cold and dark here," Judy said.

"Well…this can't be right. They wouldn't call such a gloomy place the Lover's Beach. There is warm sunshine on the other side around the point. Let's go there." I maneuvered the dinghy around the rocky point to the beach facing the sun and the Pacific Ocean.

A long stretch of white sand shimmered in the morning sun. Small waves from the Pacific were rolling in regularly. We took beach landings seriously, because a careless mistake could get us swamped. I was wearing on my wrist the kill-cord attached to the throttle of the outboard engine. All I had to do was pull my wrist away from the throttle and the murderous propeller would be shut

7

off. I would shut off the engine before we hit the beach. The kill-cord was to stop the propeller if by chance I fell out of the dinghy.

We studied the beach for quite some time and I picked out a spot where the surf activity appeared to be minimal. There was some surf action along almost the entire length of the beach except for that one short stretch. It had the least amount of surf.

The way to land a dinghy through the surf is to gun the outboard to build momentum and then ram the dinghy straight onto the beach. Once committed, there is no turning around.

I drove the dinghy at top speed, aiming at the selected spot. All went according to plan until we had just passed the point of no return. To my horror the beach sand suddenly shifted, displaying a small cliff at our intended landing spot. Some sand was still collapsing from the cliff. The dinghy was riding on top of a big swell moving in fast. There was no turning back. "Oh no...we'll just have to keep going," I said as the dinghy continued moving fast towards the beach.

We hit the sand hard, but didn't land nearly high enough on the beach. We both jumped out of the dinghy to pull it to high ground. It was a rather heavy dinghy. We pulled and pulled, but couldn't budge it more than a few feet.

While we were struggling to pull the dinghy, a giant wave came thundering in, crashing over us. The surf liquefied the sand. My feet were sinking deep into the beach with sand up to my knees. My lower legs were totally buried and I was completely immobilized. I couldn't pull my legs out of the sand. If another wave knocked me over, my knees would snap like chicken bones. Judy, shorter than I, was not in any better situation on the other side of the dinghy which was now super heavy, filled to the brim with seawater and impossible to move.

In that split second, I remembered reading about one of the lessons gleaned from the Sydney-to-Hobart-Race Disaster in 1998. The lesson was that there is an invisible thin line that separates a yacht race from a struggle for survival. The skipper must be aware when that line is crossed.

That lesson was applicable to our situation. Here we were, still trying to rescue the miserable dinghy to keep it from destruction, but our own survival was at stake. We were not in a race, but there was no doubt that we had "crossed that thin line." Our lives were in jeopardy.

"Judy, forget the dinghy, save yourself," I shouted. I still couldn't move, with my legs buried and immobilized by the sand.

Before I even finished those words, another monstrous wave roared in and engulfed us, sending Judy and me tumbling in the surf. The wave that sent me spinning also loosened the sand and released my legs. I tumbled head over heels in sand and briny water. Somewhere in that boiling turmoil were Judy, the outboard, and the dinghy. I was quite sure the dinghy and the outboard had gone inches over my head as we went headlong into the surf.

When I surfaced I was in deep water, caught in a rip current heading fast out to sea. I surmised dimly that, after hitting the beach, the giant wave was washing us off shore in the fast-flowing undertow. I could see our lifejackets floating not twenty feet from us, but they might as well have been a hundred miles away. Judy was next to me, looking very pale.

"Swim parallel to the beach," I said urgently. "We are in a rip current." I couldn't be sure she heard me as I was out of breath.

We both made it back to the beach by swimming along the shore crosswise to the current, but I was deathly tired by that time. Despite the exhaustion, I managed to crawl a few feet. Judy had already collapsed in a heap on the wet sand next to me.

"Judy, keep moving up the beach. If another wave hits us, we are going to drown. I won't be able to help you." I had no idea if she understood the precarious situation we were facing. Another big wave…it would be the end of us.

"I can't move…tired." She was barely audible.

It was clear to me that Judy was as totally and utterly drained of any strength as I was. I could barely crawl one limb at a time. Each movement of my arm and leg took enormous willpower and effort. It was excruciating but, in my mind, safety was to have dry sand under me…to get away from the huge swells. We crawled slowly, more dead than alive, struggling for survival in slow motion.

No more monstrous waves came for the remainder of our time on that beach. In time, we managed to stand up to survey the damage. The dinghy was at the water's edge, upside down. The outboard had fallen off the transom where it was clamped, but still attached to the boat by a 10-foot anti-theft steel cable. It rested like a dead fish in the shallow water.

Our handheld radio had gone to the bottom of the ocean. We recovered one wooden oar, but the other was still floating somewhere in the Pacific. We also recovered the lifejackets and found one of our backup canoe paddles.

We noticed that there was a motor fishing boat just outside of the surf zone, waving at us. It was clear they wanted to know if we needed help.

Of course we need help. We have no way of getting off this beach.

We waved back at them. They had no way of crossing the surf line to reach us. Apparently they called the Mexican Navy because soon there was a panga with someone in a khaki uniform. There was also a civilian panga just off the surf line. None of them dared to venture close to the beach and we were not about to swim out to them.

Suddenly there was movement far up the deserted beach. We saw a young man and a woman, with two children, running toward us. It was a dream-like moment to have someone coming to help, reminding me of scenes from a western movie where the cavalry suddenly appears. The young people were on the beach that morning to do some photo shooting at the sunny side of the large boulders. They saw that we were in trouble.

The woman was distressed when she saw Judy. "How terrible, you are bleeding."

Judy, all covered with sand, hadn't even noticed that she had suffered a gash on her leg and blood was trickling down. The young man suggested that we let the navy panga tow our dinghy to the marina and that Judy and I could ride back in the other panga. With all hands, we righted our dinghy and put the drowned outboard in it.

With only one oar and a single paddle, I couldn't row the dinghy past the surf zone before it was spun around. The first attempt almost broached the dinghy in the surf. I couldn't create enough forward speed before the surf knocked the dinghy sideways.

"I know how to get the dinghy to the panga," the young man volunteered. He took the single paddle and leaned over the point on the bow so his arms could paddle, first on one side of the bow and then the other. That way, he was able to propel the dinghy

10

perpendicularly to the surf line. We were all holding our breath after we gave the dinghy a mighty push off the beach.

Before long he came back by way of the side entrance to the beach...the landing place in the shadow that we had rejected earlier. The young man refused any offer of compensation for his time and effort. He was happy that he could be of assistance. He had learned how to move boats off the beach when he worked as a lifeguard. We were very grateful and have good memories of these people. Unfortunately, in our traumatized state of mind, we never learned their contact information.

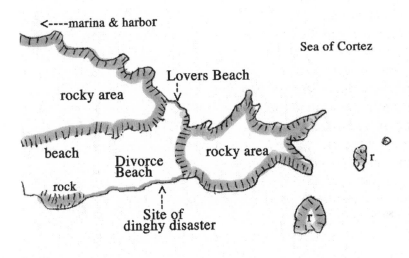

Pacific Ocean   Lands End, Cabo San Lucas

When we got to the side entrance to the beach, the civilian panga was waiting. Soon the navy panga delivered the dinghy and outboard to our dock at the marina.

We washed an enormous amount of sand off ourselves. There was sand in every orifice of my body. I tried to resuscitate and preserve the outboard by washing the sand off with fresh water and then saturating the internal engine parts with as much WD-40 as I knew how.

The near-death experience taught us something:

1. That particular dinghy was too heavy for the two of us to pull up the beach.

2. We needed to wear our life jackets at all times.

3. Any surf activity can be dangerous in a beach landing.

4. We must research local information before venturing into unfamiliar places.

Even an innocuous tourist beach can lead to danger. I discovered too late that the little beach in the shadow facing the Sea of Cortez was indeed the Lover's Beach and the beach facing the Pacific was called, ironically, the Divorce Beach. Locals knew about the dangerous rip currents and erratic waves on the Pacific side. Approaching the beach from the Pacific side was a bad mistake; I learned to always land the dinghy on a sheltered beach. Experience is a harsh teacher; I hope not all lessons will be so punishing.

We departed Cabo San Lucas the next day. Both Judy and I were emotionally exhausted by our near-fatal incident on the beach at Cabo. We were so traumatized we couldn't even talk about the event to each other for more than a year. It was two years before we told anyone else.

How did we get ourselves into this mess?

To answer that question, we need to start from the beginning. The story of this little jaunt around the world began many years ago, long before we went to sea. Seemingly unrelated events propelled us, little by little, into this adventure of a lifetime.

2. The Beginning

Santa Cruz, California (36 58.280 N, 122 03.252 W), May 1990. Anacapa Isle Marina, Oxnard, California (34 10.386 N, 119 13.646 W), April 2004.

Years before the Journey

There I was trapped in a hospital bed in the Coronary Care Unit (CCU) after a myocardial infarction. Never in my adult life had I so much free time with so little to do. I had experienced a heart attack, but my brain was still churning at full speed. Call it an epiphany or "Eureka" moment, but I understood something significant at that instant. *Life is not infinite.*

I didn't die in the emergency room at age forty-eight. *How can I make the remaining days and minutes count?* There was no panic, but I was no longer on autopilot. That was 1990, thirteen years before my wife, Judy, and I bought our sailing catamaran.

Judy brought me CDs and books to keep me occupied while I was in the hospital. One book, *Maiden Voyage*, was by a teenager, Tania Aebi, who had sailed around the world single-handedly on a 26-foot sailboat. She didn't have much sailing experience before embarking on her oceanic saga at age eighteen, but she did it.

I had learned to sail during summers as a student and had sailed off and on, but I never expected to sail across oceans. Every time I flew on a commercial airline, I would take a good look below at the unending ocean from horizon to horizon. *How could any sane person cross the vast ocean in a tiny boat?*

The decision to sail away didn't happen all at once, but the seed of an idea was planted by Aebi's book. It grew slowly and quietly, even as I recovered from my heart attack. I continued paying our mortgage and going to work. Studying for a ham radio license seemed like a good thing to add to my repertoire. Boat shows provided more ideas. Judy finally took her first sailing class at age 50. I wasn't sure she would ever go sailing off shore, but she decided to find out what sailing was about.

Judy had trained as a Registered Nurse and worked in the emergency department for a number of years. We both went on "Medicine at Sea" and "Medicine Far from Help" seminars. As my obsession gathered momentum, there were cruising seminars for both of us, followed by a skipper-guided charter trip to the San Juan Islands north of Seattle. Judy went to a Women's Sail Training class in Canada. It took us some time to discover the US Power Squadron classes...the weather class, engine maintenance, and seamanship classes came in very handy.

In the beginning it was never my intention to circumnavigate the world or to break any records. When I told our friends that Judy and I were planning to sail to Mexico, they were astonished.

One wrote, "Howard, have you gone crazy? When did you learn how to drive a boat?"

On a pre-departure medical, my cardiologist asked, "How long will you be gone?"

Judy replied, "Oh...maybe three or four."

"Three or four months, that's nice."

"No, three or four years!"

We didn't have a detailed plan except that we would live the boating life for a few years. Even if I had thought of sailing around the world, I wouldn't have boasted about it. It was not my habit to announce a grandiose plan, because then any accomplishment short of that plan would seem like a failure to us. We were trying something different one step at a time.

Buying a Boat

"If you had a chance to live your life over again, what would you do?" I asked at breakfast.

"What? It's too early in the morning for that kind of nonsense," Judy retorted.

"No, I'm not kidding," I said. "I'm getting close to retirement, there's still some good years left after that. We can do something completely different...it's like a second life."

"Well, I like to travel. In all the years we've been married, we've never gone anywhere for a long time that was not work related. Mostly you were wrapped up in your lab."

"Mmm...when the kids were young we did a lot of backpacking and skiing...and even sailing," I said. "Now with my heart attack behind us, we should make some plans...not to squander what's left. How about a sailing trip?"

"I didn't do any sailing. You and the kids came back cold and wet...sometimes bloody. It didn't look like fun."

"That was in a small boat...dinghy sailing. You remember the book you got me when I was in the CCU? That teenager knew hardly anything about sailing. She sailed all over by herself."

"You know I get seasick. Besides boats cost a lot of money. I'm not keen on the idea."

"Maybe we can work something out...like you can fly and meet me when I sail to an interesting port. That way you can travel too."

Buying a boat is like getting married. Falling in love first will make it easier to face the challenges sure to follow and the expenses. Unlike marriage, the mariner's life will literally depend on getting the right boat. The vessel must be structurally sound, able to hold together in one piece to preserve body and soul in a bad storm. A quality boat is not inexpensive.

The cost of buying a boat is not the only obstacle to boat ownership. When buying a home, the husband and wife are usually of the same mind. They are in agreement in making a major investment in their future. Buying a sailboat is often the dream of only one of them and it is often the husband's.

I knew in advance that Judy had no fondness for sailboats, much less sailing in one. She loved traveling, but in comfort and safety. Risking life and limb to explore *where no one has gone before* was all well and good to experience in a book or movie, but not in her person. Buying a boat and having to live on it struck her more like a nightmare.

Judy knew that this was my dream and I had no doubt she would try to help me if she could. She was caught between her self-interest and her desire to help me fulfill my dream. We cared deeply for each other, but we still negotiated constantly within the marriage, as we had done for the past forty years. It had always been give-and-take and never-ending compromises. This time it was going to be tough. Buying a boat was a biggie.

Definitely, I knew better than to try to get my way by strong-arming Judy. She had always been strong willed and no pushover. It wouldn't take much for me to wreck everything. More than a few marriages have ended up on the rocks over boats. It would have been ironic to shipwreck before launching the vessel.

On the plus side, by that time we both had considerable exposure to sailboats. We had looked at boats together at shows and by walking the docks. On a number of occasions we had sailed on chartered boats. We also had taken classes from the Ventura Power Squadron. Thus, we had a shared knowledge base and enough common ground to discuss the issues.

So far, Judy hadn't said "No." That was important because I knew that if she didn't want to do something, she would have said so and that would have been the end of the discussion. If she thought the trip was too risky, the proverbial wild horses wouldn't have been able to drag her on board.

"Perhaps you can try going on a short passage and see how you like it," I said.

"I won't sail on a mono-hull. I don't like to sail on my side," she replied.

Well, that is what sailboats do...they heel. "We can look for a catamaran, but it will cost a lot more," I said.

We did go on a skippered catamaran in the Caribbean during a medical seminar sponsored by West Marine. That was when Judy and I first learned about catamarans. They offered a more stable platform and minimal heeling under sail.

We didn't find an affordable catamaran we liked in the Caribbean or Florida. Then we saw an ad for a catamaran by a respected designer. We flew to Seattle to see the boat. A nice couple took us sailing on Puget Sound on a cold blustery day. The boat was light and designed for speed at the expense of structural ruggedness. It was especially uncomfortable for Judy, because it had hardly any handholds in and around the cockpit. The boat was not suitable for us although it was a high-performance catamaran.

"If you are looking for a used boat, you should look in the San

Diego Harbor," a sailor at a swap meet was telling me.

"Why San Diego?" I asked.

"Lots of couples buy boats to sail to Mexico, but something happens on the way. They break up...a lot of them don't make it past San Diego. They end up selling the boat where they left it." That didn't sound too good, but I let it pass.

After spending all day in San Diego looking at catamarans with a yacht salesman, we found nothing suitable. The good ones cost too much and the affordable ones were lacking. One cat we looked at didn't even have an anchor locker. By that time I knew a boat needs an anchor when there isn't a marina available.

"There is a catamaran that is not yet on the market...a strong boat, but it's not new. It's docked in the Channel Islands Harbor near where you live," said the salesman.

It seemed amazing that, after looking across the country as well as from Seattle to San Diego, a suitable catamaran was docked within 15 minutes of our home in Ventura, California. As a scientist, I tried hard not to be superstitious, but it seemed to me like an auspicious twist of fate.

Renovating a Cat

Both diesel engines acted like dying drug addicts. They wouldn't start without puffs of ether shot through their air intakes. Apparently their cylinders were worn with inadequate compression. The ill-fitting main sail drooped like an oversized bed sheet hanging out to dry.

The previous owner had a habit of making "temporary repairs" without following through. As a result there were multiple disasters waiting to happen. The prize was a full roll of toilet paper used to prop up a bird's nest of electrical wires behind the navigation panel. *Toilet paper among live electrical wires!* It would have been hard to find better kindling for incinerating the boat to the waterline. All it would have taken was an errant spark.

As I stood in the boatyard amidst toxic paint dust, I felt overwhelmed. *Was there anything on this boat that worked? Did we hire a blind surveyor? Did he see any of the problems?*

We met the surveyor at a class about boat buying. He seemed knowledgeable about catamarans and taught a good class. So we hired him as our surveyor to check out the vessel. The survey report mentioned none of the many deficiencies on the boat. As it turned out, the surveyor had ulterior motives.

He had the temerity to assume complete charge of the renovation project without even asking for my permission.

"Hi, I'm Mike, I'm the mechanic," said an older man who approached me at the boatyard. "You're Howard, right?"

"Yes, I'm Howard, have we met before?" I was puzzled.

The surveyor had engaged Mike the mechanic, a friend of his, to show up without even consulting me. I sent the mechanic away. *What audacity!*

"I am in the business…I can save you money and hire the best people," the surveyor said later. "My church sponsors kids from the inner city, they can do the scraping and painting. It won't cost anything, you just take them sailing afterwards. The physical labor will be good for them."

"Are you sure there are no child-labor laws against dragging kids into this kind of work? Just being in the boatyard is pretty dangerous, you know," I replied.

"Look, you're not paying them. They're fixing the boat so they can go sailing…just like the Boy Scouts," the surveyor argued.

"You do know that the anti-fouling paint is toxic…like it's poisonous. That's why it's used on the boat bottoms to keep barnacles from growing."

"Ah…you worry too much," the surveyor insisted. "It's free labor and I'll keep my hours to a minimum. It will be a top-notch catamaran when it's done."

First he turned in a sloppy survey report. Now he wants to profit from the many unexpected repairs…so he can get paid for his incompetence. It's unbelievable chutzpah to assume he could use my boat for his religious charity.

"Look, I can't afford the insurance if you bring in the kids," I said. "If one of them falls off the scaffold, it'll be all hell to pay. Besides, I'm sailing away as soon as the boat is ready. I'm not hanging around taking kids sailing."

"Don't worry, I'll keep an eye on the kids. I already promised them. You only have to take them sailing once or twice."

I could see that I wasn't getting through to him by being diplomatic. "Look, I don't want you to be involved with this project in any way," I said firmly. "This is not a job for you or the kids. Please go away; I'll tell the yard manager not to let you come close to my boat."

He went away with an injured look as if I had wronged him somehow. I don't think he realized how pushy and self-serving he had been. In dealing with some people, being nice is a weakness.

Laelia hauled out for survey in Ventura Harbor

I hired separate people to do the refit. It was important for me to be involved with every aspect of the renovation. I learned as the project moved forward and got to know the boat from stem to stern. I worked with the mechanic about installing new engines and the sail-maker on new sails. I asked them to explain their ideas and suggestions. By watching how things were done and what tools were used, I became more knowledgeable.

I learned from the painters as they applied the layers of paint. The "prop-man" taught me all about matching propellers to the engine and the need to torque the propeller blades. People loved to teach if anyone would listen, and I was all-ears. Our lives would depend on this boat's seaworthiness. It did cost money...nothing is free when it comes to boats. Sometimes the cost was not money, but time, patience, and the humility to admit my ignorance.

Judy worked with the sign maker and came up with a design.

On the bow the boat name was emblazoned in giant red letters, *"Laelia,"* the name of Judy's favorite orchid. The renovated vessel looked ravishing, like its namesake.

Near the end of all the major projects, Judy decided that there had to be odorless vacuum toilets on Laelia. Her rationale was that by eliminating sewage odor, there would be less seasickness.

How can I argue with that kind of logic?

I did the plumbing job myself. It was hard work and I learned much more than I ever wanted to know about marine plumbing. The advantage was that I became the world's foremost (and only) expert on Laelia's sewage system. That knowledge was to come in handy later.

Over the years, we had known vessels, including catamarans, demolished on the Pacific Coast and the crew hoisted out of the sea by the Coast Guard. *Is Laelia up to snuff? Will it be able to cut through the waves and skim over the sea?*

We needed a shakedown cruise, a trip to test the boat's seaworthiness. *Imagine Laelia in full canvas, finely trimmed, sailing under the Golden Gate Bridge into the San Francisco Bay. What a grand entrance!*

When we mentioned our plan to an experienced sailor on the dock, he said, "Why are you going north? You are supposed to sail south...go down wind."

An old salt, a live-aboard, said, "You don't want to go north...you'll just get all beat up."

A few days later we met an English sailor at the clubhouse in the marina. In his inimitable British fashion he said, "I think it's a capital idea! It would build confidence in you and test the boat and crew." Each of the three persons we had talked to seemed to make sense. They were all correct.

The prevailing wind on the Pacific Coast here is northwest, as is the overall orientation of the coast. If we headed for San Francisco Bay, Laelia would be sailing against the wind, which is always more difficult and tougher on both vessel and crew.

For recreational sailing or racing, it is exhilarating beating upwind even if it is wet and rough. Upwind sailing is exciting when one can return to the marina to dry off, have a beer in a warm bar, and recount the adventure. For long passages, wind on the nose for an extended period is unpleasant and tiring.

There are also a few difficult passages along this coast that have proven to be calamitous. Point Conception west of Santa Barbara, Point Sur south of Monterey, and Point Arena north of San Francisco are notorious for strong winds and nasty waves. The heavy fog along the coast is another hazard. Even the entrance to San Francisco Bay requires some degree of knowledge and caution to avoid fatal mishaps.

"The trip north can be pretty rough," I said. "They tell me that the sailing conditions on the Pacific coast of North America are as difficult as what we might encounter anywhere in the world."

"Then, if we can sail here, we can sail anywhere," Judy said. "But do you want to have it so tough on our very first trip?"

"Well, I don't want us to chicken out just because it's rough. It's not supposed to be easy. What good is a shakedown cruise if it's not a real test?"

"Then we should go," said Judy. "We can show our kids our new cat, Laelia, when we are in the Bay."

We set a date for the shakedown cruise north to San Francisco Bay.

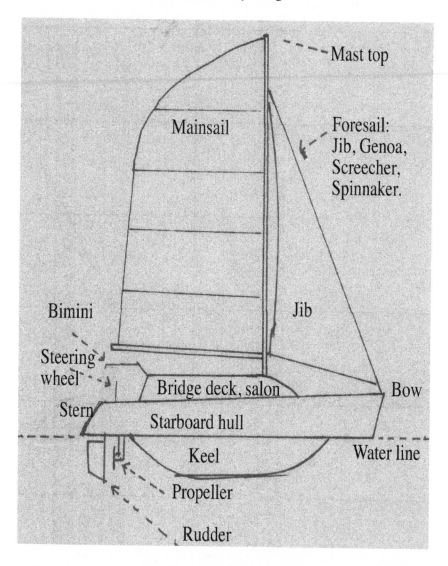

Mast top

Mainsail

Foresail:
Jib, Genoa,
Screecher,
Spinnaker.

Bimini

Jib

Steering
wheel

Stern

Bridge deck, salon

Bow

Starboard hull

Water line

Keel

Propeller

Rudder

Our catamaran, Laelia, is 42 feet in length and 24.5 feet in width. Its mast is 60 feet tall from the deck or 65 from the waterline. In the upper bridge-deck salon, connecting the two hulls, is the navigation area, the galley, and a semi-circular settee. Four en-suite staterooms are in the two hulls. In 2003, the catamaran was 12 years old, originally built by Kennex in Marseille, France. The vessel was solidly constructed. We renamed the catamaran Laelia, the name of Judy's favorite orchid.

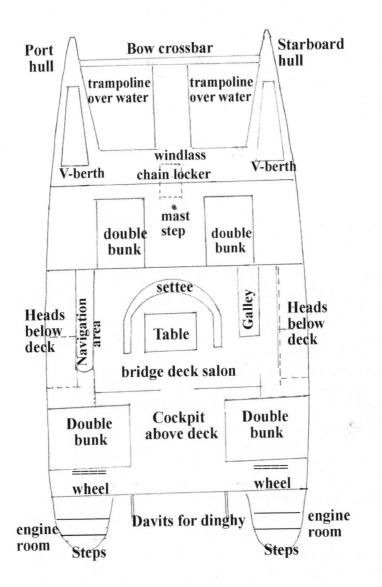

Drawing of Laelia's deck plan: the catamaran has two hulls connected by the bridge deck. The navigation area, galley, and settee are at above deck level. The engine rooms are accessed through hatches at the back steps.

3. The Shakedown

Round trip, from Anacapa Isle Marina, Channel Islands Harbor, Oxnard (34 10.386 N, 119 13.646 W), to San Francisco Bay (37 48.998 N, 122 28.685 W), April 2004.

Rounding Point Conception

The shakedown cruise was to assess the boat and crew, but little did we know how harshly we were to be tested. It was a sunny morning when we departed the Channel Islands Harbor.

"Goodbye and good luck," waved Harry and Kit, my brother and his wife.

"Thank you, we'll see you in a few weeks," Judy waved back.

The swells were waiting for us as Laelia lurched into the turmoil just outside the breakwater.

One mountainous swell roared and crashed against the barrier breakwater, flinging white spume and spraying salt brine high up in the air.

Is this an omen?

I had a premonition of an imminent struggle for survival. Whitecaps were everywhere, a gale wind was howling from the bow. The small craft advisory was bleating incessantly on the radio.

Despite the bright sunshine, this would have been the day to go to the marina to inspect the dock lines and secure the boat. It was not a day to venture out for a pleasant spin over the water.

Turning back to the comforts of the dock was a tempting option. I looked back wistfully. No one would know except the two of us. No, the problem was that we would know. We are our harshest judges.

We can't quit just because things are tough.

It definitely was not the gentle breeze that I was anticipating, but Laelia had two new engines with adequate power to maintain a decent headway against the wind. The GPS showed that we were traveling at about five knots relative to the ground, which was not shabby. It wasn't comfortable, but the boat kept moving.

As we approached the sea offshore from Santa Barbara, the swells got bigger and the wind became more intense. We had been to Santa Barbara Harbor before, but never so far offshore nor under such hostile conditions. I looked fondly at the row of drilling platforms receding astern as we headed further out to sea.

"Maybe the wind will calm down a little in the evening," I said.

Judy looked up at the clouds overhead, but said nothing.

As the sun was nearing the horizon, the wind and waves only seemed more ferocious. I could hear the gale shrieking through the rigging. The thought of turning back gnawed inside me. A comfortable berth for the night in a safe harbor had serious appeal, considering the pandemonium surrounding us.

My heart was pounding. Was that from fear or excitement? The difference between the two is a fine line. Knowing every inch of Laelia from the renovation, I had confidence that the boat would hold together.

I looked over at Judy, my wife of forty years. We could read each other's minds by now...well, most of the time. She showed no fear. Being the verbal one in the family, she would have sounded the alarm if she had any reservations about our safety. She also knew all the work we had put into the boat. Perhaps that knowledge had translated into confidence and even optimism.

At this point the nearest anchorage ahead of us was Cojo Bay, just before Point Conception. The chart showed kelp symbols surrounding the bay, which reminded me that the kelp beds could be a hazard. I would hate to have the propeller fouled by thick kelp or have the anchor tangled in a kelp holdfast.

"We have a couple of options," I said. "We can try to anchor in Cojo Bay, but with no guidebook, I don't know what kind of condition is waiting for us."

"It's getting pretty late. It'll be dark when we get there," Judy replied.

"That's true. It's a bad idea to navigate an unfamiliar anchorage in the dark. We know Santa Barbara Harbor, but that means going back and giving up quite a few miles."

"We worked hard for those few miles against the wind," Judy said as she took a deep breath.

"We could just keep going."

"Yeah, why not."

"It's going to be rough and not comfortable, but I think we'll be safe enough," I said. "Besides, we can always turn tail and run if we can't take the beating anymore."

The decision was by consensus. Perhaps that was not exactly the nautical tradition. It was important to me that Judy was consulted. As skipper I was still solely responsible for all aspects of the vessel and our safety. Also, I trusted her survival instincts. Her opinion is important.

Judy was becoming seasick and went to sleep. In the meantime, the waves were growing bigger. The boat would climb steeply up a wave, only to be tossed back into the trough with a mind-numbing crash. The heavy table in the center of the salon seemed to bounce up and smash back down with an ear-splitting bang. I held on to any firm handhold to keep from being tossed around too much.

Now and then, the boat smashed into a wave, came to a complete stop, and shuddered as it recovered itself. There were occasional loud smacking sounds from waves hitting the bottom of the salon. There was the rattling and banging of anything not firmly secured.

I either stayed in the cockpit or went in the salon to check the instruments while Judy slept on the settee in the salon. I avoided going below where I couldn't see the horizon. I didn't want to become seasick.

During the night passage around Point Conception, trying to scan the forward horizon was no easy task because despite the clear sky above, it was hard to see past the sea spray at boat level. The big waves would roll toward the boat and break, and then the wind would pick up the foam and catapult it across every surface. The wind-driven spray hitting the hull with a staccato rhythm sounded like bullets from a machine gun. With each wave, the boat smashed down in the trough and sent water over the deck and across the length of Laelia.

After the heavy sea spray had passed, I poked my head around the protective canvas to take a peek at the forward horizon. Each time I was smacked in the face by icy-cold seawater. The wind-driven spray was without mercy. Finding a piece of cloth to dry my glasses was hopeless. Everything was wet, salty, and sticky.

Occasionally, an extra-large wave would wash over the entire boat. It was fascinating to see surf roaring over the forward deck against the bridge windows. A few waves even went over the Bimini top. The boat creaked and groaned. The wind whistled in the rigging. It wasn't the "Perfect Storm," but it was our first time out at sea in perilous weather.

How many times can the boat endure these big waves? Structural failures have been known to happen in storms. I suppose we will know soon enough.

Much later, I discovered a lot of black splotches on the salon roof, which I surmised had been left by a school of angry squid. There was also a dried up pipefish in the cockpit.

Throughout the pandemonium, the boat held up well structurally. That was reassuring. The oversized autopilot worked like a charm. We didn't have to do any manual steering in the howling wind and punishing wet spray.

The boat did leak in a few places. In the bow, the self-draining vents on the deck had their limits. It seemed that when the bow was buried completely in the bigger waves, the submerged vent allowed water to flow in instead of out. There was a lot of water in the port V-berth and in the hull under a hatch, evidence of a weak gasket. After that we always taped the vents on passages and, of course, installed new gaskets for leaky hatches.

I got a fix on our position as Laelia went by the famous Point Conception. I saw the landmass looming in the dark and the Point Conception Light. It was comforting, as the light was identified in the dark of night by its single white flash every 30 seconds. Each lighthouse has a unique repeating sequence of flashes as indicated on the navigation chart.

By morning the wind was still strong, but we were no longer pounded by the waves. When we rounded Point Buchan just south of Morro Bay, the conditions had become quite mild. By the first light of the morning, a feeling of peace fell upon me like a warm fuzzy blanket. Judy and I could see the shore with trees draped in low-hanging fog. I thought I heard dogs barking on shore.

We learned some important lessons that served us well as mariners:

1. Always study the weather forecast before leaving port.
2. Never keep a firm sailing schedule.
3. There is no shame in postponing a departure on account of bad weather.

We had taken a weather class offered by the Ventura Sail and Power Squadron. Our mentor, Bruce Thompson, taught us how to forecast and check for weather conditions. We should never have attempted Point Conception in foul weather. Many boaters had rounded the Point in mirror-smooth seas with no wind at all.

From that time on, checking the weather was almost a daily routine for us on Laelia. Waiting for the "weather window" would become an important pastime requiring patience. On the positive side, we learned from the shakedown cruise that both the vessel and its new owners could endure inclement conditions at sea.

Yes, we can do it! Indeed that knowledge forestalled fear and contributed to our confidence throughout our journey.

Close Encounter with a Leviathan

After the first leg of our shakedown cruise, we were more confident and felt relaxed. We decided to visit a few of our favorite cities on the coast.

As Laelia neared Morro Bay, we saw whales frolicking in the distance, but couldn't be sure which kind they were. The infamous fog at Morro Bay was only wispy as we approached the harbor. Judy hailed the Coast Guard buoy-tender, USS Charles Cobb, on the VHF radio. The Coast Guard on the radio was most helpful in providing information guiding Laelia through the harbor entrance.

We tied up at the dock in Morro Bay. It took us three days to dry out. We didn't mind the delay and were happy to spend the extra days at dock before continuing north.

A motto for life on the water is "expect the unexpected." Our sail north from Morro Bay was not exactly what we had anticipated; we encountered a whale close up.

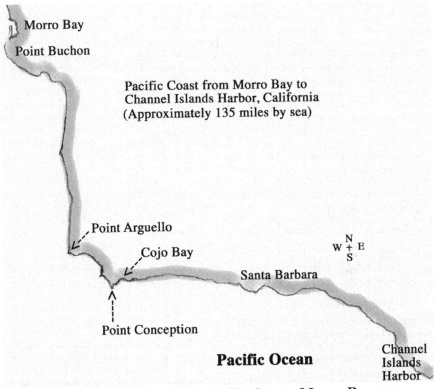

Morro Bay

Point Buchon

Pacific Coast from Morro Bay to
Channel Islands Harbor, California
(Approximately 135 miles by sea)

Point Arguello

Cojo Bay

N
W + E
S

Santa Barbara

Point Conception

Pacific Ocean

Channel
Islands
Harbor

Pacific Coast: Channel Islands Harbor to Morro Bay.

South of Point Sur, we saw a whale ahead of us on a course crossing our path. We were motoring in calm water.

A short time later, Judy became alarmed, "I think we are on a collision course. You better check."

"Yeah, you are right. I've been watching," I said. "It looks like we would cross paths at just short of a right angle."

By then we could see clearly that the whale had a black dorsal surface like that of a Humpback. It was large, perhaps as long as our 42-foot boat. A whale that large could weigh as much as thirty or forty tons, which was considerably heavier than Laelia. A collision could damage the hull or flip Laelia upside down. *What would happen if the whale becomes enraged by the collision?*

"What are you going to do?" Judy asked.

29

"I'm not sure…right-of-way rules say nothing about whales that I know of," I answered, "but the Marine Mammals Act requires us to stay clear."

"He's coming right at us," Judy said.

At that moment, the whale was about fifty feet on our right, heading at about a right angle from our course. It was clear that Laelia and the whale were about to crash into each other. There was no time to waste. I pulled the throttle back, almost by reflex, to slow the boat down so the whale could pass ahead of us. It seemed like the right thing to do.

Simultaneously the whale, apparently aware of the impending collision, also took corrective action by turning toward the stern of our boat. Had I maintained our boat speed, the whale would have passed exactly behind our boat, but now with our boat slowing down, an imminent collision seemed unavoidable.

"We're gonna be T-boned by the big guy! Hold on," I yelled.

It was good that Judy and I were both wearing our inflatable life jackets. The collision would hopefully fling us clear of the rigging. Getting entangled in the water with all the lines and wires on a sailboat meant death by drowning…a bad way to go. If we could be thrown clear into the cold seawater, we would have perhaps thirty minutes before hypothermia became an issue.

It seemed almost like telepathy…I sensed a feeling of annoyance emanating from the whale as it dove under the water, leaving its huge flukes in the air for a long moment very near us. It didn't splash much as the flukes entered the water, leaving a pool of smooth water swirling on the surface. The agility exhibited in that sudden diving maneuver was a further sign that it was a Humpback whale. Due to its long pectoral fins, the Humpback is known for its quick maneuverability.

I learned much later that we should have maintained our course and speed because whales are better helmsmen than boaters.

A Busy Morning in Monterey

We made an overnight stop at Monterey. By contacting the Harbor Master by email via the single-side-band (SSB or shortwave) radio, we were able to secure the use of the dock at the Fisherman's Wharf. It was easier to dock without having to negotiate the narrow entrance of the Monterey Bay Marina. Since we planned to stay only overnight, we thought it would be more convenient to dock at the wharf. Besides, there were good restaurants there, and we had a good Italian dinner and an even better breakfast.

The next morning, after we finished with our leisurely breakfast, we stopped by the Harbor Master's office to pay the docking fee. We waited for the Harbor Master, who returned a little breathless and somewhat agitated.

He said, "It was a long night for me. There was a shooting not fifty feet from your catamaran."

"I am sorry to hear that. What happened?" I was hoping he would continue with the story.

Instead, he sighed. "The ambulance took him, and more paperwork." Then he pulled up our check-in papers. "The reason I was late was because I was on a chase. There was someone on your catamaran."

We perked up our ears. He was chasing someone off our Laelia. "What did he want?" We asked in unison.

"Damn if I know. He either wanted to steal your boat or take something off the boat. Anyway, he got away."

Someone was trying to steal our boat while we were eating breakfast.

It had been an eventful morning. All that excitement was right around us, but we had missed it all.

Night Departure from Santa Cruz

From Monterey it was only a short hop to Santa Cruz, where we previously had lived for thirty years. We tied up at the Santa Cruz Harbor fuel dock to fill up on diesel. Immediately adjacent was their new guest dock and the Crow's Nest Restaurant. We didn't stay long, but visited with those friends whom we were able to reach by phone.

On that same day we departed Santa Cruz at 2200 hours. We decided on a night departure because the head winds would be much lighter at night and it would put us at the Golden Gate Bridge with a flood tide in the morning light.

The two primary hazards along this coast are thick fog and a strong offshore wind. The locals call it the Santa Ana wind that blows from the interior towards the sea. It is a hot, dry wind on land, but creates havoc at sea, rushing down from hills and through canyons with gale force. Anchored vessels need to seek alternate anchorages sheltered from the blow.

During the summer months, the entire coast could sometimes be shrouded in thick, blinding fog, creating a "white-out" condition. It is not unusual for the advection fog to blanket the entire coast from Santa Cruz to San Francisco. Perhaps we had been punished enough earlier at Point Conception; this part of our trip was rather uneventful.

North by Northwest to San Francisco

As we approached San Francisco, we entered the shipping channel for the bay at one of the earlier buoys instead of cutting the corner at the entrance closer to shore. It took longer, because the channel buoys extended a considerable distance to deeper water.

It was tempting for small boats to enter the bay by way of the shallower water closer to shore. The risk was that there are occasional rogue waves in the shallow water. Boats attempting to cut the corner at the bay entrance had been capsized and crews killed by unexpected big swells.

We arrived at the Golden Gate Bridge at mid-morning in bright sunshine with a following wind and a flood tide. These conditions contributed to an exhilarating sail under the Golden Gate at a fast clip as we entered the iconic San Francisco Bay.

We had arranged with the Benicia Marina to dock Laelia, because that was the nearest marina to where our daughter was living. She wanted us to call her when we sailed close to the Carquinez Bridge so she could take a photo from shore.

As we approached the Benicia Marina, we saw from a distance what appeared to be hundreds of small watercraft. They were small run-abouts and speedboats, plus a liberal sprinkling of jet-skis. The situation was worse as we got closer to the commotion, complete with revving engines and darting boats. It became clear that a boat race would be starting shortly.

Why are they blocking the entire navigable waterway with a racecourse?

"Get the hell outta there." All of these boaters had a beer can in hand and healthy vocal cords. "Take your stinking sailboat to where you belong!" It was getting personal.

They wanted us to move along the back where there was lots of seaweed. Laelia was already in very shallow water. The depth meter was showing no more than a foot of clearance under Laelia's keels. The last thing I wanted was to run aground. Then we would have to wait for the high tide in the dark to refloat the boat. Laelia needed to get out of there before the start of the race. At one point, there were no more than a few inches of water under our keels as we maneuvered our way to the marina.

We had fun in Benicia visiting with our daughter. We also took a course on "Medicine Far from Help." We learned how to inject local anesthetics before suturing a wound. Of course the anesthetic didn't do anything for the pig's foot from the supermarket on which we practiced. It was cold and the skin was so tough it bent my suturing needle.

We also learned skills that I never intended to use. Drilling holes in the skull to relieve intracranial pressure seemed rather desperate. Splinting broken bones was more practical. I favored chemical attacks using drugs to treat a variety of problems such as anuria. *Let's not go there.* We learned the different levels of antibiotic usage and the problem of antibiotic resistance.

Weeks later, I had a good scare after we arrived at the Ballena Isle Marina in Alameda. By that time, we had been in San Francisco Bay for some days and the black-water holding tank was full. There was a sewage discharge station at the marina. We attached Laelia's sewage tank to the discharge hose and opened the station's vacuum valve. The hose gave a loud whoosh as the suction went to work. I then went into the engine room to check on the holding tank.

"Oh, no...the holding tank collapsed," I gasped, realizing the potential calamity as I saw the shrunken plastic.

The holding tank was made of polyethylene plastic that was old and brittle from age. The vacuum was too powerful. The tank was all scrunched up and in danger of cracking. The tank was designed to have a small opening at the top to relieve the vacuum while the sewage was being suctioned out of the bottom, but the opening was blocked by spider web or corrosion. Had the tank cracked open, the remaining sewage would have been all over the engine room and I would be mopping up for days afterwards. I quickly turned the vacuum valve off. The tank remained deformed for many weeks, but didn't exude any unpleasant content.

Return to the Channel Islands Harbor

We departed on a Sunday when the San Francisco Bay was a madhouse of floating objects and boats of various sorts. There were windsurfers, small and fast like mosquitoes, buzzing all around. All we could do was to keep a moderate speed and make no sudden turns. We crossed our fingers that windsurfers would look after their own wellbeing and not collide with us. A few of them just had to show off by cutting across close to our bow at high speed. Not surprisingly some of them would crash in the waves dead ahead of Laelia. We slowed to avoid running over them. It was an unnerving experience.

As we traversed the Bay, there was also the weekend sailboat traffic. Some of these boats were perhaps in a regatta. We had at least one near collision with a fast moving racer.

Another mistake we made was sailing out of the Bay with the wind at our back, but failing to consider the incoming tide. Swells were generated by the strong wind against a contrary current. Our exit from the bay was uncomfortable as we bashed against wave after wave under the Golden Gate Bridge to the Pacific Ocean.

Along the Pacific Coast, we had strong NW winds blowing anywhere from twenty to thirty knots all the way to the Channel Islands Harbor, where our shakedown cruise had begun. We flew only the jib. The waves were huge and it was often difficult to control the boat as Laelia surfed down large swells. At one point we noticed that the boat's speed was 16.4 knots. With this roaring wind in our favor, it was a fast trip. Laelia made it home in record time and completed the shakedown cruise in one piece.

4. Southbound

At home in Ventura, California (34 17.143 N, 119 11.513 W), June 2004. Departing Anacapa Isle Marina, Oxnard (34 10.386 N, 119 13.646 W), 18 October 2004. Departing San Diego Harbor (32 42.550 N, 117 14.103 W), 25 October 2004.

Home No More

"After we sell the house, we'll be homeless," Judy said.

"Well, I know what you mean, but the boat will be our home. We'll buy another home on land when we come back."

Her anxiety was real and distressing to her, while my sense of loss was less intense. The two of us had different upbringings. Judy had a stable home all her life. She was born and raised in Long Beach, California. When she went to the School of Nursing at LA County General Hospital, she could ride the Red Car home on weekends. After five years of marriage, we moved from Los Angeles to Berkeley. That was the first time Judy moved away from Southern California; it was a shock to her.

On the other hand, I was born in Shanghai in 1942. War had made me a refugee from the moment I was born. In 1949, when I was seven, my parents fled Shanghai to Hong Kong with the family. For many years afterwards, I had a fleeting yearning: *When are we going home?* It was more an ache or longing for a faraway home. Even as a child, I had to remind myself that our family was never going back to that home in Shanghai.

When I was fourteen, my parents immigrated with the entire

35

family to the United States. All that relocation created in me a love for travel. To this day, my heart beats a little faster upon hearing a train whistle or a ship blasting its horn at departure.

It was not until Judy and I made our own home in California that the yearning for that far-away home subsided, but the feeling of loss was never forgotten. Perhaps that was what I meant by "home," a place that was lost and found again. For me, home is not a physical structure...it is a place in the heart.

We both realized that it didn't make financial sense to keep an empty house while we sailed away on our boat. It was a good time to sell, and our bank account, seriously depleted by the boat renovation, needed to be replenished.

After selling the house, we were without the entire inventory of "stuff" from our kitchen and garage. In contrast, there was not even a pantry on the boat. We dealt with that deficiency by eating out a lot. When we went from three cars to one, we had problems.

"When are you coming back? I need to go to the hair salon."

"Bring the car back soon, I need to buy parts for the boat."

We adapted to the limitations of owning only one automobile. It was a big change for us. When our last vehicle, a Honda Odyssey, went away, it brought a strange feeling of helplessness. It was also the biggest change to our quality of life. Every little errand required a lot of walking.

Of course, we were made of much sterner stuff, we didn't whimper and whine...well, we might have wondered a little, in secret: *Good grief! What am I doing? These are pretty irreversible changes.*

By then, Judy had taken to telling people that we were "homeless, unemployed, boat people."

Misadventure at Santa Catalina Island

It started as an uneventful sail from the Channel Islands Harbor. Upon arrival at Santa Catalina Island, we decided to tie up at a mooring in Emerald Bay.

Judy and I knew the drill. It required me to pick up an upright whip linked to the mooring line. As soon as the bow mooring line was hooked on the cleat, I would pull hand-over-hand a smaller line that was connected to the second mooring line. Once we had the second line hooked onto the stern cleat, we would have the

36

boat tied "bow-and-stern." No matter what direction the wind blew, the boat would stay in about the same orientation. That is how they are able to pack so many boats in the harbors at Catalina during the summer.

Having been through all that before, we knew that it required a pair of gloves, because the line that connected to the two moorings was not only full of slime from sitting at the bottom all the time, it was also encrusted with razor-sharp barnacles.

While I was trying to hook the mooring lines on the cleats, Judy was at the helm using the engines to keep the boat in place. We thought it lucky that we were the only boat in Emerald Bay, it being October and well past the high season.

The wind was brisk, and the mooring line we grabbed was for a longer boat…as we discovered too late. I hooked one mooring line on the bow cleat easily, but was unable to hook the other line on Laelia's stern cleat. It would have hooked on if Laelia had been a few feet longer. I had to drop the line when the stern drifted sideways.

As the mooring line went down, it swiped across the underside of the boat where the starboard propeller was still turning, keeping the boat in place against the wind. I knew instantly what would happen when the spinning propeller met that mooring line, but it was too late to correct the mistake.

The engine all of a sudden groaned to a stop and the low-oil alarm started shrieking. My stomach dropped to my toes. I knew what was happening under the boat. It didn't take much to imagine the propeller snatching the mooring line and reeling it in with the power of the diesel engine. It whirled the rope taut around the hub until the engine died.

Damn! This has gotta be damaging to the transmission. Maybe we'll need a tow to the boatyard…the trip has not even officially started yet. No matter what…the line has to be untangled from the propeller.

A wave of panic swept over me. I felt sick as I kicked off my shoes and fumbled for the swim flippers.

Am I crazy? That water is frigid! What's gonna happen to my cardiac pacemaker in cold water?

I knew for sure that Judy was not going to dive under the boat. Someone had to do this job. Quietly, I dropped overboard. The cold water didn't take my breath away, which I considered a good sign. I held onto the boat for a brief moment.

"Judy, could you please get me a knife?"

This was just in case I needed to cut the mooring line that I knew was wrapped around the propeller. Judy brought *a kitchen knife!* The image of Johnny Depp with a knife between his teeth diving under the pirate ship came to mind. Somehow, a kitchen knife from the galley dashed that bit of fantasy.

I dove under to investigate and made a mental note to buy a good rigging knife for the boat at the first opportunity. A sharp rigging knife could be used in emergency situations where an arm or a hand is tangled up in a jib sheet or halyard under tension...well usually they would cut the rope, not the body part that was caught.

I took a deep breath before diving under Laelia. *If I don't get myself entangled under the boat, I could surface when I run out of oxygen.* The boat was not going anywhere...it was held in a death grip by the mooring line around the propeller. There were many coils of ¾-inch polypropylene rope wrapped all over the propeller and its hub. The rope was spun and twisted on with such force that it felt like a steel cable.

I knew life on land could be a tangled web. I had hoped that we could be spared of such complications at sea. Alas, it was a mess under the boat. Just as on land, all I could do was to deal with it one strand at a time.

After some studying, I was able to turn the prop in the reverse direction. As the hub was turned, the rope gave a little slack. The extra freedom in the rope allowed it to be released one loop at a time. In between, I coughed and choked after each surfacing to get air. There was no need to cut anything. It was fortunate that there were no other boats around to watch this melodrama.

Ugh, this water is salty. Is it safe to drink?

It was a good thing that Catalina had strict rules against sewage dumping within three miles of its shores.

After the propeller was freed, with some trepidation I turned on the engine for a test. It purred as if nothing had happened. I scrambled into the engine compartment expecting to see a flood of water coming through the damaged transmission...nothing. All was well.

"You are shivering! Get down below, take a warm shower and put on some dry clothes," Judy ordered.

Tomorrow we would tie up at another mooring in Avalon Harbor with lots of boats all around waiting for the show. I could see that this was going to be a long, long trip because we were having so much excitement already and the trip had barely started.

A Death at Sea

We were sailing south en route to San Diego. Suddenly, we heard a woman screaming over the radio on Channel 16.

"Help me...help me." She was crying incoherently and the voice was audible only intermittently. It was obvious that she was not accustomed to using the radio.

"Ma'am, you have to hold down the button on the mic to talk and release the button to listen." A male voice came on the radio. He repeated the instructions a few times.

"He's dead...he's dead, and I don't know what to do," the woman cried and screamed.

"Tell me what happened, Ma'am."

"He went to take a nap and never woke up," she replied.

"Anything happened before he took the nap? Did he eat or drink anything?"

"No, he was talking to a mechanic on the radio about a leaky exhaust pipe. He was told to wrap it with duct tape until we could get to the shop at the harbor. Then he decided to take a nap." The woman seemed to be recovering her composure somewhat. The conversation continued to arrange for bringing the boat to shore.

It was sobering to listen in on a tragedy striking so swiftly. We both thought that it was likely that the man had died of carbon monoxide poisoning.

On many small boats, the engine block is in close proximity to the bunk. A leaky exhaust pipe could easily create a dangerous level of the invisible, odorless, poisonous gas. It was something I had worried over during the renovation. I installed not only smoke alarms, but also carbon monoxide and propane alarms on Laelia.

Although we didn't know the boater who died, we felt a sense of loss and sadness. The fear and anguish in the woman's voice stayed in my mind for a long time. *Life is fragile and the sea is unforgiving.*

39

Departing the San Diego Harbor

The sailing magazine *Latitude 38* organized the annual Baja-Ha-Ha Rally to Mexico. "Ha-Ha" conveyed the laid-back and non-competitive nature of the rally. The rules allowed starting early or late and, if necessary, turning on the engines as much as desired.

We paid to join the Baja Ha-Ha Rally as a way of putting a little pressure on ourselves to untie the dock lines from our home marina and to begin the daunting journey to ports unknown. I also thought that it would be fun to join these other like-minded people on such an adventure.

There were 160 boats in the armada, all departing San Diego Harbor on the morning of 25 October 2004. I kept Laelia in the back of the fleet to avoid the heavy boat traffic. Starting at San Diego, the first leg of the rally would end at Turtle Bay (Bahia Tortuga), Mexico, the second leg at Bahia Santa Magdalena, and the final destination was Cabo San Lucas.

The Grand Pooba of the rally told us to fly our spinnakers at the starting line just outside the harbor. The idea was to have a colorful display of the entire fleet.

We were not set up to fly our spinnaker at the time, but we did have the red-and-white screecher up and ready. As luck would have it, soon after we had unfurled the screecher the *Latitude 38* photographer overflew us in a helicopter. Later, we were able to buy the digital photo from the magazine.

We sailed and motored three nights against a headwind blowing around 25 knots. Some of the boaters were whining bitterly on the radio that it was rough and horribly wet. The going was slow and uncomfortable, but we were managing. Actually, it was nothing compared with our shakedown trip north to San Francisco.

We enjoyed the trip from San Diego, despite the persistent swells and the strong contrary wind during parts of the passage. The temperature was warmer and the conditions not nearly as ferocious as on our shakedown trip north.

The sky was sparkling with stars until the full moon dominated. Standing watch at night was becoming more enjoyable. When we were far enough offshore to lose sight of the coast, we had stars overhead and the ocean lapping at the hull. There was absolutely nothing around except the wind and the waves. The boat was sturdy and braved the swells with only periodic groans that boats like to emit from their depths. Despite 160 boats in the rally, we saw only a few sailing past.

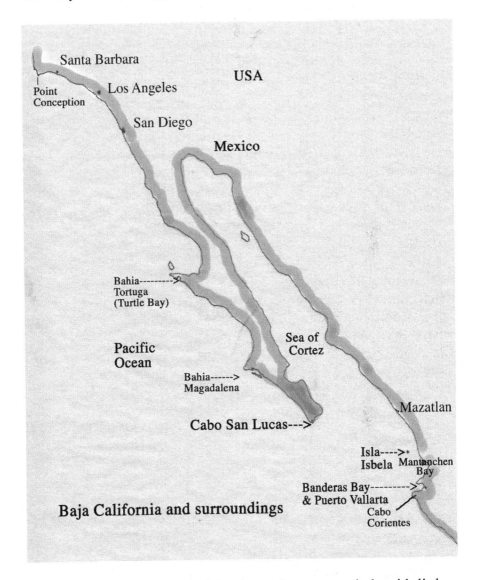

Baja California and surroundings

When all is well on a cruising boat, there are periods with little to do. I had time to set up a 50-foot tuna cord and a wire leader attached to a green-yellow-red artificial lure I had bought in San Diego. I had the tuna cord dragging behind the boat. A few hours later, there was a fish flopping on the surface. *We have a fish.* I brought in the line hand-over-hand. It was our first catch on this passage, a Dorado or Mahi Mahi.

To stop the fish from struggling, I poured a little beer on its gills. The alcohol acted as a general anesthetic and was absorbed quickly. The Dorado had a stunning green color pulsating in the fins when first caught, but all that vibrant liveliness faded suddenly when the fish died. There was a brief moment of sadness in me to see life ebb.

We saw three sea turtles swimming past the boat during this passage. I quickly hauled the fishing lures out of the water so there would be no chance of snagging a turtle. The same precaution had to be carried out when sea birds hovered over Laelia. These birds could see the lure in the water and could become hooked if they tried to dive for it. That would have been a serious problem. These birds are strong and would fight my efforts to remove the hook.

Besides, we didn't have much in the way of a freezer. In order not to waste what we caught, we would have to eat fish for three- or four days straight. As time went on, we fished less and less. With all our provisions on board, we didn't need to fish to survive, but I learned that we could sustain ourselves by fishing if necessary.

5. Passage to Mexico

Laelia at sea, sailing between San Diego (32 42.550 N, 117 14.103 W), 25 October 2004, and Cabo San Lucas (22 52.855 N, 109 54.652 W), 04 November 2004.

Medical Emergencies at Sea

It was the urgent tone in the voice late at night over the radio that prompted our extra attention. On Laelia, as with most vessels, the VHF radio is always turned on to Channel 16. VHF frequencies are for short-distance, line-of-sight communication at about fifteen to twenty miles. Channel 16 is for hailing and for emergency use. If the Coast Guard wanted to board Laelia for an inspection, we would hear them hailing us on that channel.

On that particular night, someone in the fleet was seriously ill and requiring immediate medical attention. Not much was revealed over the radio because we could hear the transmission from only one of the two vessels, Sea Gem, which was closer to us.

"This is Sea Gem, en route to Turtle Bay. Over."

There was only silence from the other vessel.

"...that's possible...you want to give me a little more info on the patient's condition? Sea Gem, Over."

We heard static.

"That's affirmative on the emergency evacuation...ETA about two hours to reach your location..." We heard Sea Gem's reply.

Silence.

"Diverting immediately...Sea Gem standing by 16..."

We knew the vessel Sea Gem, a large motor vessel in the rally fleet that could travel at high speed.

Next morning, we learned over the radio net that the patient had been transported ashore. Subsequently, his condition was stabilized at a clinic near Turtle Bay, and he was airlifted by helicopter to San Diego. No name or detail was mentioned on the air to protect the patient's privacy.

Only much later were we able to piece together through scuttlebutt what had happened. The patient had a preexisting gastric condition, probably an ulcer, which was further aggravated by seasickness. Internal bleeding from the ulcer had become life threatening. The story was sketchy, but it was sobering news to us. Had the boat been at sea far from help, the outcome could have been very different. It was a lesson not missed by many of us going to sea for the first time.

Several days later, we heard over Channel 16, in the early evening, an anxious woman's voice: "Any doctor in the Ha-Ha fleet, any doctor...this is sailing vessel Star Light, Star Light." The airway remained silent for several minutes.

"Any doctor in the fleet, any doctor...this is Star Light, Star Light," the voice repeated.

"Star Light, this is sailing vessel Voyager. We have a physician on board. Over."

"I have a question...I hope you can help. My right pupil is dilated. I am worried. Over."

"What are your other symptoms? You have any headache, double vision, or dizziness? Over."

"No...I feel okay. I know from first aid that a dilated pupil can be a symptom of brain injury. Over."

"You feel any nausea or have any memory loss? Over."

"No, I'm feeling pretty normal..."

"Did you bump your head, or do you feel any lumps on your head? Over."

"No..."

"Have you been seasick ...are you using scopolamine patches?"

"No, I am not seasick and I don't need the patches....Uh...wait. I did help someone else with putting on his patch, but I washed my hands afterwards. Over."

"Did you wash hands immediately afterwards? Over."

"Oh...I couldn't get to the head right away...I think that must be it...I must have touched my eye on the way... Over."

"Hopefully that's what happened. The scopolamine should wear off by morning. Over."

"Oh, thank you. I feel so much better. Thank you. Over."

"You are welcome. Good night. Voyager out."

"Star Light out." That was a happy ending.

Our friends Rick and Alice were in the same Medicine-at-Sea class with us a few months earlier. Rick recounted to a small group how he got hit just above his eye by the spinnaker pole at night during the passage.

"It was terrible," said Alice. "There was blood all over his face and it kept gushing out in spurts. All I could do was press a towel hard on that side of his face."

We were all suitably impressed.

"So what happened next?" someone asked

"The towel got all bloody, but the bleeding slowed to an ooze. I had to get out the suturing kit. The pre-threaded sutures were the best. I could never have threaded the needle. My hands were shaking and the boat was rolling and bumping...and the blood was making everything slippery and sticky."

"Did Rick scream when you sewed him up?"

"No, that went pretty well. I injected him first with lidocaine like we were taught in class."

"That was the only part that had a sting to it," Rick said.

"With Rick it was nothing like sewing up the pig's foot in class," Alice continued. "The pig's foot held still, but Rick kept squirming. The blood made the skin slippery and I couldn't see the cut too well. I poured saline straight from the bottle to wash the blood away so I could see. It was just over the eyebrow...I got five stitches in there."

Later, at the final party of the rally on land, Rick didn't win the worst-injury award. The stitches over his eyebrow were done so well, they hardly showed. It was not nearly as dramatic as the expanse of purple bruise on the large rump of the winner. I thought Alice should have won the prize for the most heroic performance. She put her knowledge to work in a trying situation.

Anchoring for the First Time

Laelia was now in Mexican waters on the Pacific side of Baja California. We were at sea day and night. There was no marina where we could take refuge. Two stops were planned for the rally fleet. The first was at Bahia Tortuga (Turtle Bay) about 350 miles south of San Diego. We arrived at the bay in early morning to navigate the harbor in daylight.

Judy and I had taken a class about anchoring and had watched the instructor going through the routine on his 36-footer. We had also watched the charter captain anchor a catamaran in the Caribbean. Our own shiny new anchor had never been dropped in the water except to test the windlass at the dock in the marina. I knew how the electrical controls worked for the windlass. Both of us knew the theory, but deploying an anchor for real was another matter.

The theory said nothing about the boat heaving in the waves or the stiff wind and swift currents. If we didn't set the anchor properly, the boat could drift away in the middle of the night or drag anchor when we were away from the boat. It would be a shame for Laelia to end up on a pile of rocks or on top of some other boat.

We needed to drop the anchor at a "good spot" and let out enough chain to give the rode enough scope. What that meant was that in order for the anchor to dig into the sea bottom securely, we must let out more length of chain than the depth of the water. The minimum scope had to be 3 to 1, meaning three times as much chain as the depth of the water. That way the boat, when being blown by the wind, would pull on the anchor with the chain parallel to the bottom of the sea instead of pulling the anchor up and away from the bottom. Of course, the more scope the better.

If we had the entire bay to ourselves, I could put out as much chain as I liked. It could be a scope of 10 to 1, but there were many other boats around. It was necessary to make sure there was enough "swinging room" so we wouldn't bump into other boats when the wind shifted.

The more chain that is let out, the more swinging room is needed. For that reason it is considered very bad manners to drop anchor too close to another anchored boat. Finding a good spot was not as easy as it sounded while we were circling around, trying not to collide with other boats. I had to pick a spot that was not too deep and not too close to another vessel, and then quickly calculate the scope according to the depth.

All of that needed to be done decisively, as the wind was gusting and the current pushing the boat in the wrong direction. I was on the bow picking the right moment to drop the anchor while Judy was at the helm maneuvering according to my hand signals.

"Have you dropped the anchor yet? Now we are too close to the blue ketch."

I could barely hear her. The wind was blowing and the engine was humming, plus the fact that my hearing was not the best.

"Go to the right." I also pointed to starboard, knowing that she couldn't hear me. When Laelia was clear of other vessels, I used hand signals for Judy to stop the boat and then I squeezed the remote to lower the anchor.

Once the anchor was dropped with enough chain, we set the anchor by backing the boat slowly under engine power to make sure the anchor was digging into the substrate. The finishing touch was to test the holding by backing at higher engine revolutions per minute (RPM) to make sure the holding was secure and the anchor was not dragging. This was always a tense moment when the anchorage was crowded or when the wind and the currents were rough. At Turtle Bay, Judy and I were anchoring for the first time. We had no choice. There was no dock for us to tie up to.

Laelia was securely anchored. *We did it. Whew!*

Turtle Bay

The village of Turtle Bay is not a metropolis, but it was our first landfall in a foreign port. After several days at sea, even a small village is a safe haven.

Looming over the beachfront was a pier built of heavy timber left over from better times. We saw other dinghies at the pier, so we decided that must be the best place to land. I plowed the dinghy into a mass of other dinks already tied to the pier and grabbed on to a rusted ladder to climb about twenty feet up, Tarzan style.

A bunch of local kids, around 10 or 12 years old, were scampering up and down that same ladder. They helped, whether or not help was wanted, to pull in the dinks and tie them up. Presumably they also looked after the dinks while everyone was ashore. Needless to say they expected to be compensated for their service. What would happen if I didn't pay them? Under the circumstances, common sense ruled: it was best to pay the dollar.

The pier had been built during more prosperous times and was, by then, patched together to keep it barely serviceable. The ladder was quite old with parts rusted away. The irregular metal ladder steps reminded me of a metal bear trap. The deck of the pier had wooden planks missing. We all learned quickly to look where we put our feet as we walked over the pier to the village.

We learned later that there had been a cannery here some years earlier that had gone out of business. Parts of a huge heat exchanger were rusting in the surf zone. Presumably they were left from the cannery. I never figured out how the village residents made their living, aside from the few tourists who showed up from time to time. We were all amazed to see not one, but at least two Internet Cafes in the village. Also, there seemed to be quite a few SUVs.

The rally organizers threw a no-host dinner at one of the restaurants. There were plenty of margaritas being served up from a big ice trough. Unfortunately, the restaurant had no way of coping with a few hundred people when it came to serving real food. After waiting more than an hour for food while drinking more and more margaritas, I went to investigate. It became very clear to me that the kitchen had no way of preparing anything listed on that menu, such as lobsters, steaks, and other mouthwatering items that many cruisers had ordered in their exuberance of having survived the first leg of the passage.

All the orders were in a pile on the kitchen counter untouched. The idea of serving food had been abandoned as the cooks sat dejectedly in the kitchen. They explained to me in Spanish that they could only do a simple combination dish that night, and I could see even that was done one tortilla at a time with a small 6-inch frying pan.

It dawned on me that if we wanted to eat anything at all, we'd better settle for whatever they were able to produce. I told them to not worry about the orders, just give us the "combination" dish.

As the plates were prepared, I personally carried the dishes to our table. Waiting tables was how I had supported myself for four years as an undergraduate. Without question, everyone in our party was so famished that anything would taste good to them. There were nine or ten of us. When we left, there were still lots of people from other boats drinking margaritas and waiting. Perhaps with enough margaritas, they might forget all about the food.

Rumor had it that the Grand Pooba, our glorious leader, had gone to a different and better restaurant. He had a good quiet meal without the company of several hundred starving diners drowning their sorrows in margaritas. *Hmmm...the fleet's unwashed masses have been betrayed. Is my paranoid mind reading too much into this?*

One of the really great things about being with the Baja Ha-Ha fleet was the camaraderie among the boaters. Help and advice were available from sailors with special skills or equipment. The mainsail halyard on Laelia had shredded. When Judy asked on the radio about a replacement halyard, we had three offers. One of them delivered the 110 feet of halyard to our boat and would not accept any form of payment.

In a similar spirit, we helped by giving another boat 15 gallons of diesel and 10 gallons of water. I gave our benefactor a bottle of Grand Marnier to say thanks for the halyard. Unfortunately, we never got back our only fresh water container.

Boats Passing in the Night

On the second leg of the trip, we had a very pleasant downwind sail all the way south into Bahia Santa Magdalena. It is a wild bay with little development, only a few fishing huts visible. Seawater was in different shades of green and blue depending on the depth. I sought the shallower green water to drop anchor.

After some circling, Laelia was anchored in 30 feet of water not far from the mangroves. I wanted us to be at the far fringes of the fleet in order to stay clear of other boats and to have plenty of swinging room.

There was a celebratory party planned by the rally on shore. To get ashore, we had to land the dink on the beach. There was incentive to go ashore because lobster dinners were available. Getting ashore seemed easy enough at high water, but the surf became a bit nasty at low tide.

We watched from a distance how the others were managing the landing. We saw one inflatable getting swamped by the swell as his outboard failed him. Another got stuck on a sandbar at low tide. A successful landing with even small swells required good timing. It involved gunning the outboard at full throttle just as one swell had passed and before the next swell rolled in. Once the dinghy was stopped as it hit the beach sand, everyone had to jump out and pull the dinghy to higher ground through the shifting sand as the next surf chased from behind. We watched a number of them being swamped and getting soggy, falling in wet sand. I imagined that it was not nearly as hilarious to the actual landing party.

I decided that we would ride to the beach in a "panga" piloted by local fisherman. These pangas, serving as water taxis, were heavy wooden boats powered by big outboards. It saved us from getting all drenched in seawater and covered with sand. I knew Judy was just as pleased as I to forego the beach landing exercise.

Once on shore, we waited in a queue for more than an hour before we got our plate of lobster and corn on the cob. It was tasty and we conversed with others while standing in the queue. Soon after we ate, it was getting late in the afternoon, and we decided to look for a panga to take us back to our boat before dark. There were still others in the queue when we left.

Later we heard some unhappy people on the VHF radio. Apparently, the kitchen ran out of lobsters and there was nowhere else to eat. Then the hungry people found out that the pangas were all gone. We never heard what happened to the people stranded on the beach.

The day after the party we got up at four in the morning to pull anchor, depart, and prepare for the five o'clock roll call on the VHF radio at sea. The Grand Pooba wanted assurance that all boats were accounted for and that the entire fleet had departed the anchorage.

By now we were getting the hang of talking on the radio. Perhaps I should say that Judy was getting quite good at it. She was now the Communications Officer on Laelia. There is definite etiquette in using the radio. On the rally, due to the short distance, the net was by VHF radio. The Grand Pooba, the net controller, began the radio net with a weather report. Various boats reported their GPS positions, injuries on board, and damaged boat gear, as well as bragging about the number of fish caught.

It was an uneventful sail with the longer and faster boats sailing ahead and the smaller boats trailing. Some boats sailed farther offshore, seeking stronger wind. As time went on, the fleet separated. For most of the day, we saw only a few other boats, although there were more than one hundred vessels in the fleet.

As we approached Cabo San Lucas at the tip of Baja California, the density of sailboats around us increased. The rally boats were all converging towards the same point for the landfall. We had a north wind coming from the stern and Laelia was sailing "wing-on-wing." Both the jib and mainsail were extended as much as possible, with the mainsail held securely in place by a preventer. (The preventer was a safety measure to prevent the boom from swinging across suddenly in an accidental jibe.)

Sailing with this configuration was not as fast as if we had sailed at a slight angle from the wind on a reach. All sailboats sail faster with a following wind on a reach, with the wind more to one side, but that would require jibing back and forth. With wing-on-wing, we kept the wind dead astern and saved having to jibe regularly. It saved a lot of physical labor. Our autopilot was steering well. We were making good enough speed.

All we had to do was to watch out for hazards. There were commercial cruise ships with all their bright deck lights on. It was impossible to see which way they were going, because the deck lights had obscured their navigation lights. On the plus side, these cruise ships were idling at very low speeds, waiting for daylight to approach the port. Apparently it was cheaper for cruise ships to spend the night at sea rather than paying harbor fees. It was not difficult to keep our distance from them.

As we were sailing dead downwind while other sailboats were jibing back and forth across our path, there was a chance of collision. On one occasion, a light-colored sailboat appeared out of the dark. It was quickly closing in on Laelia. I turned on both engines as a precaution. I could see the other boat very clearly by that time and knew that we were on a collision course. *What should I do?* I released the autopilot to manual and turned the wheel away from the other boat to avoid a collision. Soon after I turned, the other boat passed Laelia at about ten or fifteen feet. *That was a little too close!*

The most frightening part was that the other boat never made any attempt to avoid the near collision. I didn't see anyone on watch on the other vessel. It was fortunate that Laelia's sails were all secured. The jib flapped a little, but nothing slammed hard across and nothing broke. We were back to normal. My heart quit pounding like a drum, but my mouth was still dry.

It is not unusual for sailboats to approach very near each other in a tight yacht race. Racers often come within a few inches of a collision while rounding a mark. In a regatta, there is usually a full crew keeping the vessel under tight control. There are also observers and rescuers in the event of a serious collision. On the other hand, cruising boats at sea are usually heavier and less maneuverable, requiring greater separation.

In a collision at sea, there would have been no help. No one would even know we were missing until morning roll call on the radio. It would be days before anyone could find out what happened, if ever. Not keeping a watch is an unforgiveable sin and a violation of good seamanship.

6. The Sea of Cortez

Departing Cabo San Lucas (22 52.855 N, 109 54.652 W), 11 November 2004. Arriving at Marina El Cid, Mazatlan, Mexico (23 16.166 N, 106 27.845 W), 13 November 2004.

Crossing the Sea of Cortez

Judy and I enjoyed the magical light show at sea on our passage from Cabo San Lucas to Mazatlan. There was no wind and the sea state was kindly. The air was warm and sultry. On night watch we could see two trails of illumination stimulated by Laelia's twin hulls cutting through the water. There were occasional larger flashes produced by jellies or salps that had been ingesting lots of luminescent plankton or were capable of producing luminescence independently. It was the turbulence in the seawater that excited the bioluminescence.

The coruscating show reminded me of the bioluminescence from the "red-tide" that happens during summer months when algae blooms take place on the Pacific coast. Some of these microorganisms contain neurotoxins. The high concentration of toxins in filter feeders such as mussels and clams make them unsafe to eat during warm summer months.

We were running one engine at a time at a moderate RPM to conserve fuel. So there was one dazzling trail behind the catamaran and another trail of fainter intensity, because the propeller on that side was not churning. A few times I noticed that the engine RPM was going up and down a little. I was puzzled and hoped there was nothing wrong.

Several areas of the horizon showed a white glow in the sky. I checked the magnetic bearing of the direction where the glow originated. I didn't understand what caused the glow. After plotting the boat position on the chart and the bearing where the glow originated, it seemed that, in each case, the glow led to a town or city. *Ah...it's the reflection of city lights from the sky. It's the glow of civilization!*

Seasoned mariners would no doubt laugh at my naiveté, but this was my first time away from the coastline on my own boat. I never would have guessed that the glow of city lights was detectable from hundreds of miles at sea. I felt pretty good that I had learned something new. Also, it was surprisingly comforting to see signs of humanity, even from afar. While I was still shrouded in that satisfying glow, the shrill scream of the engine alarm startled me.

Oh, my Gawd! What's wrong now?

The engine RPM was at zero and the boat was gliding slowly to a halt. I turned the engine key off to stop the ear-piercing alarm and started the other engine without delay, so that Laelia could continue her progress.

I scrambled down to the errant engine compartment. Everything looked in order. There was no fire and the engine block felt to my hand about the right temperature. I knew without looking that there was enough diesel fuel in the tank.

"Wait… why is the fuel filter looking so murky?" I pointed the flashlight for a closer look.

"Yuck, it's full of gunk and maybe a little water too. Well, maybe that was the problem." I switched to the spare filter by turning a couple of valves.

I was very glad that I had asked the mechanic to install dual filters for each engine so that I could switch to a clean filter immediately without delay. I tried starting the engine again and it came to life as if nothing had happened. *Problem solved...engine doesn't work unless the filter allows enough fuel to flow through.* I made a mental note to change the dirty filter out in the morning and have it available on standby.

I understood in theory the dirty fuel problem from my readings. Apparently it is a common problem for diesel tanks to collect water and grow fungi and bacteria. *What kind of desperate organism would thrive on diesel fuel and a little moisture?* All that growth becomes a mass of brown-black slime. Normally, nothing happens while the water-saturated slime settles at the bottom of the fuel tank. So the engine starts fine and the boat has power. Disaster only strikes when the skipper needs his engine not to fail. It can be during a sudden storm or as the boat is encountering rough surf towards a pile of rocks. The heavy wave action stirs up the sludge in the fuel tank. There is no time to install a new filter. The boat can meet its demise for want of a clean filter.

Having dual filters seemed like a good plan. Of course it would be even better to have a clean fuel tank. I did drain and clean the fuel tank several times before leaving California. Apparently these microorganisms thrive on a diet of diesel even better at tropical temperatures. With that bit of insight, I started putting bioactive inhibitors to poison the little buggers in the fuel tank with every fill-up. There was plenty to learn at every turn.

I slept a few hours while Judy was on watch. When it was my shift again it was almost dawn. We were getting close to our destination, but I didn't know the harbor entrance to Mazatlan. It was clearly shown on the electronic chart, but we had learned that charts for this part of the world were not always accurate and could be off by some miles. Electronic charts, with data copied from the original paper charts, were no more accurate than their paper counterparts. Our GPS unit gave very accurate coordinates for Laelia's position on earth, but I couldn't be sure of the location of the harbor. I wanted to see that harbor with my own eyes before closing in to shore.

There was considerable morning mist, and some lingering fog was obscuring the horizon. I could see faintly a blinking white light in the direction we were heading. It could be the navigation aid for the harbor entrance. We were gaining on the light. Soon we were close enough to study it with binoculars. The visibility was still poor. Something about that light didn't seem right.

It took a little time before it suddenly dawned on me that the white strobe light was on the mast of a sailboat. It gave me a cold sweat thinking that I had made such a dangerous error. At least I had realized my mistake before Laelia was in serious jeopardy. The fact that the boat in front was flashing a non-standard navigation light, in serious violation, was of little consolation. We were at sea depending on our wits to survive. Mistaking a moving light for a harbor beacon was an error that could lead us into fatal danger. Another lesson learned.

Eventually we did find what could be the harbor entrance. It had a dredge blocking the opening. That helped with the identification, because the guidebook had mentioned the dredge as a possible obstacle. Somebody on the dredge was waving. By now the visibility was better. We went as close to the entrance as we dared to take a peek.

At that moment, a motorboat roared out of the entrance, but it was a shallow-draft boat that could squeeze by easily in a narrow channel. The dredge in the middle of the entrance left little room for our catamaran. We waited until the dredge was moved to the side and tied up. As we entered the channel with only a couple of feet of clearance from the dredge, I was glad we had waited. By that time there was a swift current in the channel. I had both engines running in order to have full control of the catamaran. We tied up to a dock at the El Cid Hotel Marina.

Life in Mazatlan

That evening, we decided to celebrate with something better than my cooking. We walked through the grand hotel lobby where there were uniformed concierges to help us. They explained to us the difference between a "pulmonia" and a real taxi. A pulmonia was a small three-wheeled, motorized vehicle about the size of a golf cart with the driver in front. It was just about right for two passengers at a fraction the cost of a taxi. Of course the passengers were exposed to the tropical night air. The taxi drivers considered these transports a scab competition and warned that passengers would catch pneumonia from the exposure, hence the nickname "pulmonia."

"Wow, these little run-abouts are the cat's meow," I said.

"Well, we'll see. I am not that convinced," Judy countered.

The important thing was to negotiate the fare before settling one's bottom inside the pulmonia. It was necessary to haggle. That was part of the charm of being immersed in a foreign culture.

For people who really wanted to save money, the Mazatlan municipal bus was the best option. It was cheap and the bus would stop anywhere along its route to pick up a passenger if a wayward hand would simply waft in the air.

We took a pulmonia to a little palapa and ate tasty shrimp and chicken fajita. The price was a fraction of what we might have paid in California. True, the restaurant was literally "a hole in the wall" with very little space for a few rickety tables.

They performed some kind of magic to transform shrimp and chicken wrapped in tortilla into a heavenly feast. I was enjoying the food, but Judy seemed a little dubious.

I said, "Well...there's no tablecloth...but it's the food that counts...right? This food is scrumptious." I really liked the place. That was our first meal in Mazatlan.

"I think we better take the taxi back. The air is much cooler in the dark," Judy said.

"Well, it didn't cool off all that much, did it?"

"It's dark now. There aren't many people around the water front."

"Ok, I suppose taxi drivers have to make a living somehow," I said, not insisting on having my way. We had a good dinner and there was no point getting into an argument over nothing. Besides, she did ride along in the pulmonia earlier. She was probably more worried about safety than the cool air. It was an easy compromise to keep the peace.

Life for us in Mazatlan was agreeable and leisurely, a time for recuperation from our bad beach landing in Cabo. Unlike Cabo San Lucas where there was a glaring divide between the super wealthy of the marina district and the rest of the town, Mazatlan was more homogeneous. It was still distressing to see women selling trinkets with their children in tow, a form of glorified begging. Yet, Mazatlan appeared to be a prosperous town. There were many shops full of merchandise and plenty of restaurants.

We engaged a local canvas maker to sew a mosquito net for the boat. It was very good workmanship at a reasonable price.

The Mazatlan marathon was a big event in town. There were runners as well as people who came to watch others sweat and suffer in the hot sun. The vendors of course loved the event as they sold their wares. We loved it because of the yummy brunch put on by all the restaurants for hungry runners and the rest of us sedentary spectators.

Life was good in Mazatlan and the boat kept me busy. The inverter/battery-charger on Laelia stopped charging not long after our arrival. After troubleshooting to no avail, I asked for help on the morning radio net. It was a local net on the VHF radio, providing the weather report and whatever information local cruisers sought.

One of the long-time cruisers was available to help with the battery charger. The problem turned out to be loose nuts in the electrical system. Warmer temperatures in the tropics and repeated heating and cooling cycles had loosened the nuts at the battery terminals. Apparently this was a common problem for boats freshly arriving from temperate climes.

Our outboard that had tumbled and drowned in the surf at Cabo San Lucas was resuscitated here. The outboard mechanic told me that he recovered at least a whole liter of sand from the innards of the outboard engine.

Our neighbors on the dock were interesting people. One couple lived on a 50-foot cement sailboat. It was a big boat with plenty of comfortable accommodations. The most amazing part of the amenities was a big hot tub on the foredeck. Consequently, the boat was heavy and probably slow unless the wind picked up. They didn't take the boat out very much and seemed quite content to use it as their retirement home. They introduced us to the eateries in the street stalls of Mazatlan. Good food at rock-bottom prices where most locals can afford to eat. I loved the food there.

Another neighbor, an avid fisherman, gave us fresh fish all cleaned, filleted, and wrapped. A couple from Canada on a well-equipped traditional vessel was all ready for ocean cruising; except that the skipper was waiting to get his cardiac operation from the Canadian Health Service. Apparently there was a waiting list for that particular procedure in Canada.

He volunteered as the net controller for the local radio net. To get better reception, he and his wife would take the boat out for a morning sail away from the interfering masts in the marina. We learned from them that there was a "Puddle-Jump" group in Puerto Vallarta preparing to cross the Pacific Ocean.

We could have stayed in Mazatlan indefinitely, and many did, but the knowledge of the Puddle Jump group in Puerto Vallarta kept tugging at me. We studied local weather and followed the weather report for the Sea-of-Cortez broadcast from Oxnard, California, by Don Anderson. He had the station call sign of "Summer Passage," which was the name of his boat.

Anderson's story would be a book in its own right. He had cruised throughout this area and was an avid ham radio buff. His weather reports covered not only the general weather pattern for the Gulf of California, but also the microclimate for particular bays and harbors in California and throughout Mexico. He could do it because he had personally sailed these waters and knew the specific local variations under general weather conditions. We benefitted from his weather reports not only in Mexico, but also much later in some of the more treacherous waters of the Pacific.

Matanchen Bay

We didn't make detailed plans on when to arrive and depart any particular location, but we knew we needed to heed the cyclone (hurricane) season. Visa restrictions often set the duration we were allowed to stay in any particular country. I had met one skipper who made detailed schedules down to the exact date for each port.

"Why do you make such detailed plans?" I had asked.

"Well, that way we won't overstay at one place then short change other ports." It was important to him not to miss any of the places on his list.

We were less disciplined and would leave early if it felt right, or stay longer if there were more interesting things to do. It's a big world with more places than we can ever visit in a lifetime. We didn't keep a list, but did plan to cruise in Mexican waters.

Despite the comfortable life in Mazatlan, it was time to depart. We figured that, if the group at Puerto Vallarta called the great Pacific Ocean a "puddle," they no doubt knew a lot more than we did. Perhaps we could learn something if we joined them. The idea of crossing the Pacific was intriguing. We left for Puerto Vallarta, about one hundred nautical miles (NM) south of Mazatlan, to check out the "Puddle Jump" group.

En route we had hoped to stop at a large rock called Isla Isabel. The main attraction was the roosting bird life at this isolated rock. The guidebook didn't inspire much confidence regarding the anchorage. Not only was it described as "rocky and deep" with space for only two vessels, but there were hazards. One was the mast of a sunken boat sticking out of the water that could hole an unsuspecting vessel.

Upon arrival, we saw that there were already two boats crowded in at the rock. My first reaction was: *How could anyone anchor so close to a huge rock?*

It was high water at flood tide. We couldn't see any mast poking through the surface. I was reluctant to drop anchor around this place. It would be very inconvenient to snag Laelia's anchor on some steel shroud belonging to the sunken vessel. It would be like getting grabbed by a ghost reaching out from the deep. We circled around a couple of times, but didn't find any shallower water where we could drop anchor.

"I don't like this anchorage," I said. "It's still early in the day. We can look for some other place on the coast."

We checked the guidebook and the chart to conjure up a Plan B for the night. There was Matanchen Bay within striking distance.

Along the way we saw fish jumping, schools of dolphins, and giant flocks of pelicans diving and feeding. It must be a very rich body of water for sea life. The frenzy we saw over the water was no doubt matched by the pandemonium below the surface. After all, the Sea of Cortez is known for its biodiversity, in contrast to the almost desert-like rugged landmass of Baja California. There is richness in the harsh beauty of the Baja terrain (*A Forgotten Peninsula* by Joseph W. Krutch). For the incredible underwater sea life during an earlier time, *The Log from the Sea of Cortez* by John Steinbeck is still current and memorable.

We practiced coastal navigation as Laelia sailed along the shore and we identified Piedra Blanca de Tierra as well as the lighthouse at Punta Camarones.

"We are learning Spanish," I said to myself.

The bay is huge, with enough space to accommodate more than a hundred anchored boats. Yet, Laelia was the only vessel there. This circumstance gave me a puzzled feeling and a gnawing doubt.

"Where is everybody?" I asked, "What do they know that we don't know?"

There wasn't any tsunami warning this morning. Nothing appears to be amiss on the beach. Perhaps this is not the season for boats to come here?

Laelia was securely anchored in muddy substrate. Our trusty

little catamaran was the only vessel in this big bay. We could see some palapas on the beach.

No doubt there are restaurants among them?

We lowered the dinghy into the water and put on our lifejackets to make the beach landing. The shacks on the beach were indeed restaurants, but no one was there. None were open for business, because there were no customers.

What a disappointment! No food.

We did find a few residents living in one small lean-to. They indicated that we could leave the dinghy on the beach and pointed to the direction of the little town of San Blas.

It was a short walk. We could tell immediately that this was a very poor little community. Even the church was in dire need of repair. Mexicans in general are very devout and would repair the church before their own homes.

We looked for the Port Captain in order to check in. At that time, Mexican law required all cruising boats to check in at every port in Mexico. Often the port captains would try to extort extra money from passing boats.

There was a rumor that an expatriate and the Port Captain were squeezing money from cruisers. I had no information on whether that was true or not. Perhaps that was the reason we were the only boat in the huge, magnificent bay.

The guidebook had mentioned a tour into the tropical jungle on local pangas. We managed to find a taxi driver who knew where the pangas were docked. From there we rode a heavy wooden panga powered by big outboards. The driver went at high speed through a twisting waterway in the jungle.

The waterway was not more than a narrow creek at many sections, with occasional pangas approaching head on from the opposite direction...also at high speed. The approaching pangas were not always visible around blind turns. The roar of an approaching outboard was drowned out by our own ear-splitting engine noise. A collision would have been spectacular, probably with no survivors. All I could do was to hold on, sit tight, and try to focus on the scenery while the jungle vegetation flashed by.

At the end of the ride was a gift shop and a restaurant built over a large pool of fresh water. There was a small waterfall surrounded by tropical vegetation. A few diners were swimming in water that was known to harbor crocodiles.

The waiter bragged, "I know every croc that lives in these parts."

There was not the faintest concern with regard to safety or liability. I thought someone should send a few dozen legal beagles to shake things up a little.

We ate our lunch, but didn't see any crocodile begging for food. No tourist got snatched and devoured. So it was kind of a dull trip, but we were in a real tropical jungle.

Puerto Vallarta

How much do I have to drink to become an alcoholic?

The marina at Nuevo Vallarta was in the middle of an all-inclusive, luxury resort hotel on the outskirts of town. We could join the complimentary welcoming parties every week and enjoy their happy hour each afternoon. The two-for-one drinks were cheap and very potent.

As a result I was drinking, in a few months, more than in all my previous sixty-one years combined. Bars and restaurants at the resort didn't accept cash. All I needed to do was sign the bill.

Within the resort, there were condominiums, a small zoo with a large tiger, several restaurants, multiple bars, entertainment, shops, massage therapy, beauty parlors, several pools, boat rental, and a beach bar on the sand. Vacationers could come to enjoy a relaxing vacation in or out of the sun without ever seeing Mexico. It was a fantasy world, completely insulated from the harsh realities of everyday life in this country.

Judy's cousin came to visit early in our stay in Mexico. In retrospect, we should have waited till we learned more about the country before inviting visitors. Life in Mexico is harsh and public safety in general is not a top priority.

We took a water taxi from the marina to the Puerto Vallarta waterfront. Upon arrival, we realized that there was no provision for the boat to tie up at a dock. Passengers were expected to leap onto a slippery concrete platform while the boat was heaving three or four feet up and down in the surge. Falling in the water would certainly mean being crushed by the heaving boat against the concrete pillars.

Granted, there was more surge than usual. There were about

twenty passengers, mostly locals in the water taxi. When the operator couldn't urge any passenger to make the death-defying leap, he decided that he would make a beach landing instead, not far from the dock. He had his crew throw a stern anchor as he approached the beach full of swimmers. He nudged the bow against the sloping sand and kept the propellers turning. He told everyone to disembark quickly while he held the boat steady against the surf.

As the passengers rushed to get out of the boat in a mad scramble, Judy's cousin fell. Luckily she didn't hit her head. We didn't discover till much later that it was a very hard fall and she had sustained a huge bruise on her side.

To add to the indignities, we discovered that we were jumping into deep water. The bow was touching the sand, but the exit at mid-ship was in water above our knees. For the next few hours we were walking around in soggy shoes full of sticky salt and sand… squish, squish, squash. There was no sense of responsibility for protecting passengers from harm and injury, much less concern for their comfort.

Even on paid public conveyances, we were on our own with no assurance of safety. In Puerto Vallarta, the bus drivers appeared to have a different mindset than those in Mazatlan. Here they were engaged in speeding, racing, and yelling obscenities at others as they drove.

Much later, Judy, while disembarking a bus, was almost run over and killed by the bus. Four of us were on our way to an anchorage to visit another cruiser. It was a bumpy ride for what seemed like an eternity. Upon arrival, just as Judy was stepping off, the driver suddenly moved the bus a few feet. Judy fell as she stepped off the moving bus and was partially under it. The driver started to engage the gears again to drive away. We all yelled for him to stop and I pounded on the side of the bus.

In the meantime, Judy realized her predicament and was doing a quick scramble and roll from under the bus, away from the big tires. The bus departed, tires rumbling, within a few inches of Judy. She was rather scraped up and had grains of sand ground into her palm, but did not sustain any life-threatening injury.

We invited our kids during their Christmas holiday. Originally, we planned for them to stay with us on Laelia. After all it was a catamaran with four double staterooms plus two single V-berths. In real estate parlance: "It sleeps ten."

As the time of their visit approached, Judy and I reassessed our plan. We realized that living on the boat requires considerable behavioral alteration. Life on a small boat is a very frugal existence. Not only is electricity rationed, so is water. Of course, while we were at the dock in a marina, electricity and water were not in short supply, but there was definitely a limitation with regard to the holding tank volume. Guests would have to flush sparingly as well as using the head on shore whenever possible.

We wanted the kids to have a fun time while visiting. They all worked hard and this was their once-a-year vacation. All those limitations to live on a boat would have been unpleasant. Consequently, we were very receptive when we heard on the morning radio net that a cruising couple would like to rent out their resort condominium in the marina at a reasonable price during the holidays. It was a perfect solution.

The visit went well. *What could go wrong living in lavishness?* There was plenty of food in different restaurants every day. For fun, slithering inside a giant dragon-shaped water slide was thrilling. When it was hot, sipping drinks at the beach after a swim in the surf was easy.

We also went on a snorkeling trip and a session at the canopy tour on zip-lines to kick up the adrenalin. I checked the zip-line setup at the canopy tour and was pleased by the amount of serious safety considerations. The harness, the safety precautions, and the well-trained guides were all very impressive. Of course a fall from the treetop would have been fatal.

The marina is at the mouth of a tidal river. We got to know Charlie, a permanent resident, by his reputation. Often in the morning, there was an alarm passed from boat to boat by voice that Charlie was on the move. Charlie was a large crocodile. I didn't see him until we took a tour up river. I thought crocs would avoid the noisy motorboat, but instead Charlie approached the tour boat for a photo-op.

I heard later that the tour operator was banned from the marina. He was accused of feeding Charlie raw chicken to attract the croc and enhance his tour business. Training the croc to associate humans with food was a dangerous practice. It seemed counterproductive to train a hungry croc to lurk in the marina.

Life at the resort marina was pleasant. From sunrise to sunset, the days slipped by quickly and painlessly. Life could go on like this indefinitely...in kind of a purposeless stasis. Many expatriate cruisers stayed in Mexico for decades. That definitely was not our plan. Although not yet clearly enunciated, our goal was not to let our lives languish.

7. Planning for the Unknown

Paradise Village Marina, Nuevo Vallarta, Mexico (20 41.722 N, 105 17.612 W), 08 December 2004 to 05 April 2005.

Cruise Preparation

There is a Chinese saying: "The journey of a thousand miles begins with just one step." That is easier said than done because the first step in our journey was preparation...the most difficult step. How to prepare for the unknown? What do we need for a long ocean passage on a small sailboat aside from food, water, and fuel?

We had an adequate amount of medical supplies on board for illnesses and emergencies. Boxes of tools and boat parts were stored on board during Laelia's renovation. We even had a "sea-anchor" for deployment in the event of a catastrophic storm. There seemed to be a thousand more things to worry over. "Expect the unexpected" seemed to be the way of life on a boat.

The first leg of the journey was to Pacific islands inhabited by friendly humans, although they speak French, but to me it felt more like a one-way ride to the Orion Constellation.

Do they have peanut butter out there?

One cruiser we met had told us that her greatest fear was of running out of toilet paper at sea. To carry enough, she would flatten rolls of it to maximize storage space on board.

The manager at our marina, Paradise Village, organized a planning group and gave us ideas on how we could produce an information handbook entitled *Puddle Jump-2005*. To divide up the labor, each of us would contribute a section.

"I don't know anything about ocean cruising. How can I write about things I don't know?" I thought that sounded pretty sensible.

"What better way to learn something than by writing about it?" the marina manager replied.

I decided to do navigation charts. It was the only job left; no one else wanted to do it. I didn't have any nautical charts except the few I had used for the passage from California to Mexico. I had no idea how to select charts, but I supposed learning new things was something I could do.

I looked up Jimmy Cornell's *World Cruising Guide* and old handbooks from past years. The difficulty was in not knowing where exactly we were going, although, for the handbook, we only needed charts to include New Zealand. I made a list of the major destinations in the South Pacific and thought that New Zealand was an appropriate goal. Although the idea of a circumnavigation began to emerge, I didn't want to make the goal too grandiose.

Then I had to decide on chart scales. We would need a few large-scale charts to give an overall perspective and more detailed charts for individual harbors and ports of call. If we used too many detailed small-scale charts, the cost would be too great. So I had to compromise and make use of intermediate-scaled charts.

The photocopying shop in town would only accept charts that could be legally copied. I borrowed some charts from the Puerto Vallarta Yacht Club. We also borrowed charts from individual cruisers. The person who had the most original charts, not surprisingly, was very protective of them. I listed the ones we needed and had him accompany us to make the copies. He didn't want his charts ever to be out of his sight. We copied a set of charts for everyone who had paid in advance.

All went well, except for one skipper who didn't want to join the group and went sailing while the rest of us toiled to produce the handbook. A day after we had distributed all the copies, he arrived back and demanded a set of the charts. I was perfectly comfortable telling him that he was too late. He made a lot of noise yelling, but I ignored him.

Somehow he discovered the sources of the original charts. Like a bully, he went and harassed our benefactor. Unfortunately, the owner of the charts who helped us the most was unable to withstand the torment. He wanted me to stop the harassment. Regrettably, I had no easy way to do that. Bullies are good at picking on those who are particularly vulnerable. He had found the weak link.

The owner of the original charts was afraid to offend people. He had the idea that sailors would need help sooner or later and that offending others would ultimately lead to bad karma, I hated to appease a bully, but I thought it necessary for the sake of the person who had been helpful to me. While I made an extra set of charts from my own copy, I fervently hoped that there is such a thing as karma.

We heard months later that the bully's vessel never left that year for the Puddle Jump. Apparently, he emotionally abused his partner/crew to the point that she left him and flew home. Then, the bully had a heart attack.

Perhaps there is such a thing as karma after all.

To Wait or Not to Wait

In America, these devastating winds are called hurricanes. In Southeast Asia, they are called typhoons, and the same savage winds are called cyclones in the Southern Hemisphere. It was still the cyclone season in March for the South Pacific islands, but Puddle-Jump fever was already running high on the docks. If Judy and I were really serious about crossing the Pacific that year, we needed to make some decisions soon.

At the marina in Nuevo Vallarta, we heard rumors of discussion among more experienced sailors about this year's crop of Puddle Jumpers. I got the impression that they didn't think Judy and I were capable of such an undertaking. I knew we were green, but still I didn't like the idea that we might be judged "not capable."

One evening, I was conversing with one of the "senior" sailors.

"Do you think we are ready for the Puddle Jump this year?" I asked bluntly.

"Well, I don't think so," he replied.

"Ok, I appreciate your honesty, but why do you say that?"

He seemed distressed by my persistence as he replied, "You don't seem to show any signs of getting ready for such a trip."

"Thank you for telling me," I replied. "I'll have to do some serious thinking on that." *I thought we had been preparing.*

We had renovated the boat quite thoroughly at considerable labor and expense, although the preparation was not necessarily apparent to the casual observer. Much of the work was done while we were still in California.

Do we really want to venture out this season? Are we ready to begin a journey to places we don't know? What if we stay in Mexico one or more years, then depart later?

To wait or not to wait, that is the question!

What we lacked was experience in open-water sailing and the practical art of anchoring. We had taken Power Squadron classes in engine maintenance, weather forecasting, seamanship, and marine electronics. Both of us had attended a West Marine-sponsored Medicine at Sea class and a hands-on emergency medicine course for sailors. We could give shots, splint broken limbs, and sew up lacerations. We even had bags of sterile IV fluid on board in the event of a serious medical emergency.

We were conscious of one glaring weakness in our ability to anchor Laelia. This was important because there are few marinas in the South Pacific and we would need to anchor out frequently. We knew all about the theory. We had taken a class in anchoring in Santa Cruz, but had no hands-on experience. Our awkwardness in dealing with the anchor during the Ha-Ha Rally made it clear that we needed more actual practice.

So we took Laelia for a short sail to anchor out overnight at the La Cruz anchorage, not far from our marina. We found a spot and dropped the hook. After we had let out some chain, we realized that the boat would swing onto some rocks in the event of a wind shift. No problem, we could just retrieve the anchor and try again.

Judy was at the helm maneuvering the boat according to my hand signals, which we had agreed upon. I stayed by the windlass on the foredeck with the control switch. The windlass was a powerful 1.5-KW electric motor that turned a gypsy wheel. As the gypsy turned one way or the other, the anchor chain, draped over the wheel, was hoisted up or dropped down into the sea.

All of a sudden, as we neared the end of cranking up the anchor, I saw a section of the chain slip off the gypsy. My first impulse was to grab the chain to stop it from getting away, but I checked myself. Perhaps it was the image of mangled fingers and a bloody deck that stopped my impulsive act.

I watched the chain, now no longer constrained by the gypsy wheel, rushing into the water, link after link. The weight of the chain already in the water was pulling the rest of it along. I listened to the rattling as the chain rubbed against the boat. It sounded like a train going by. There was no way to stop all two hundred feet of chain from rattling until the last link settled on the seabed.

That was exciting, but not terribly encouraging.

I didn't lose the chain completely because a nylon backup line was tied to the last link...that was something I had learned from my readings about securing the "bitter end." I was able to retrieve the end of the chain by pulling on the nylon line.

We moved the boat to a better spot and re-anchored. That night, with no more incidents, I spent a good amount of time thinking about the runaway anchor. The chain had jumped off the gypsy because, as the retrieved chain piled up high under the gypsy wheel, there wasn't enough weight hanging down on the wheel to keep the chain engaged.

There was scant space under the gypsy wheel because the boat builder mounted the windlass below deck level, for purely cosmetic reasons, leaving little room for the chain to mound up under the gypsy.

Back at the marina, we made major changes to Laelia's anchoring system by raising the windlass higher. It involved a lot of machine work, but was necessary to make anchoring work better. This was an important modification to the boat. The deck was no longer streamlined, with the windlass sitting exposed at deck level, but the anchoring system would function better and more safely.

A couple among the "senior sailor" group asked us to take them on a day sail because they were interested in catamarans. At least that was their excuse. After a lackluster sail on a calm day, they told us that we were indeed rather green, but would be able to learn on the job. They thought that Judy and I could be safe on the high seas, though we still had a lot to learn. It was good getting a positive nod from friends who cared although it was not an unconditional endorsement.

We had to decide. I sorted in my mind and discussed with Judy all the pros and cons of jumping off that immediate season.

1. We had already weathered a serious storm on our shakedown

cruise. We could deal with the high seas in rough weather.

2. Anchoring could be practiced on the run. It was important that we had remedied the mechanical problems of Laelia's anchoring system.

3. Waiting another year or two would only deplete our bank account more. We would be older, with possibly more medical issues, as we waited. The boat would also be aging and needing additional maintenance. Except for experience, we were as ready as we would ever be.

4. Hanging around the marina had its downside. Life was easy, with too much drinking and eating. It wasn't making us more fit for the long journey. It was jumping off that season or, most likely, never.

Perhaps it is best to strike while the boat and crew are still holding together.

8. The Pacific Passage

Departed Nuevo Vallarta, Mexico (20 41.702 N, 105 17.602 W), 05 April 2004. Arrived at the equator (00 00.000 N, 132 05.070 W) at 1400 UTC, 21 April 2005.

Taking the Plunge
On April 5, 2005, we jumped off on a passage of 2,800 nautical miles (NM) to begin the journey of a lifetime. If all went well, we expected to make landfall in French Polynesia in twenty plus days. Except for a few islands near the Mexican coast, there would be no refuge in bad weather and no help in thousands of ocean miles. The two of us would be alone on our own.

There was no fanfare at Laelia's departure from the marina at 0920 in the morning. The wind was light in Banderas Bay as we departed. The shoreline receded gradually as we sailed westerly, and in a few hours the sunset brought darkness and total isolation.

Laelia didn't have sufficient diesel fuel for the entire passage. So it was necessary to use the engines only for charging the battery, for when the wind was light, or for entering harbors. While we ran the engine, it was my usual practice to also power the reverse-osmosis water-maker to replenish our fresh water supply.

It was important to be alert to the levels of water, electricity, and fuel. Life on board was necessarily frugal with every resource. In order to ration electricity at night, Judy would often wear an LED headlamp if she wanted to read after dark. The radar, GPS, and the navigation lights had priority on the electricity.

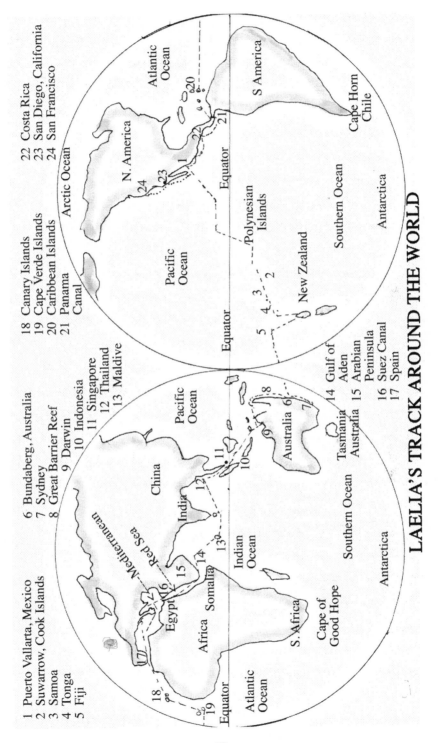

LAELIA'S TRACK AROUND THE WORLD

1 Puerto Vallarta, Mexico
2 Suwarrow, Cook Islands
3 Samoa
4 Tonga
5 Fiji

6 Bundaberg, Australia
7 Sydney
8 Great Barrier Reef
9 Darwin
10 Indonesia
11 Singapore
12 Thailand
13 Maldive

14 Gulf of Aden
15 Arabian Peninsula
16 Suez Canal
17 Spain

18 Canary Islands
19 Cape Verde Islands
20 Caribbean Islands
21 Panama Canal

22 Costa Rica
23 San Diego, California
24 San Francisco

As soon as Laelia cleared Cabo Corientes, our plan was to sail generally southwest. At some point, we expected to pick up the NE trade wind to gain ground westward before attempting to cross the equator. It was advantageous to stay in the Northern Hemisphere for as long as convenient, because the trades in the north are usually stronger than those in the Southern Hemisphere.

During the passage, we were not out of touch with the world. It was possible to send a short text by email via the single-side-band (SSB) radio (marine band or HAM radio). We could also talk to other boats on the informal radio net. The net operated every day at a prearranged time and radio frequency. The net controller would begin by checking for a clear frequency and asking for priority traffic or emergency messages. After that, various boats would call in to report their positions and local weather conditions.

When it was Laelia's turn, Judy would say, "This is Laelia with Howard and Judy on board at latitude 18 degrees and 42 minutes north, longitude 108 degrees and 09 minutes west. We have NE wind at 10 knots, waves at 4 feet with a period of 10 seconds. Cloud cover 20%. All is well on board."

After the radio net, I would make a general inspection of Laelia's condition. One morning I found a stainless bolt on the deck.

Where is that bolt from?

Based on its location, it must have fallen from the mast. It was the type of bolt used to hold the mast track in place. The mainsail slides up and down on the track and exerts a tremendous force when the wind whips through the rigging. It could be a serious problem if I found any more bolts like that.

It was also part of my chore to dispose of the carcasses of flying fish (*Exocoetidae*) and dried squid from the deck. The Pacific was teeming with flying fish. They were around six or seven inches in length with the juveniles as little as one inch in length, all with elongated pectoral fins. From a distance, the smaller fish in the air looked like dragonflies, but close up, they really were fish with wing-like fins.

They could "fly" considerable distances by springing out of the water and gliding as far as fifty feet or more at a height of seven or eight feet. Some even made zigzag patterns as they traversed the distance. Others would glide and then hit the water before taking off again, like a pebble skipping on water. Usually they were in large formations in the air. Laelia crashing through the water probably generated pressure waves that appeared to them like a large hungry predator. The poor critters took to the air to escape. Alas, they landed on deck and died.

Judy at the mic on a radio net

We caught a fish by trolling a 50-foot cord with an artificial lure on a steel leader. The fish had the brightest canary yellow fins, bluest dorsal colorations, and silvery white ventral scales. I made a sincere apology to the beautiful fish, a young yellow-fin tuna, before I turned it into four large steaks. We wrapped the tuna in foil with seafood spices, garlic, sliced onions, cooking oil, and juice from several miniature Mexican limes. It went well with baked potatoes. We had fish steak for dinner on one night followed by fish tacos for lunch the next day.

Our biggest concerns were ships. We felt safer away from the coast, far from shore in deep water, with no rocks and no shipping traffic. One night while on watch, I saw a single ship all lit up and not moving. It appeared to be the mother ship of a fishing fleet. I was not successful in contacting them by radio.

An Experiment
What would happen if I fell overboard?

It was just an idle thought on a slow day. The wind was light and the sun was beating down unmercifully. The air was humid and everything was sticky to the touch. The sea was smooth, without a ripple. The day's boat chores were already completed.

It would feel good to go for a swim in the ocean. I need a bath anyway. Laelia was drifting along sedately at about two or three knots. At this speed it seemed safe enough to swim along. The idea definitely had appeal. I stripped and soaped myself.

"I don't like the idea of you leaving the boat," Judy said.

"I am not leaving. Where can I go anyway? There is nothing around except water for hundreds of miles."

That was the wrong answer. It wouldn't be good to get her too upset over this. There had been horror stories of an entire crew jumping in the ocean for a swim, but none being able to reach high enough to get back on board. There had also been reports of a boat sailing away with a sudden gust of wind, leaving the crew stranded in mid-ocean. None of that would be the problem here, because Laelia had steps on the stern all the way to the water surface for me to climb back on board. Despite Judy's objection to the plan, I was sure she would maneuver the boat to rescue me if it came to that.

"Well, I'm going to wear a tether. And just to be sure, I'll add a loop of rope on the stern as a backup for climbing back on." Judy was still dubious about all that, but relented. I went into the water.

Wow, two knots is pretty fast!

I was swimming to keep up with the boat, but even at such a slow boat speed, I was getting dragged now and then. *The silly boat must have speeded up.* Climbing back on board was not as easy as I had envisaged. I had to stop swimming in order to reach the handhold high on the stern, but the boat kept slipping away just as I was reaching up. I didn't panic, but was grateful for the extra loops that I could use as an underwater rope ladder.

It was a short swim, but an important lesson was learned. Don't fall overboard! It would be nearly impossible to climb back onboard a boat, even with a tether, if it was moving at speeds faster than two or three knots.

I got the soap rinsed off, but didn't enjoy being dragged along like a hooked fish.

Hey, how else am I to find out about such things? There's a cost to learning new ideas.

When we wrote to family and friends about the episode, we got back plenty of comments.

One wrote, "Howard, you are a crazy man! Let me get this right...you thoroughly soaped and lathered yourself, added a tether, then threw yourself into the ocean as fish bait. What a cool experiment! All that to convince us that falling overboard is not a good idea?"

Another remarked, "Judy trolling for sharks with live bait...it would have been a good reality show!" There were also demands for a webcam to see the sudsy, skinny-dipping scene.

Hearing Voices at Sea

It was my turn to be on night watch while Judy was asleep. There were swells abeam making Laelia roll from side to side. The moon had not risen and the sky was pitch black. Suddenly I heard low voices that sounded like a chorus of people murmuring.

"Help us...help us...help us..." It was not very loud, but repetitive. The sound came from the stern, not too far away.

It can't be! There is not a soul around for thousands of miles.

I froze and listened intently, keeping very still. I shivered. The sound was eerie and unnerving.

What can it be from? Maybe it's a boatload of refugees adrift at sea? Not likely. Voices that cannot be...it's simply not possible. Is hallucination a sign of impending psychosis?

I had read reports of single-handed mariners hearing voices at sea. I always presumed that they had been at sea for a long time and were suffering from something akin to sensory deprivation, leading to hallucinations.

I looked into the darkness around Laelia. It was gloomy. Behind us was a luminescent trail, not providing enough light to see anything. The luminescence was generated by turbulence as Laelia was cutting through the water, disturbing its planktonic inhabitants. Occasionally there were momentary flashes of light.

I continued to hear the same chorus of voices repeating themselves at a regular interval. Each time it was slightly different and indistinct...kind of muffled. It sounded human. I resisted the temptation to get a flashlight.

My reasoning was that if I got a light, it would be akin to confirming that I was losing my grip on reality. Why else would I need a light to look for refugees who couldn't possibly be shadowing our boat and pleading for help in the dark?

The sound is real. I'm not sensory deprived! It's only our fifth day at sea, for crying out loud!

It was true that I didn't talk a lot. I could probably go for days without talking to anyone, but Judy needed people to talk to. We talked when both of us were awake. I was not seriously deprived of social interactions or sensory input.

I'm not hallucinating!

I decided to investigate. I went to the stern and followed the source of the sound. The dinghy was hanging from the davits at the stern. With each rolling motion of the boat, the dinghy was swinging a little. I noticed that the murmuring sound I was hearing kept the same rhythm as the swinging movements. By now it was no longer a murmuring voice, but a rubbing sound coming from the rubber dinghy brushing against the stern of the boat. I was sure that I had found the source of the sound.

Whew! I feel better already.

The only explanation I could conjure up was the following: It was a novel sound in an unfamiliar setting. I didn't recognize what I heard and there was no other sensory cue to help identify that sound. In the absence of any context, my brain incorrectly interpreted the soft sounds as human voices. During the inspection, the visual cue of the dinghy rubbing against the hull provided the context and allowed my brain to identify the sound correctly. The brain needs known references or context to interpret unfamiliar auditory inputs.

The technical term for how the brain interprets sensory inputs as familiar images or voices is "pareidolia." Examples are odd-shaped cloud formations that appear as familiar objects. Another example is the "rabbit on the moon." Similarly, people have reported hearing voices in the dark from their departed loved ones.

Judy and I discussed my experience. She hadn't experienced the same "illusions" although she was not completely immune to these mysterious auditory experiences.

"I did hear some splashing noises a few times with the breathing sounds. The sound then went away from the boat. At the time, I thought it was from dolphins surfacing near the boat and then swimming away."

Here she was alone in the dark of night, hearing heavy breathing when there couldn't be anyone around. She was probably correct that that the sound was from dolphins, because we have frequently seen large pods of them. They made audible noise when they surfaced near the boat.

First Injury

After days of anticipation, we were finally in the NE trades at about 700 miles SW of Puerto Vallarta. There was wind, but not a consistent or friendly wind for sailing. It was erratic, blowing at 10 knots then gusting to 25 or more out of the north or NNE. I thought the trades were supposed to be consistent.

With the waves pounding the hull, there was a loud crash every few minutes that jarred my liver lobes right out of their rightful niches. The boat was rocking so much it was difficult for my finger to hit the correct keys on the laptop. After each of the big rollers rumbled past, I thanked the inventor of fiberglass and the builder of Laelia for having done a good job on this sturdy boat.

Laelia had Plexiglas hatches built on the underside of the hull, intended as escape routes in case the boat capsized. With Laelia loaded down and bouncing along on big ocean waves, these hatches were under water most of the time. Not surprisingly, one of the hatches was leaking. It was nothing serious, but just enough that we had to sponge up the sea water on the port floor every couple of hours. It was a glaring reminder that disaster was lurking behind just quarter-inch thick Plexiglas.

I had worried about the possibility of the escape hatches cracking or getting torn away by waves. As a precaution, I had cut a piece of three-quarter inch plywood sized to fit the hatch opening. On a boat, survival was to think one step ahead of the next calamity.

Having the hatch immersed under water did offer certain rewards; with the high water level I could see underwater all the way to the other hull. It was like an aquarium observation window. I could inspect the underside of the other hull to see if the rudder was still there.

Early this morning while in the dark, Judy was going off watch to the bathroom before getting some sleep. When one of those big waves slammed the boat abeam, she slipped and fell on the wet floorboards next to the leaky hatch.

"Oww! My big toe hit something solid. It hurts!" Judy said slowly while controlling her breathing.

The toe appeared intact...no blood. It was not a compound fracture, but I couldn't tell if the toe was broken. It was already swollen with a dark purple toenail on the big toe. I helped her up from the floor and back on the seat in the salon.

"The throbbing pain is killing me," she said.

It seemed that the bleeding under her toenail was creating pressure causing the pulsatile pain with each heartbeat. I had heard that blood pooling under the toenail could cause serious pain. Judy was very pale. I was worried that she might go into shock.

"Would it help if we try to drain the pooled blood under the toenail?" At that moment, she was agreeable to just about anything to get relief from the pain.

It was not exactly customary surgical equipment: a paper clip held by a pair of rusty pliers. The straight end of the paper clip was heated to red-hot over the stove before touching it to the middle of the toenail. The toenail has no nerve endings so it shouldn't hurt. The idea was to touch the toenail lightly with the red-hot paper clip without skewering the toe, just burning a small hole through the nail to relieve the pressure caused by the pooled blood.

"There should be a small gush of blood and some sizzling, but no pain," I said.

Unfortunately, there wasn't any sizzle and no blood gushed out. There was the odor of burnt toenail. So now, in addition to the swollen toe, Judy sported a hole on her big toenail.

Having exhausted the "do no harm" motto, perhaps a more passive remedy was appropriate.

The small hole in Judy's toenail was plugged with antibiotic ointment and her foot soaked in cold water. That was probably the proper first aid in the first place. Judy doesn't have a very high pain tolerance, but she seemed to be holding up OK at that moment. There wasn't much more I could do to the toe, but, if necessary, we could turn to pharmaceuticals. We carried on board several levels of analgesics.

There are many inherent hazards on a sailboat, and injuries can be a serious problem. Even a small injury to a foot or hand can incapacitate a crew, and medical assistance is frequently far away and not accessible.

At the time of Judy's injury, Laelia had already passed the point of no return at almost 1,000 NM downwind from our departure port. If her injury had required medical assistance at a hospital in Puerto Vallarta or anywhere in California, it would have been a slow slog up wind. Hawaii was more than 1,500 miles away. Even somewhere in southern Mexico would be 1,000 miles, requiring at least a week. It was best not to get hurt or become ill. Judy's toe inflicted serious pain and bothered her for a long time. We never quite figured out whether there were any broken bones.

Life at Sea

To keep Laelia sailing at an optimal speed, the sails were trimmed to suit the wind conditions. The sails were opened up fully for light and moderate breezes and, with increasing wind strength, reefed to protect the rigging from damage. When the wind was already tearing at the sails, reefing the main was a major workout. I would first lower the main a little at a time by releasing the halyard, then winching in the reefing line. Little by little, back and forth between the halyard and the reefing lines, the sail was lowered and the reefing lines taken in securely.

The biting wind would be ripping at any exposed skin. The waves splashed high on the deck, soaking me from head to toe. Then a blast of icy cold air would drill through my wet clothing to make sure I knew what wind chill was all about. In strong wind, the reefing chore could take as much as half an hour or more. By that time, I would be chilled to the bone.

Whenever possible, I would reef by sundown or in advance of possible bad weather. Certainly it was not a job to do in the dark. Judy always insisted that I wear a tether hooked onto the jack-line with a carabiner when I went out of the cockpit or on the foredeck. (A jack-line is a sturdy nylon webbing secured along the length of the vessel.) Just the same, I would never trust the jack line with my life. I relied on my own ability to hang on and stay on board at all times. I always had at least one hand gripping something secure on board.

For short passages of two or three days, we could wait for a "weather window" to avoid inclement conditions. Most weather forecasts were reliable for only three to five days. For much longer passages, it was not uncommon to encounter a storm along the way. A storm at sea can be sheer misery.

A week into the passage, the storm forecast was for wind strength increasing to 30 or 35 knots. A stiff wind was already blowing and Laelia was charging ahead at 8 knots of speed with a double-reefed main. The swells were huge, anywhere from 6 to 10 feet high, slamming the catamaran bridge deck at irregular intervals.

While the storm raged, Laelia was like an empty soda-can being tossed around by the waves. The spumes were flying off ten-foot swells with the wind howling through the rigging. Everything was wet and damp in the cockpit. The boat pitched and rolled, then it crashed and shuddered. We could hear the rushing water next to the hulls and waves banging against the sides. From time to time a wave would slam the bottom of the salon in a numbing, crackling explosion.

It was just the two of us riding out this storm. Laelia, not much more than a small scrap of fiberglass with an aluminum mast, was lurching in a boiling cauldron.

Are we having fun yet?

Judy got seasick under these conditions and went to sleep. She has the uncanny ability to be asleep as soon as her head hits the cushion. Obviously, she was not fearful about a possible shipwreck. For someone who was never interested in sailboats, she appeared to be taking these nasty conditions in stride.

When a wave slammed the bottom of the salon, the loud crash was accompanied by a shock wave that traversed all the way to the top of my head.

Instead of standing, I should have been sitting down on a soft padded cushion.

Could such shock wave cause a brain concussion? I tried to think of the list of symptoms for a brain concussion, but could not concentrate.

What is the date today? I didn't seem to know that either. *What did I eat for lunch?* Well, it was sandwiches of overly ripe avocados with Kirkland canned chicken. *I remember lunch! I still have memory...must be OK...no concussion.*

It is best to keep activities to a minimum when things are so unsettled. Even sitting still, my muscles were tense and were reacting to every movement of the boat. It was uncomfortable and very tiring. There was no fear. We just needed to endure. *Conditions will improve and we will see the sun again.* There was hope. Judy was sleeping soundly; she was more interested in not becoming seasick than being fearful. *That's good, because fear can dissolve away the ability to reason.*

I had the dry retch from time to time. Surprisingly, I discovered that eating something helped to settle my stomach. Well, I suppose I had to keep my strength up. Keeping busy also kept my mind from dwelling on how terrible I was feeling.

Conditions in the Northern Hemisphere were getting rougher, it seemed. We were still in radio contact with our weather guru, Summer Passage, in Oxnard, California. He had a gigantic Yagi directional antenna raised over the roof of his home. From Laelia, despite the distance, we could converse with him and receive the most reliable weather forecast for our location. He was checking the condition of the ITCZ (Intertropical Convergence Zone, or the doldrums) for crossing the equator at a safer longitude.

It was preferable for us to cross the ITCZ at a longitude with the least convection activity, in order to minimize the chance of encountering crippling electrical storms as well as stagnant conditions with no wind. These "holes" or regions of less thunder and lightning in the ITCZ are not static, but are variable and on the move. Even the ITCZ itself is not static but can move north or south.

For early explorers, becalmed and trapped under the unmerciful equatorial heat with no wind to power the ship, the doldrums could mean death to a good portion of the crew. Fortunately, on Laelia we were armed with diesel auxiliary engines for calm days, but a lightning strike could destroy all electrical instruments on board and possibly fry the crew in an instant.

We were still in the Northern Hemisphere, but could hear, on Summer Passage's radio frequency, another vessel somewhere in the Pacific passage. The skipper couldn't tolerate the rough conditions in the Northern Hemisphere and had headed south early, against advice.

"There is no wind for the last twelve hours out here,"

complained the skipper on the radio.

Summer Passage, our weather guru, replied, "Who's to blame for that? I told you not to cross the equator so soon. If you can't listen to advice, you only have yourself to blame." That was the only time I detected exasperation in his otherwise calm demeanor.

Following the advice from Summer Passage, we had planned to tack and head south at longitude 130 degrees west. At the time, we were still at 12 degrees 36 minutes north, 124 degrees 44 minutes west (12 36 N, 124 44 W). It would be around another 350 NM, in about three days, before we could turn and head south for the equator, but our spirits were buoyed by the prospect of crossing the ITCZ and the equator.

The storm had blown over, but the wind was inconsistent. It shifted from NE to N then back again at twenty-five or more knots of wind. On top of that, the waves were pushing the boat off course. The jib luffed and flapped hard, trying to beat itself to pieces. As the boat speed dropped, the autopilot was unable to hold a course and went into alarm mode. I would then scramble to regain sufficient boat speed to get the autopilot to do the steering again. I did what was needed and tried to sleep whenever Judy was well enough to be on watch.

One night I had to go up to the bow to retrieve the topping-lift line that was flying loose in the air. I discovered the problem by chance in the dark when I stepped on the shackle pin that should have been holding the topping lift to the boom. Somehow the pin had unscrewed itself from the shackle. I had to climb out on the end of the boom in the morning to reposition the line with a new shackle. I did have a tether on, but a fall onto the deck would probably break something and end the journey.

We had a juvenile Brown Booby (*Sula leucogaster*) land on the boat. It probably got blown off course by the storm. We had Boobies landing on Laelia before, but usually on the upper spreader of the mast. With their webbed feet, it was difficult for them to hold on against the aluminum cross bars. They never failed to leave a calling card on the deck to show their appreciation for the ride. I didn't mind them hitching a ride, but cleaning up all that sticky mess was a chore. This latest one landed on the sun deck and almost joined us at dinner in the cockpit. It seemed unafraid, but cautious and stayed only a few hours.

On long passages in good weather, life on board took on a regular rhythm. I would do a little more night watch because I was not sleeping well at night. Instead, I slept more during the day while Judy preferred to be awake. After many days at sea, as we acclimatized, there was also less in the way of seasickness.

Most of our fresh vegetables were being used up. Onions kept really well without refrigeration. Apples and carrots lasted a long time in the refrigerator. Avocados had a habit of ripening all at the same time. Potatoes when rotten had the most fetid odor. When necessary, we grew bean sprouts. We also made yogurt overnight to be used for breakfast.

One day at a time, we continued our journey. Judy checked in with the radio net each day to report our position. She talked to some of the boats we knew from when we were in Mexico. As time went on, we also picked up radio signals from boats that came by way of Panama and Galapagos. We frequently listened in on conversations of other vessels we didn't know as they joined in on the radio net.

There was a vessel called Imagine with several children on board, and another vessel manned by a single-hander named Harry.

"How come you are all by yourself?" asked the children on Imagine. "Don't people like you?"

"People like me OK. I just like to sail by myself," Harry replied.

"Aren't you lonely all by yourself?"

"No, I'm not lonely because I have my imaginary friends to talk to."

Crossing the Equator

We were finally in the dreaded doldrums. If I had thought the word doldrums meant calm or stagnant, I was mistaken. The condition here was erratic at best. The warmer ocean temperature means more evaporation and greater convection activity or more updraft. Together with the vertical air movement is plenty of electrical activity. Sometimes there was wind in the doldrums, but not consistently so. On the other hand, we always experienced strong winds and a heavy deluge within squall cells.

One early morning before daylight, we were at about 07 degrees north and 129 degrees west. Judy had already put our spare GPS and handheld radio in the oven to protect the equipment from lightning strikes. The oven, being all metal and electrically grounded, was what physicists called a Faraday Cage. It is a safe place for storing electronic equipment. I was typing some notes on the computer, but decided to put the laptop in the oven for safekeeping. A lightning strike would very likely destroy all unprotected electronics on board. We had read reports of boats struck by lightning. In one particular case, the high-voltage current path had traveled down the aluminum mast and struck from the base of the mast straight to the engine block.

The sky was clear, but the horizon looked pitch black. I could feel the static electricity in the air. Judy and I both sensed danger. For a while there was no wind, so we turned on the engine to continue our way south. There was lightning and later squall after rainsquall. In between squalls, we had several rainbows. The squalls were visible from a long way away as giant columns of black clouds rising straight out of the water. We looked forward to those squalls only in the very beginning when we needed rainwater to wash the accumulating salt crystals off the boat.

We learned quickly to be apprehensive of the electrical activities in the squall, but we couldn't outrun some of them. Immediately before the squall arrived, the wind speed increased by 10 or 15 knots and shifted direction by as much as 40 degrees. The autopilot couldn't follow the sudden wind shift, got off track, and started a screaming alarm. This was on top of the usual sounds of water swishing by, waves pounding, and things crashing somewhere in the boat. It was quite a noisy time.

As the squall engulfed the boat, the sky suddenly went from sunlight to complete gloom with wet mist and dark clouds overhead. At first it was a few large drops, then it opened up with a torrential downpour. Soon it was no longer raindrops, but streams and sheets of water. It lasted for as much as half an hour before we ran though the squall. It was more likely that the squall had passed over us. Then it was instant sunlight and clear blue sky. It was quiet again.

In the distance, we could see another squall. Sinister pink glows flashed inside the dark cloud column. It looked like a fiery inferno inside a curtain of black smoke. There must be fierce electrical activity in that squall column. I checked the wind direction and changed course, hoping to avoid that particular squall and possibly electrocution.

It was during one of those sunny moments between squalls that we were overtaken by a huge pod of Common Dolphins. There must have been over a thousand of them. They didn't bother to come and ride the bow waves. Laelia was probably not moving fast enough. They just passed us by on both sides. It reminded me of a Hells Angel bike convoy passing our slow VW bus on the highway. As they passed, some surfaced and took a look at Laelia. At any one time, there were seven or eight of them surfacing near our boat on either side. Due to the favorable lighting and the clear water, we could see them under the surface as streaks of light color and could detect many more of them that didn't surface. They passed us in groups of perhaps 50 to 100 as a rough guess, because it was not possible to count them. Soon after one group tapered off, the next group would begin.

As we got closer to the equator, I was wondering what it should look like. There probably should be a sign like one of those that the National Park Service uses to mark the Continental Divide. A friend sent me an email telling me to look for the yellow line drawn along the equator. Another told me to watch out for a bump at the equator as the boat went over it. That would be nice.

How else would I know when we had crossed into the Southern Hemisphere? One friend told me about "Chevron Island," where we could dock our boat for the night, fuel up, and get something to eat. Well, I must have missed the "island" completely, for I had not seen much of anything for the last 500 miles.

It is a time-honored tradition to celebrate when a person crosses the equator for the first time. I read somewhere that people who have not yet crossed the equator are "Pollywogs" and they become "Shellbacks" after the crossing. Crossing by airplane doesn't count; it has to be by boat or ship.

Aren't pollywogs tadpoles? How come pollywogs don't become frogs afterwards?

It certainly was hot. We were in the doldrums where there was little or no wind, just sticky humidity. We couldn't sail, so we were running the diesel auxiliary engine. To save fuel, we ran the engine at low RPM moving the boat slowly. As the middle of the day approached, the air temperature went up. The engine hummed monotonously and I could detect a faint odor of exhaust. There were swells about two or three feet high, but they were slow and gentle. With no wind, there were no ripples on the water surface. The sea was glassy.

We tried to stay in the shade; the sun was intense here. A few days before, even with my natural sun protection, I received some sunburn on my back. I was rather upset about that, not so much about the burn, but about the carelessness. I could ill afford any careless mistakes thousands of miles from help. Thinking clearly and avoiding mistakes is a good part of survival.

It was not a comfortable boat motion, but we were excited about crossing the equator. All eyes were on the GPS as the latitude ticked down to zero (00 degrees 00.000 minute N). We took pictures of the GPS screen for the record. It was a little like the dropping of the Big Apple at Times Square on New Year's Eve with everyone (all two of us) counting down in unison.

Four, three, two, one...We are now in the Southern Hemisphere!

We crossed the equator at longitude 132 05.070 W. It looked just like the Northern Hemisphere and anywhere else as far as the eye could see. We turned the engine off and just let the boat drift. We opened the Champagne with a nice smart pop and toasted King Neptune. We poured some Champagne on the bow of the boat and in the ocean for the occasion, because King Neptune is fond of such drinks, or so we were told. Judy also opened the box of chocolate truffles and each of us savored one piece...well, actually more than one.

After all that celebration, we thought a little wind would be very nice for sailing, but there was none. We let the boat wallow around in the windless humidity.

Good grief, sweat is oozing out of me all over. Maybe I should go for a swim?

The water proved refreshing. While I was in the water, I checked the bottom of the boat and discovered a lot of little creatures attached. They looked like some kind of *Mollusca,* probably the pelagic gooseneck barnacle *Lepas anatifera,* but I couldn't be sure. How could these larvae attach to the boat while we were moving? They must have some kind of instant super glue.

A current took Laelia back north, so we had to cross the equator again and had another glass of bubbly. We are not big drinkers and, on an impulse, I poured the rest of the bubbly for King Neptune.

There wasn't much wind until we got to latitude 001 degrees south, sixty nautical miles and one day later. When the wind did return, it was variable, blowing ten to fifteen knots from the west or southwest. It seemed that whoever was responsible for managing the wind around this part of the world was being playful or drunk.

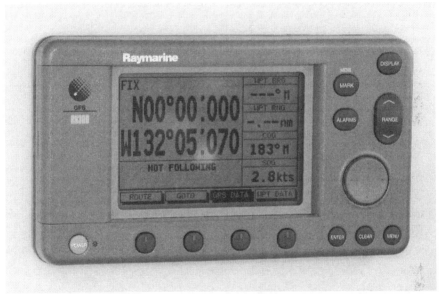

Laelia was at GPS coordinates 00 00.000 N, 132 05.070 W and traveling at 2.8 knots on a heading of 183 degrees magnetic.

Perhaps I shouldn't have poured the rest of that bottle of good Champagne into the ocean.

With the slow progress, I had time to check email over the radio. Our friends George and Rosemary, in Tasmania, wrote: "Shellback is the nautical term for an old sailor and a type of turtle." Another friend in Santa Barbara told me that, after crossing the equator, I had to wear a gold ring in one ear. *Well, I don't have pierced ears. So that is one tradition for someone else to continue.*

9. The South Sea Islands

Arrived Taiohae Bay, Nuka Hiva, Marquesas (08 54.982 S, 140 06.201 W), 27 April. Departing Taiohae Bay, 19 May 2004.

Landfall in the Marquesas

"Land Ho!" Judy was the first to sight land just before she went off watch at dawn. She saw a small bump on the horizon that turned out to be Ua-Huka Island. She checked the chart and looked through the binoculars to make sure. It was an exciting moment after 22 days of nothing but waves and more waves. We gave each other a kiss and a hug. On mighty tall ships of yore, the crewmember that first sighted land got an extra ration of rum, but never a kiss. So following tradition, Judy would receive an extra ration of chocolates when we finally arrived at our destination.

Our destination was the largest of the six inhabited islands in the Marquesas. It took until late afternoon for Laelia to arrive at Taiohae Bay, Nuka Hiva Island (Baie de Taiohae, Ile Nuka Hiva).

Wow, we are finally in the fabled South Pacific. This is the Marquesas, the islands of tropical fantasy. Am I in a dream?

I felt a little giddy. Perhaps it was from the lack of sleep. The landscape was a lush green with coconut palms easily recognizable. There were other big trees that we learned later were breadfruit. Houses were noticeable on the hills. We didn't smell land and vegetation as described in books. Instead, there was a pungent odor of smoke from burning garbage

Our first welcoming party was a spotted eagle ray (*Aetobatus narinan*) about eight feet in width. I had never seen a ray that size before. Pretty exotic. It came and circled Laelia a few times to examine us as we dropped anchor. Apparently, we passed inspection. It was probably wondering why these people were making such a racket. We went below to get some sleep soon after we secured the boat and celebrated our arrival with the remainder of the chocolate truffles.

The town of Taiohae on Nuka Hiva Island was where we needed to check in with the Gendarmerie upon arrival. It was the largest town in the Marquesas Islands. Nuka Hiva at that time had a population of somewhere over 2,000, and about half lived in Taiohae. The islands were volcanic in origin; some peaks soared to several thousand feet in elevation. The bay that formed the harbor at Taiohae was the remains of a caldera where its seaward boundary had subsided. It was a large bay with a sandy bottom that provided secure substrate for anchoring. In the morning we circled around in the crowded anchorage for a better spot to drop anchor. Finally Laelia was secured a long distance from the dock, which made coming and going to shore by dinghy inconvenient.

As we drove the dinghy to shore, we discovered that there wasn't really a dock. The "landing" was a vertical concrete seawall with a dilapidated wooden ladder hanging off its face. There were 15 or 20 dinghies amassed in front of the ladder. To land, we had to scramble across a series of dinghies before climbing up about 10 feet of ladder.

Clambering from dinghy to dinghy was not like walking on the sidewalk or even hopping on rocks across a creek. Dinghies move unpredictably as they bob up and down and roll one way or the other. At first I wobbled awkwardly from one craft to another while concentrating carefully to avoid falling. Later, I stopped thinking about falling and just ran across the five or six dinghies quickly, stepping away from each dinghy before it had time to move. It was not unlike running across a creek in a movie by stepping quickly on the backs of crocodiles.

The decaying ladder didn't protrude above the ground level as we climbed up. There were no handholds to negotiate the final ascent onto the ground so it required some amount of physical groveling. To finally get ashore, we had to use our hands, then knees, and then go on all fours before standing up on two feet. Often the ground was wet so it was hard to arrive clean and dignified.

Judy especially didn't enjoy this manner of arrival. She considered the final landing on terra firma especially humiliating, "This is terrible, crawling in like beggars. It's so undignified."

"You are right, it's not an elegant arrival to the South Sea paradise, but we are not in California anymore. There is no OSHA (Occupational Safety and Health Administration) and no handicapped access ramps. You and I are on our own," I replied.

We got in touch with our Polynesia Yacht Service (PYS) agent, Alain, by radio to do the check in paperwork. After the papers were filled out, he told me to try the Gendarme myself. The way things worked was that when the Polynesian Gendarme was on duty, everyone got the desired 90-day visa extension. Polynesians in general were friendly and easygoing. When I went in, the French duty officer was hardnosed and "by the book." He said a lot, but my French from my elementary school days didn't cover such excited bureaucratese. It took our agent, Alain, another half hour before we got our 90-day extension. Alain not only smoothed our check-in, he saved us a bundle of money. PYS provided us with a letter guaranteeing repatriation in lieu of an expensive bond. At that time, cruisers were required to post a huge bond in French Overseas Francs to prevent overstaying. It was to discourage "hippies" from hanging out forever and living off the land.

A woman who had been at Taiohae Bay some weeks before us informed Judy that there would be a Saturday market early the next morning. Since we were running low on fresh produce after the long passage, we thought we should go and check it out. At five o'clock in the morning, it was still pitch dark. We dragged ourselves out of bed, braved the salt-spray, and headed out across the harbor for the dinghy dock in the dark. Judy was the first to climb up the ladder, peeking over the concrete embankment, and spied masses of people and stalls.

Passers-by with big boxes of pastries and a sack of fresh vegetables announced with triumphant glee, "You guys are too late...all the good stuff is already gone."

There were actually not more than a dozen makeshift stalls as we rubbed the sleep out of our eyes. Judy was quick and homed in on the French pastry stall. She scored us the last couple of almond tarts while I bought a stem with several tiers (hands) of green plantain bananas on it. The minimum purchase was by the stem. This turned out to be a mistake when all thirty pounds of bananas ripened all at once a week later. We learned that the market started around four o'clock. I took photos of the market as a consolation prize.

We bought some coconut bread and a couple of donut-like sticks and two big mugs of coffee from a permanent stall. The locals were seated around the outdoor picnic table with a few places remaining; I asked if we could join them. They motioned us to take the seats. We were the only foreigners there. One of the gentlemen had a vest on with Maori designs; I asked him what it represented. He told us that he got the vest while on an official trip to New Zealand to learn the Maori language. He explained that the Maori language was the closest language to the original Marquesan tongue. Most of them were speaking Tahitian and French these days, but there was a desire to restore the original Marquesan culture. We learned much later that in schools, at least on some of these islands, including Mo'orea, the kids studied French, English, and Spanish. I suppose restoring a culture is a good thing, but it appeared to be an uphill effort.

There were markets called *magasins*. They were small, but were full of canned and frozen foods as well as drinks and a few vegetables. The most important items, however, were the baked goods. The baguettes were so yummy when fresh and their aroma was heavenly.

We confirmed, as eyewitnesses, that the movies were telling the truth...people do buy their baguettes and tuck them under their bare armpits. The store actually provided long plastic bags useful for those of us who hauled baguettes into dinghies and occasionally got salt water splashing all over. The problem is that baguettes become rubbery if left in the plastic too long. They also become hard and dry if left too long in the open. The only solution is to eat them as soon as possible. We became very fond of fresh baguettes.

What will become of us after we depart French Polynesia to uncivilized lands with no baguettes?

More immediately, we had problems. Judy was giggling, "I

can't walk a straight line."

"I can't either. It feels like the ground is moving under me. Hey, you are bumping into me," I protested.

We were walking side by side, but collided with each other. *My! What a couple of dweebs.* It was just like the drunkards in the cartoons. For several days, we avoided walking too close to the water's edge. It would have been embarrassing to fall in the water for no apparent reason. It took almost a week for the ground to settle itself. Apparently, we had adapted to the motion of the boat at sea. We had to re-learn how to walk a straight line on land again.

By the next week, my problem was how to deal with thirty pounds of ripening plantain bananas that I had purchased. Judy insisted that plantains are for cooking, but I happened to like the slight tartness that comes with these tasty treats. Unfortunately, thirty pounds of banana was a lot, no matter how much I liked it. I learned the hard way that eating bananas morning, noon, and evening could cause severe distress of the digestive sort. I got through only about a third of my supply before I admitted defeat. The upside of this experience was that we created a recipe for banana jam, which could come in handy next time I overdid on bananas.

Along the entire waterfront there was a park with coconut palms as well as hibiscus and mature trees providing shade. Fruit trees abounded along roads and around homes; breadfruit, mango, banana, papaya, noni, lime, pamplemousse (pomelo or *Citrus maxima*), and a variety of green-skinned orange were most common. We learned not to walk too close under the palms because a coconut could drop at any time. Just as a reminder, one dropped with a loud thud within ten feet of Judy. One direct hit on the head, by a coconut dropping from a hundred feet up, would probably be terminal.

There were also a number of stone statues, called *tikis,* at the park, but they were reproductions or gifts from other islands. Many of the antiquities had been damaged or destroyed when these islands converted to Christianity. The Marquesans seemed only recently to have realized the importance of preserving their culture.

We took a guided tour of Nuka Hiva Island. The steep slopes surrounding the harbor were unable to hold much topsoil and were covered primarily by shrubs and low growing plants. A little inland, the jungle took over. In the higher areas, it was primarily an Acacia forest with fern undergrowth punctuated with clusters of balsa and kapok trees. There were also *Pandanus* palms (*Pandanus tectorius*) that were useful for roofing and for making ropes. We came across orchids growing among ferns as well as in forested areas. Pigs, chickens, goats, cattle, and horses grazed all over the island and kept the plants from re-claiming the roads.

We even saw the endangered "imperial pigeon" (*Ducula galeata*) found only on Nuka Hiva. There were about three hundred of these birds left in the world. Our tour group saw 1% of the population that day. We tasted the cattle and pigs from the island in restaurants, but didn't get around to the goats. Horses were useful for hauling coconuts out of the steep hills and therefore were much desired by many families, next after automobiles.

The Marquesas Islands were just about the ideal landfall for cruisers after a long passage. Marquesans are as easygoing and friendly as the land is rugged. There was no petty crime that we noticed. People seemed comfortable with leaving things unguarded in the back of pickup trucks. Cruisers could get a ride from passing vehicles easily if they would ask.

There were many late model four-wheel drives and pickup trucks. We noticed one or two accident sites where vehicles had gone over the embankment at night, allegedly because of drunk drivers. These islands were no longer primitive, but we got a glimpse of what a simpler life might have been like in a bygone era. Even Gauguin probably missed the original Marquesas as described by Melville in his novel *Typee*. Melville based his story on the actual escape after he deserted his ship. His descriptions were considered a good first-hand account of Marquesan life before disease decimated the population. Most of the original culture was wiped out when the Island converted to Christianity.

Only fragments of the earlier customs were still noticeable. A pretty waitress we met at the restaurant was later seen dressed as a young man working at a coffee shop. Then we saw her again as an accomplished Polynesian dancer at a performance. His name was Romeo. This was completely accepted by the local culture. In earlier times, the islands had cycles of famine and violent conflict.

The population was divided between warring tribes that practiced cannibalism. It was not uncommon for families to raise one son as a girl in order for at least one male offspring to survive what must have been fierce battles. There was a dark side to the idyllic existence.

School Fundraiser

Having a stomach was definitely a financial liability in French Polynesia. Food was expensive on these islands. A medium-sized zucchini cost two dollars and a small cabbage was six dollars at the market. Paying seven or eight dollar for a bottle of beer made temperance almost attractive. Judy and I ate on board as much as we could, but we wanted to check out the local cuisine too. After all, what was the point of traveling to exotic cultures?

We were on our way to a little restaurant for lunch. We had heard that it was the only place on the island that was open on Sundays and had great Chinese food. On our way there, we met our new friend Alain and his wife. They were en route to a school fundraiser lunch and we were invited. We figured a school fundraiser was a worthy cause and we might get to meet more of the local people.

It turned out that it was a Catholic school fundraiser. The school was not far from the church because we could hear the loudspeaker blaring away. We made our way to the table where Alain and his wife, Odile, introduced us to another couple. The hundred or so tables were all under several big red and white tents pitched in front of the school. It was a local social event! Probably half the town was there. Of course many were parents of school children, but even people without children were there to support their neighbors and friends.

I went over to the food booth and was told that there was a choice of seafood or roast pork. That sounded pretty good and I figured that I would eat the pork and Judy could have the seafood. That was what she would often order at a restaurant. I also got some drinks for both of us.

As I placed the plastic boxes of food down on the table, I heard Judy pipe up, "I'll have the pork!"

Something about the tone and the rapidity of her voice led me to suspect that I was getting the short end of the stick. It didn't take long for me to discover how right I was. There were crabs in the seafood mix, but these were not the big Dungeness or Alaskan King variety. What I saw were the same little critters that scurried sideways on rocks at tide pools. Their shells were still that algal greenish brown instead of the red color of cooked crabs. The critters didn't try to pinch me because, mercifully, they were already cut in half. I had always prided myself on being adaptable and able to eat any food. These little guys didn't have much meat in them and I didn't want to make big slurping sounds. All I could do was crunch their poor little legs and bodies and got a taste of the tide pool.

I looked deeper into the box and came up with six or seven ...*what is this? Chitons?* I knew about chitons from my marine biology class eons ago, but never, not even when I was famished, had I the remotest inkling of eating one.

My gawd... it's like eating raw slugs.

Chitons are marine mollusks with eight transverse plates of articulated dorsal exoskeleton. Its foot was like that of a slug or snail. Normally, chitons cling to rocks in the intertidal zone, surviving by scraping any digestible matter off of rocks with their radulae. These critters were bigger than the ones I had met in California; they were almost two inches long. Still, they had no resemblance to big chunks of roast pork...drool. I tried to scrape the poor little devil off its exoskeleton with my front teeth and got only part of its anatomy.

There was more in this seafood tray. I found something that resembled chopped up tentacles of an octopus. The suction cups were still identifiable.

*Mmmm...the tentacles must have cartilage in them...*crunch, crunch, crunch. *What do you know! It's raw.*

Then there were pieces of boiled taro that at least were filling some of the empty spaces in my stomach. I got my hopes up when I saw small pink sausages at the bottom. Alas, they turned out to be red fingerling bananas. Cooked, but very mushy and slimy.

"Yum, this pork is so good. It just melts in my mouth. I wonder what they use to make it so good? It has that mouthwatering quality." Judy was enjoying the roast pork.

"It must be how they cook it in the pit for hours. There is a special aroma that adds to the flavor." She seemed to have forgotten all about her seasickness during our passage. I was glad she had a chance to make up for those hours of misery. My thoughts were interrupted at that moment as my stomach growled in protest.

She was eating roast pork cooked Marquesan style. It started with a fire in the pit that heated volcanic rocks to red-hot. Then, banana leaves were laid down over the rocks before the pork wrapped in more banana leaves was put in there, layered with more leaves and covered with sand to cook for several hours. We noticed that Marquesans and Polynesians in general were big eaters; the plastic tray had a very generous serving of everything. The amount was much more than Judy could eat...I thought that was rather fortunate. She took pity on me and gave me her leftovers. At least I didn't go away hungry.

Clearly this was a community where kids came first. Little toddlers would wobble up to the microphone while the older kids were singing. Nobody was concerned. We didn't see any child getting reprimanded even when some of them were getting a little loud and rambunctious. It was apparent that the average age of French Polynesia was quite young reflecting an upswing in the population.

After the official events were over, everyone picked up and disposed of their trash. The kids started running around on the field with soccer balls. Many of the men started a game called Petanque, a game from the south of France. It was played with two competing teams of one, two or three people on each team. First, a small ball was tossed on the ground, and then each team would toss the larger balls to as near the small one as possible, from six meters away. They could knock the opponent's ball out of the way to improve their teammates' positions. If the second team couldn't toss closer than the best toss of the first team, they lost. If they succeeded, the game continued with the other team trying to better their situation. The game resembled bocce ball or lawn bowling.

Alain said that I could ask to join in on the game and I would be accepted. It would have been fun, but then I saw how deadly accurate their tosses were. One man, while practicing, tossed three balls in a row hitting the target at 6 meters. This game was very popular in the Marquesas. We saw men and boys play this game every Sunday.

All commerce closed on Sundays. Except for attending church functions, there was very little else to do except play. For historical reasons, Marquesans were predominantly Catholic. We saw a few small Protestant churches; they had all been built more recently. In the rest of French Polynesia, the religions were more diverse, with numerous Catholic and Protestant churches and a very strong presence of Mormons and Seventh Day Adventists. I suppose nothing stimulates religious zeal better than a chance to save primitive savages on some remote island...the more remote and savage the better. The fact that many of these islanders had practiced cannibalism in the not too distant past must have been the reason for the large influx of missionaries.

Daniel's Bay

This was our best opportunity to see the third highest waterfall in the world. The guidebooks all insisted that it was a "must while visiting Nuka Hiva." *How could we resist?* We sailed the five or six miles over to Daniel's Bay (Anse Hakatea) on the southwest shore of Nuka Hiva Island to check out the 300-meter waterfall. The nickname "Daniel's Bay" was because Daniel and his wife Antoinette had lived there for many decades. They had been welcoming cruisers and maintained a visitors' logbook that ran into volumes. He was an icon for visiting "yachties" around the world.

To enter the bay we had to trust the GPS and the electronic chart with our lives, because the entrance was not obvious by eye. On the chart screen, we could see that the boat was heading towards a bay, but visually, on deck, all we could see was a rocky cliff with crashing breakers. We could hear the rumbling of the breakers and see them smashing onto the rocks. The cool mist from the spray and the smell of the sea foam told us we were too close to shore. Judy was usually at the helm when we were that close and when we needed to maneuver quickly. It was not a job for the autopilot. Laelia, with both engines engaged, inched forward until we were almost on top of the rocks.

"There's the entrance!" We both yelled involuntarily as we spied the passage to starboard. The entrance was not visible until Laelia was far enough into the beginning of the channel sandwiched between similar looking rock walls.

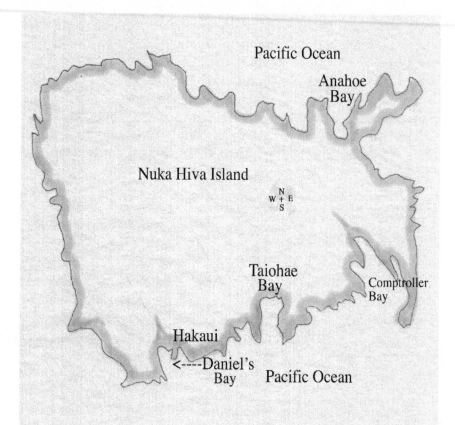

Steep cliffs lined the entrance. As Laelia traversed against a surging current, we discovered a bay that looked like a small lake surrounded on all sides by tall jagged peaks. The seething water and the tumultuous noise outside was suddenly cut off as we navigated the short passage. We anchored Laelia in the bay with steep cliffs all around, making us feel like we were floating inside a gigantic wine barrel. There were goats grazing along the steep wooded cliffs. The sunlight, the greenery, and the silence composed an oasis of serenity. I was entranced and elated by a sense of wellbeing.

A few hours after we arrived, Alain came over by dinghy to

invite us to a barbeque lunch the next day at Daniel's new home. We were glad to get a personal introduction to Daniel, the namesake of Daniel's Bay.

A TV crew had used this cove for filming "Survivor Marquesas." When the crew left, they built a replacement house for Daniel and his wife. Their original home that Daniel had built was torn down during the filming.

We were also pleased to revisit with Odile, who is usually very busy. She was the only medical doctor for this group of islands with a total population of around 8,500. There was a modern staffed clinic in Taiohae, but it was difficult to recruit new doctors to stay for extended periods. .

Alain built his own cruising sailboat when he was a young man. He converted an open life raft by adding a deck and installing a mast. He had sailed all over these Pacific islands over the past thirty years. He now owned a blue-water catamaran that he would charter to visiting boaters.

On the day of the barbeque, we had planned to hike to the waterfall and then join the party at lunch on our return, but we started late and took a wrong route. Everything went awry.

Soon after we landed at Daniel's Bay, a tiny, emaciated kitten came meowing at us. We had heard that there was someone nearby who owned animals, but didn't feed them. This kitten must have spotted us for a couple of soft touches and came chasing across the beach at us.

We tried to ignore the kitten and went on our way, but the silly thing followed us...well, not exactly "followed." This was the first time that I had ever experienced walking along with some furry shuttlecock zipping between and around my legs. The kitten would follow along behind me for a few seconds, and then all of a sudden it would jump ahead between my legs to land in front where I was about to put my foot. One step by my hiking boot, the kitten would have been history. While trying to avoid stepping on the kitten, I lost my balance and almost tripped over myself. Of course the cat would somehow manage to drop back and repeat the dopey stunt again...and again.

Why can't we outwit this little monster? It was inconceivable for two sensible humans to be driven mad by a defenseless kitten. Eventually, we came across a man who was working by the trail.

He seemed to like the kitten and held it while we absconded. Soon after we were granted our freedom, Judy's left hiking boot became unglued with the front part of the sole coming loose.

Certainly it was better for the boot to become unglued than having the two of us driven unglued by the silly kitten.

Judy couldn't walk far with the front half of the sole flopping wide open with every step. It reminded me of a hungry little feline opening and closing its jaws and baring its teeth. We tied the sole to the boot with a string and limped back to the trailhead. This was not the kind of trail that could be negotiated without some kind of decent footwear. Clearly this wasn't the day for us to see the waterfall. On the positive side, we did make it back to the barbeque lunch in plenty of time.

According to Daniel, he was 77 years old at the time and Antoinette had just celebrated her 75th birthday. Daniel, at a height of around five feet eight, appeared to be in excellent health and could lift barrels of noni fruit that I couldn't budge. He had a handshake that was like a steel vise as he gripped my hand. I gritted my teeth to avoid crying out in pain.

"Nice to meet you," I said.

Alain introduced him, "Daniel used to be the strongest man on the island."

He's not kidding! Reflexively, I flexed my right hand.

Daniel's only regret was that he no longer could chew meat like he used to, due to his dental problems. When Daniel was younger, he had owned several fishing boats and used to catch plenty of fish, but he didn't go out to sea any more. He still had a full head of salt-and-pepper hair. Looking at his grizzled beard and sun-beaten face, I thought of Ernest Hemingway's *The Old Man and the Sea*.

Daniel and Antoinette had met and gotten married on some other island, but had returned to Daniel's ancestral home forty some years earlier and never left. Antoinette had developed arthritis in recent years that severely limited her mobility. She couldn't walk very well and stayed confined to the house. Odile's visit was social, but it was also a house call to check on Antoinette. Their genuine fondness for each other was transparent. It was a joyous occasion for both as they kissed right cheek then left, as was the custom on the island. Judy got along well with Antoinette who seemed to be taken with Judy's blond hair. The two of them talked for a long time.

The barbeque consisted of a modest campfire started with a small amount of kindling and a few pieces of coconut husk. In the middle of all the burning coconut husks was a breadfruit (*Artocarpus altilis*). Before coming to the Marquesas, I had never seen a breadfruit, although I had read about it. There were many different varieties with different flavors. What I saw was about the size of a large cantaloupe with rough, nodular-textured, green skin. It didn't take long for the fire to consume nearly all the coconut husks and the breadfruit was charred all over. Daniel deftly removed the last charred, glowing breadfruit skin with a knife without getting the center all sooty. Amazingly to me, the center was not burnt, but looked much like the inside of a baked potato with a similar texture. It tasted like something between a baked potato and a roasted chestnut. There was also a pleasant smoky flavor that came from the campfire. It was delicious and aromatic. Unfortunately, it was the last breadfruit from Daniel's tree. The breadfruit season was pretty much at an end. Otherwise, I would have provisioned the boat with breadfruit and cooked them in the grill on board Laelia.

Breadfruit originated in New Guinea, but was propagated throughout the Pacific Islands by the seafaring Polynesians during pre-European times. The HMS Bounty was en route from Tahiti to the Caribbean with a thousand breadfruit plants when the crew mutinied.

A grill was placed over the remaining glowing embers for cooking the shish kabobs of tomatoes, onions, peppers, and beef liver and heart that Alain and Odile had prepared. The beef was from the hills of Nuka Hiva, from cattle that were as range-fed as any animal could ever be. All these animals roamed freely on the island. Alain also brought cooked plantains. Both the plantains and Judy's chocolate brownies went over well, especially with Daniel and Antoinette. It was quite a feast, washed down with freshly squeezed lime juice from Daniel's tree.

The next day, we returned to get water for Alain's boat from Daniel's spring water tap. Daniel brought out a bowl of pork that he had cooked the night before for us to taste. A German woman and her Marquesan guide made it to Daniel's Bay on horseback overland and were camped next to Daniel's house overnight. They caught a young pig in the hills with the help of Daniel's dog. Daniel cooked the pork and shared it with anyone who was around. The pork was very tasty. The skin, fat, and meat were all cooked so tender that it seemed to just melt in my mouth.

Daniel said, "I just boil some onions and some salt. Then, I throw the two-legged-pig in the pot."

I had read that historically, during times of cannibalism, Marquesans referred to humans as "long pigs." Perhaps it was the puzzled look on my face; Daniel laughed uncontrollably at his own joke and explained that he slaughtered the pig lengthwise and ate half the pig with only two legs.

I certainly hope it's a joke. Cannibalism was indeed practiced on many of the Pacific Islands. When the last incident took place was still a matter of debate, but it was well into modern times.

After we loaded the water from Daniel's tap in jerry cans and carried them to Alain's dinghy, we noticed a whole bunch of kids perched in trees and standing on boats at the water's edge. It took me a while to realize why they were so happy, laughing out loud in anticipation. As our dinghy went by them, they all jumped into the river making as big a splash as they knew how. They are trying to get us wet. It was a good-natured prank as a little river water felt terrific in the tropics.

The children were certainly happy and the land was peaceful as well as plentiful. Besides the many fruits he could pick from trees, Daniel had a large patch of sweet potatoes. We also saw squash vines belonging to Daniel's relatives up the valley not far away. The spring water in front of Daniel's house was potable straight from the tap. In recent years, the Marquesans exported noni fruit that brought in considerable amounts of cash, which accounted for the many late model pickup trucks on Nuka Hiva.

This was our first encounter with the noni. It was a fruit the size of a small avocado, but looked like a green pinecone. When ripe its odor was most foul, but it contained very high amounts of antioxidant. The locals picked and shipped the fruits in barrels to the State of Utah by way of Tahiti for processing into fruit juice. Americans would pay to drink this juice, hoping to live longer.

It was an idyllic life with few modern trappings. Daniel and Antoinette had no electricity, but did have a battery-operated radio. They were happy and Daniel said that he would not go anywhere else. Except for Antoinette's declining health, they were content.

Daniel said, "When you come to visit next time, you should come by helicopter…it's faster than a sailboat." He gave me a thoughtful look then continued, "But you better not wait too long, maybe no more than two or three years."

Breadfruit about five inches in diameter

At that point, I had a lump in my throat and was unable to speak. When I recovered, I thanked him for the visit and bid him au revoir. As was the local custom, Judy bid Antoinette and Daniel au revoir with the right-cheek and left-cheek kisses. I bid Antoinette au revoir similarly. Daniel gave me again one of his bone-crushing handshakes. The incredible strength in those hands was indelible in my mind. The strongest man in Nuka Hiva was an unforgettable giant of a man. Navigating our way to these different places in the world was not easy, but departing was even more difficult.

I received an email from Alain that Daniel had died a few months after our picnic and Antoinette followed him a year later. To Alain and Odile, Daniel and Antoinette's passing was like losing members of the family. Even years later, it was still difficult for them to return to that place where we gathered. A young couple, Ma'i and Maria, are now welcoming visiting cruisers at Daniel's Bay.

The Third Highest Waterfall in the World

We had not yet made our homage to the third highest waterfall in the world because of bad weather. Not long after the barbeque, the sky turned dark and the wind intensified. Cloud after cloud raced overhead at Daniel's Bay. A storm was brewing. We were not concerned because we knew Laelia was anchored in good thick mud that had excellent holding power. The mountains surrounding Daniel's Bay provided good shelter for us to sit comfortably. We felt secure, but were startled by the crackling of lightning and the instantaneous rumbling thunder overhead. I thought I detected a whiff of ozone, a distinctive pungent odor, in the air immediately following the flash. The presence of ozone meant the lightning had struck close by us inside the protected anchorage.

That was a close call!

The rain began to pour. Most rainsqualls in the tropics lasted no more than thirty minutes or an hour, but this one was different. It rained almost continuously all night. It wasn't just a drizzle, but a torrential downpour. I had left a 5-gallon paint bucket on the deck; it was filled to overflowing by morning. Where we could see only one waterfall the day before, there were now eight or nine waterfalls visible all around the little Bay. The water in the bay was all muddy from the runoff. Everything on the boat had a nice fresh look because the salt crystals had been washed into the sea.

Judy and I were determined to see the famous waterfall. We had gotten up extra early that morning to make sure there was time for the hike. We took the dinghy around the sand bar across the river mouth and landed not far from the trailhead. In the beginning, the trail was wide enough for a four-wheel-drive or pickup truck. We met one of Daniel's relatives. We introduced ourselves and asked for permission to go to the waterfall. We gave him our boat card with a picture of Laelia as a token gift. That was the local custom, although we already had Daniel's blessings.

He wanted to know where we were from and how long it had taken us to sail from California to Nula Hiva. He thought twenty-two days was a long time to be at sea. Of course his ancestors were famous for paddling their longboats across extensive stretches of the ocean. The Polynesian diaspora navigated the Pacific and settled as far as Hawaii and New Zealand. The journeys were incredible feats of bravery and fortitude. Many were successful, but history will never know all those who perished.

At the beginning of the trail we encountered an oddity. The most incongruent installation in this jungle environment was a fully functional phone booth. There was a telephone inside with which a call to Paris was at local rates, but we didn't know anyone in Paris. It was an intrusion by the modern world of communication into the jungle, but at the same time a throwback in the mobile Internet age.

The trail followed a small river for the first mile or two in a little valley with quite a lot of trees and shrubs. We noticed that there were perhaps five or six families living in this valley now by the number of dwellings and areas cleared of the forest. There were the usual palms, breadfruit, noni, and lime trees along the path. Wherever there was a sunny spot along the trail, there often was a patch of squash vines. The trail was muddy at places due to the heavy rain during the night. The trees were still dripping and spider webs glistening in the sunlight with water droplets, but the air smelled fresh and moist as the sunlight warmed the jungle.

On either side of this rocky trail were mountains with steep slopes coming straight down to the creek, with the foot trail on one side of the creek or the other. That meant we had to ford the creek repeatedly. Some parts of the creek were shallow enough to wade or walk across on steppingstones, but there was a least one crossing that was hip deep with a swift current. The creek was about ten feet across during that segment; it was too far to jump and too deep to wade. A downed tree about a foot in diameter was conveniently lying across the water. It served well as a footbridge although at ten feet above the raging torrent. From experience, I knew I could run across if I didn't think too much. I walked most of it then ran the last few feet as I began to lose my balance.

Judy, on the other hand, thought about the possible consequences of falling into the creek. True, the power of that current could easily kill by smashing body parts against rocks and boulders in the creek.

"Just run across," I told her, but she stuck her tongue out at me.

She decided to ride astride on the log and scoot herself across. It was an agonizing process. The log was muddy and not polished like a saddle. It was taking her forever. I knew well that, at moments like these, anything I said could be used against me. Definitely, it was a photo opportunity, but Judy didn't like her photo being taken at that particular moment.

She yelled at me, "Stop taking your stupid picture!" *She is angry.*

"Ok, ok, but hurry up and let's move on."

Despite all that cool running water, the air was hot and humid. It was perhaps even a little steamy. I didn't fall in the creek, but I was soaking wet with perspiration.

Not long after the creek crossing, we came across a tree with branches stretched across the trail with something hanging down. It looked like a small snake. We approached it carefully. I didn't think there were poisonous snakes in the Marquesas, but couldn't be sure.

It was not a snake, just a vine hanging from the tree branch. Judy examined the vine and identified it as a vanilla orchid. This particular one hadn't flowered. After flowering, the mature seeds, upon fermentation, could be used for flavoring ice cream and other foods. Of course, it was only appropriate to document the finding of an orchid in the wild with a photo. Judy was too tired to object.

The trail soon narrowed to a path wide enough for two people walking side by side. The path was still lined with volcanic rocks on either side as it had been from the start of the trail. These were not small pieces of stone, but about one yard in length and one to two feet on each side. The rocks were deliberately shaped by hand, probably without iron tools. They were stacked one on top of another to form low, bench-height walls on either side of the path defining the trail. The surface of the trail was filled with smaller rocks and forest debris. We were amazed by the immensity of this trail that continued for the next few miles until a few hundred yards before the waterfall when it terminated. Locals called this trail the King's Way. Occasionally, there was a wide-open area along the trail paved with the same volcanic rocks. Some of these were maraes with sacred banyan trees growing nearby. These were ritual human sacrificial sites. Other stone platforms called paepaes were foundations for shelters. There were a few tikis (Ti'i) along the path, but I couldn't be sure they were originals.

I tried to calculate how many people and over how many hours it would take to carry one of these large rocks over uneven terrain to build the trail. Several miles of heavy rocks formed this double-walled trail. They didn't have trucks, forklifts, or large animals. Perhaps there were slaves captured from battles. Multiply the man-hours by the number of rocks.... It must have required a mind-boggling amount of time and labor. There had to be a population in the tens of thousands just in this one valley to support such a project. Why did they build such a permanent walkway? Was it for convenience during the rainy season? Or perhaps the waterfall had a spiritual significance? I didn't have an answer, but the waterfall did provide the people in this valley their only source of fresh water.

The next question was whether this valley could support such a large population? The fruit trees and palms did appear to scatter deep into the woods. So perhaps shelters and homes were all over this valley at one time, but much of the evidence had been taken over by the jungle. I tried to imagine several thousand shelters on either side of the path with people coming and going. It would have been quite a crowd. Also, I didn't detect any sewage system except for the creek; that creek wouldn't have been adequate for discharging the daily waste for a large population. It would have been downright unpleasant.

Other valleys on Nuka Hiva were also believed to have had substantial populations. Typee Valley, in Herman Melville's *Typee: A Peep at Polynesian Life*, was believed to have as many as thirty thousand inhabitants. Some estimates placed the peak population of Nuka Hiva and surrounding islands at around a hundred thousand or more. Based on the extensive constructions we saw, it seemed credible that the original population was very much larger than now. Sadly, diseases, for which the islanders had no immunity, had decimated their original population.

There were no native historical accounts available. The early missionaries found the Marquesan culture violent and savage. In an effort to suppress practices such as tattooing and cannibalism, much of the local culture was eradicated. Along with the introduction of religion, the songs carrying the island's oral history were silenced and lost.

Before the arrival of Europeans, the traditional diet depended heavily on breadfruit and very little seafood. The reason was that there were many religious taboos against fishing at certain times of the month, depending on the cycle of the moon. Also, women were not allowed to go fishing. From time to time there would be a bad breadfruit harvest due to drought, which meant famine. There were tribal wars for resources between valleys and islands. It was sobering to imagine the hustle and bustle of humanity as well as the sound and fury of battles in the distant past at these exact spots of immense beauty.

We continued up the path and arrived at a meadow with few trees. The waterfall named Vaipo or Ahuii, with water source from higher slopes, came straight down the face of a sheer cliff. It was a long way down, but not much more than a few meters wide. It looked like a ribbon to me, but it would probably be classified as a horsetail fall. It was given as approximately 350 meters high, but its exact height probably had never been confirmed. So its status as the second or third highest waterfall was just whatever was in the guidebook. Close up it was not possible to see much of the waterfall except the lowest portion.

I waded and swam across the small nameless lake to the several rock columns that received the falling water at the base of the fall.

Judy started wading. "Yikes, some critter is biting my leg." She turned and went back to shore.

In between the tall rock columns there was an inner pool that constituted the very center of the waterfall. The water came down with a frightful force and it was frigid. I felt chilled and didn't stay long for fear of falling rocks.

As I reflected on the way back through the jungle, it seemed that our struggle along the trail was the journey and the reward. The waterfall turned out only to be the incentive. Much of life is no different.

Departing the Marquesas

We became very attached to the island of Nuka Hiva, but it was time to move on. There are many islands in French Polynesia, but we were allowed only a 90-day stay in the entire territory. There were other islands to visit.

Before leaving Nuka Hiva, there were chores. We needed to

replenish our water tanks, but the water supply at Taiohae Harbor was contaminated because of all the cattle running loose on the higher grounds. The island's leaders spent their money on improving the roads instead of securing safe drinking water. The priority seemed misplaced to us. There was good water at Daniel's Bay where the spring water was piped to a faucet in front of Daniel's house, but at the time we didn't have jerry cans to haul the water. We had lost our only jerry can to another boat that was desperately short on water during the Baja Rally.

We could run the reverse-osmosis water maker on the boat, but at 6 gallons per hour that would mean running the diesel engine for 20 to 30 hours to produce enough water to fill Laelia's fresh water tanks. The amount of fuel expenditure would make that option uneconomical.

As luck would have it, we found jerry cans in the local hardware store in Taiohae. They were selling at an exorbitant price equivalent to US$22 for each plastic jerry can, which would have cost around $5 at a Walmart. We bought seven of those jerry cans. We heard that there was a good source of drinking water right at the beach in Anaho Bay on the north side of Nuka Hiva. So that was worth a sailing trip.

Along the way, we visited Comptroller Bay, where the rival-group in the TV show "Survival Marquesas" was encamped. Historically, this was where the British and the French navies fought to control the Marquesas Islands. This was also the area where Melville had jumped ship and hidden among the natives. We didn't go ashore here because we had already visited the area by a four-wheel drive vehicle when we first arrived.

As we sailed north along the east side of Nuka Hiva, we ran into a huge pod of Pygmy Pilot whales. It was a very large pod of as many as a few thousand whales. These were not huge animals. Most were about the size of small dolphins with dark coloration and blunt noses. Laelia and the whales were traveling in opposite directions. We kept our course and they kept theirs, moving past us on both sides of Laelia for about 45 minutes. There was a tourist fishing boat in the vicinity; the people on that boat jumped in the water to swim with the whales.

It was becoming pretty popular at many places for people to try to mingle not only with marine mammals, but also sharks. I wasn't sure it was such a terrific idea to intrude so intimately into the habitat of wild animals. Perhaps the Park Rangers at the Yellowstone National Park in the U.S. could tell a bear story or two as a warning to divers in the Pacific. The lessons learned on wildlife management involving bears would certainly be applicable to sharks in the ocean.

At least the people from the fishing boat didn't try to feed the pilot whales and the whales paid no attention to the swimmers.

Anaho Bay was not very big, with only a few dwellings visible from the water. There were already five boats anchored in the protected part of the Bay; we had to anchor in deeper water. The beach was protected by a fringe of coral heads lurking just below the surface at low tide. We took the dinghy to the beach by weaving through a narrow channel through the coral reef. The water tap was just on the beach at the tree line not far from the water's edge. Unlike most other water sources, this tap was not owned by anyone and we didn't have to ask for permission.

Judy took our laundry to the shore and washed it by hand with fresh water and dumped the wash water farther up on land for the plants. It's life without washing machines. We then took the wet laundry back to the boat to dry. The laundry looked like pennants flying in the air and made the boat appear very festive.

I filled the seven 5-gallon jerry cans at the tap and carried them across the beach to the dinghy, then transported them to Laelia before pouring them into the fresh water tank. It took five trips to load 175 gallons of water onto the boat…that added up to 7,306 pounds.

I couldn't say hauling water was a barrel of fun as it took the good part of a very hot day to do that job. Of course I worked slowly…after all, I was in the tropics, there was no hurry for anything. I was comfortable with island time and the job was not going away.

The cruising life was in many respects not unlike living in a third world country where immense amounts of time were required to secure the basic necessities of living. Managing water, food, and shelter all took time and effort on a daily basis.

We went back to Taiohae one more time to attend a Polynesian dance festival, a fundraiser for the Polynesian Dance School, and to get fuel. It was quite a big occasion with a large tent set up to accommodate fifty or so big tables. Before the dancing there was food in large quantities, including Marquesan roast pork, roasted chicken, kumara (Maori sweet potato), potatoes, and Poisson Cru. Of course there were assorted sweet pastries for dessert.

Poisson Cru was one of the mainstays of Polynesian cuisine. It was not unlike ceviche. Traditionally it was fresh tuna cut to about half inch cubes and marinated in lime juice and coconut milk before mixing with finely chopped cabbage and carrots. It was surprisingly delicious. The tuna was always so fresh that it had no fishy taste whatsoever.

The dancing was by students at the school, ranging from six- or seven-year old girls to their moms. It seemed quite incredible that human hips could be so disjointed from the rest of the body as they shook, swiveled, and vibrated. The dancers wore frilly skirts around their hips, which amplified the motion. There was traditional Polynesian music with drumbeats in synchrony with the dancing action. There were also modern adaptations of Polynesian dances as well as modern dances. We recognized some of the dancers. One of them was Romeo, who worked as a waiter at the coffee shop and as a waitress at one of the restaurants. Many cruisers were quite taken with her long silken black hair and expressive eyes. At the dance she was one of the most enthusiastic and skilled dancers.

Some of the very young dancers, not more than seven or eight years of age, did excellent dancing. The moms were the most accomplished dancers and appeared to enjoy their performance. Normally, there would also be male dancers dancing as males, but they didn't participate in this particular festival. It was quite a family-oriented occasion with many children and seniors around. At the end of the dance a birthday cake was brought out for one of the moms. So it all ended with applause, smiles, tears, and lots of hugs.

We needed to fill the fuel tank before departing the Marquesas. Alain had noticed that I was reluctant to back my catamaran against the concrete wall to get fuel. It was not just the solid, concrete wall with no fenders or protective barrier, but it was the five-foot ocean surge smashing against the wall that was terrifying. As each incoming swell roared towards the fuel dock, there was a torrent of water crashing into the wall then leaping straight up into the air. A boat getting too close to that wall could easily be pulverized in short order. There was no possible way for me to bring Laelia to that unforgiving solid wall in such a seething cauldron.

Alain came on board to show me how it could be done. He said that it was not part of his service as an agent, but it was a personal favor to a friend. He asked me to get ready to drop the anchor as he stayed with Judy at the helm backing the boat towards the wall. When Laelia's stern was still more than 70 feet from the wall, he signaled for the anchor to be dropped. As the anchor dug in and the propellers continued to power in reverse, Laelia was holding in place at about 25 feet from the wall. Needless to say, all I could hope for was that the anchor would hold while Laelia continued to pull hard towards the concrete wall. Alain then whistled for the attendant who came out at a leisurely pace and threw a leader line to us. A stronger line followed before the nozzle for the diesel fuel was dragged through the seawater and hauled aboard.

We dried the seawater off the nozzle before filling Laelia's fuel tanks. Alain then asked Judy to observe the process of how I retrieved the anchor at the bow while he took the helm. Up to that point, Judy had never watched the anchoring process on Laelia because the two of us were always at opposite ends of the boat when we dropped or retrieved the anchor. It was important for Judy to know the process at the bow so we could work together better. Alain had been a help to us in many ways. We felt very fortunate to have met someone like him at our first distant landfall; it started us on an upbeat trajectory for the rest of our journey.

We bid good-bye to Taiohae Bay and set a course for the Tuamotus Archipelago, at about 850 miles to the southwest.

10. A Sudden Storm

Atoll Rangiroa (14 55.990 S, 147 42.750 W), 25 May 2005.

Our destination was Atoll Rangiroa, the second largest atoll in the world. We had never seen an atoll before and wanted to step foot on one. Judy had an added incentive to make landfall at Rangiroa on her birthday in May. She studied the guidebook and picked out a likely sounding restaurant in the Avatoru Village. It would be pretty cool to have a birthday celebration on an atoll.

Darwin proposed that atolls were formed by fringe coral reefs around volcanic islands. The corals continued to grow even as the island sank, giving birth to a lagoon. The string of coral reefs, islets (or *motus*), together with the lagoon, became an atoll. There were hundreds of *motus* and reefs at Rangiroa, but only two of them were permanently inhabited. The total population was a little over two thousand in 2005. To get in or out of the Lagoon, vessels navigated between islets through two narrow passes.

We received an email via the SSB radio from our friends in Tahiti on s/v (sailing vessel) Sage. They wrote:

Dear Howard and Judy,
We arrived here in Papeete on Saturday. It was a five-day-five-hour passage from Daniel's Bay. s/v Corona arrived here on Thursday. We had wanted to stop in the Tuamotus, but winds and seas had different ideas. s/v Corona had winds of 51 knots apparent and seas that seemed to come from three directions at

once. We had 31 knots true with seas of 15 feet at 7 seconds and 3-to 4-foot wind waves that seemed to be everywhere. This is not what you want when trying to enter a tight pass. We decided to play it safely and came to Papeete. For the last two days we have had winds in the high 30s, squalls that have dropped inches and inches of rain and lightning storms to keep us from getting too comfortable. The lightning at times had been right on top of us. Apparently this happens about twice a year.

The skipper of s/v Rambling Star, who tried the pass at Rangiroa, felt lucky to escape with the boat intact when it was spit back out of the pass. All in all it was an eventful week.
Bill and Joan

We felt bad that our friends had a nasty passage. I figured the same storm that went over us at Daniel's Bay was what hit them. When I collected that full bucket of rainwater in a single night, I wondered then if they would see that same weather system. It was good that they were now safely recuperating in Papeete, Tahiti.

On our passage to the Tuamotu Archipelago, we had light wind for the first several days after leaving the Marquesas. Laelia managed only a pitiful 50 NM on each of those few days. We then had a few average days with 100 plus nautical miles. Finally, we were getting close to our destination. It was still dark when I told Judy that we were within six hours of entering the pass at Rangiroa in the morning. I went off shift to get a few hours of sleep before we were to navigate the pass. These more difficult navigation jobs required both of us.

While I slept, the wind picked up, blowing 25 to 30 knots, and the swells heightened. Judy reported following waves that towered over Laelia's stern threatening to bury the whole cockpit. The condition was unsafe for navigating a narrow pass at the atoll.

A "pass" for entering an atoll is not necessarily a well-defined, straight waterway with concrete banks, but is formed by reefs and islets. The channel could twist and turn around submerged rocks and coral reefs that might or might not be marked by well-maintained buoys. Locals traverse the channel by rote, but I had only a vague notion of the pass from the guidebook. I didn't have a clear idea on how to navigate either of the only two passes, Avatoru and Tiputa, at the Rangiroa Atoll. At the time, strong winds and heavy wave action made it hard to see reefs lurking below the surface. A bump with a coral head and Laelia would become the next derelict sitting high on the reef.

Our friends had already warned us that s/v Rambling Star was "spit out of the pass by the current." The conditions were bad and we needed to make a decision. We could take a risk and attempt to enter one of the passes at Rangiroa. Laelia's maximum speed was greater than that of Rambling Star. I thought perhaps Laelia could overcome the adverse current.

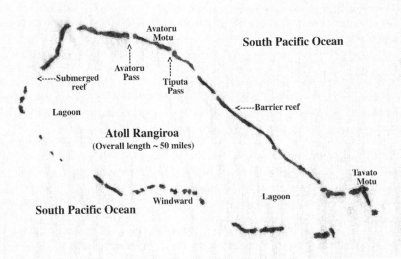

winds and heavy wave action made it hard to see reefs lurking
South Pacific Ocean

Avatoru Motu

Avatoru Pass

Tiputa Pass

<-----Submerged reef

Lagoon

<-----Barrier reef

Atoll Rangiroa
(Overall length ~ 50 miles)

Tavato Motu

Windward

Lagoon

South Pacific Ocean

Aside from the difficulty of navigating an unfamiliar pass in a storm against a strong current, we would also have to contend with anchoring in punishing conditions in a crowded anchorage with poor holding substrates. The guidebook had at least warned about the poor holding in the atoll. The situation was not appealing.

"Well, how do you feel if we bypass the Tuamotus?" I said.

"Even if we managed to get in, there isn't much we could do in this weather." Judy detested getting all wet making dinghy landings.

"Well, it's too bad, but I guess you'll just have to settle for a birthday dinner on Tahiti."

With that decision, we changed course and were blown past the

Tuamotus. The lousy weather continued. Laelia was taking a heavy beating as we hunkered down in the boat waiting for better times. While we endured, we did only what was needed to survive and to keep the boat moving. The big waves were making quite a ruckus. One big wave rolled the boat so much it flung the teakettle onto the floor. Catamarans are known for stability; we were not accustomed to having this much rolling motion.

More email came to us during the storm. We learned more details about the near disaster suffered by s/v Rambling Star.

Navigable passes at most atolls are on the leeward, or downwind, side relative to the prevailing weather. When a storm hit, the swells driven by the wind would surge into the atoll over the low reefs on the windward side into the lagoon. The excess water would tend to exit through the passes leeward. As a result, the current flowing out of the pass could be as much as five or six knots depending on the storm. A sailboat with a length less than 40 feet could normally power at a speed of five or six knots in still water. In the case of s/v Rambling Star, the boat had been motoring at its maximum RPM, but not making much headway in the pass. It was moving fast relative to the water, but with the current moving against it, the boat was making very slow progress.

It was a very dangerous standoff. The skipper could see that there were carcasses of boats wrecked on the reef not far to one side of the pass. He also noticed that his engine temperature was rising towards the red line on the gauge. Rather than waiting until his engine seized from over-heating, he backed off the throttle. Not surprisingly his boat was "spit out" of the pass by the raging current. In order to steer the boat, the flow of water must exert a force on the rudder. When the boat was spit out with the current in the midst of a storm it would have very little steering control. With diminished steering control in a storm, just about everything bad could happen.

The skipper of Rambling Star was indeed very fortunate; he should rename his boat Lucky Star.

11. Island Hopping

Arriving Marina Taina, Tahiti (17 35.200 S, 149 36.991 W), 26 May 2005. Arriving Cook's Bay, Mo'orea (17 29.7 S, 149 49.4 W), 08 June. Arriving Taha'a (16 38.208 S, 151 29.227 W), 06 July. Arriving Bora Bora (16 29.344 S, 151 45.665 W), 10 July. Arriving Suwarrow, Cook Islands (13 14.902 S, 163 06.623 W), 24 July 2005.

Tahiti

After many hours of a punishing storm at sea, the weather finally cleared as Laelia approached the exotic Island of Tahiti, the best known of the Polynesian Islands. We had reserved a slip by email at the Marina Taina not far from Papeete, the largest city on the island of Tahiti. Entering the harbor at Papeete was more involved than most other ports. The Island is enclosed in a barrier reef and all traffic including fast ferries, ships, and slow sailboats enter the lagoon at the Papeete Pass. To avoid collision, vessels had to report to the Port Control fifteen minutes prior to arrival. We saw ferries from a distance. They certainly didn't slow down and they were not bashful about taking their right of way.

Nearby there is a historical site of interest, Point Venus, about six nautical miles to the east from the Pass on the coastline. Captain Cook, Charles Green, and Daniel Solander among others were there to observe the transit of Venus in 1769. For their time, the expedition was a big deal, not unlike a space shuttle launch, an

119

undertaking of great risk and expense to study the universe around us. Charles Green, the astronomer, died on HMS Endeavour on the return voyage. At Point Venus they collected data to determine the distance of the sun from the earth. They were off by about 2%, an incredible accuracy considering the tools available at the time. Cook did have his sextant, his crewed ship, and the latitude and longitude of the newly discovered island of Tahiti. Most important of all, he had the newly invented chronometer, Model H4, by John Harrison. On the other hand, he didn't have weather reports, the GPS, accurate charts, or even a radio. In contrast, on Laelia we had the GPS to fix our position exactly and radios to contact the world around us.

At the time, an official exchange on the radio, from the vessel in front of Laelia with the Port Control, was loud and clear, but the skipper couldn't remember how to spell his vessel's name by the phonetic alphabet. The Port Controller roundly reprimanded him. It was embarrassing with hundreds of people listening in over the same radio frequency. We were ready when it was our turn and Judy had the job of talking to the Port Controller on VHF Channel 12.

Judy said it slowly and clearly, "Port Control, Port Control, this is sailing catamaran Laelia. Over."

There was a pause. Then someone with a French accent, "Port Control, boat name?"

"This is Laelia spelled: Lima Alpha Echo Lima India Alpha. We are 15 minutes from the Papeete Pass. Requesting permission to enter. Over."

"Permission granted. Make contact again 5 minutes before crossing the east end of the airport. Out."

"Laelia, standing by channel 12."

That wasn't too bad, but we had to contact them twice more. It seemed like a lot of bureaucratic bother, but we followed their procedures meticulously.

The charts showed all manner of coral beds, big and small, scattered throughout the channel between the shore and the outer reef. It wasn't easy figuring out where we were on the chart even with the help of occasional numbered channel markers. To make things more confusing, there were sailboats anchored everywhere, so it was not easy finding the deep-water channel. This was where the GPS and the modern electronic chart plotter performed wonders. It would have taken much too long to sight a bearing and fix the positions on a paper chart by hand. The electronic chart plotter showed, almost instantaneously, Laelia's position accurately within ten to fifteen feet. The French charts, used to create the electronic chips, were also exceedingly accurate.

Docking at the Marina Taina was a new adventure. It was our first try at Mediterranean mooring. Sailors call it Med-tie or Med-moor. Instead of docking alongside, boats would dock stern to the dock. We first had to drop the anchor from the bow as Laelia backed towards the concrete wall. It was not unlike our previous attempt at the fuel dock in Taiohae Bay except, this time, we had to approach much closer to this concrete wall. A big motor yacht was nearby, so we had to take care not back into it. When we were sufficiently close to the concrete wall, lines were thrown ashore from the stern to people on the dock to secure the boat. With the wind and the current, it was not easy to back a straight line without hitting something along the way. Of course there were a lot of people watching and offering suggestions. By that time, we were pretty thick skinned and didn't care.

I just want to dock the damn boat and get some food and sleep.

When we were tied up at the wall, I thought we were all done.

"No, you are not done yet," said the marina manager. "You need to have ready two 70-meter dock lines on the bow."

"Seventy meters? Did I hear you right?" I was in disbelief. The manager spoke good English, but with a French accent.

"Yes, it's your responsibility to secure the lines to your bow cleats and my divers will secure the other ends to under-water moorings." He talked fast and went on to other urgent business.

Seventy meters is about 210 feet each. Where do I find that much rope?

I realized that because we were docked on the outer wall there would be a lot of surge. If the anchor ever gave way, Laelia would smash her stern onto the wall. The extra lines tied to the underwater mooring were security for Laelia.

I had to cannibalize my stern anchor lines and another rope reserved for the sea anchor. More lines were gathered by tying together a bunch of old dock lines that I hadn't thrown away. The divers took the ends of the lines and secured them underwater.

We spent most of the day hosing down the salt deposits on the deck and reorganizing inside the boat. Laelia was a bit of a mess with things strewn everywhere by the storm.

The boat also needed some serious repairs. During the passage, with the storm raging, one of the hatch covers at the stern got washed away. A two-foot square of curved fiberglass was needed as a replacement. Our agent told us that he would find someone to do the job. Apparently, despite the large population of Papeete (around 125,000), it was difficult finding people willing to perform manual labor at prices we could afford.

It was a relief to find good security at the marina. We learned that a family of cruisers on s/v Sea Bear had all their cash, electronics, and cameras stolen on a Sunday afternoon. It happened when they were ashore leaving their boat tied at the free public quay not far from the town center. Papeete is a big city requiring caution as in large cities anywhere in the world. Apparently no one expected a brazen daytime burglary such as that. We saw the victims interviewed on television asking to have their photo-chip returned with no questions asked. As far as we know, no one ever responded to that plea.

The motor yacht next to us in the marina was from Australia. It was a charter boat for deep-sea fishing trips. They were completing some engine repairs before departing in a few days. While we went ashore, the crew on the yacht dumped their bilge water into the sea. There must have been a couple of gallons of sooty, gunky oil floating all around Laelia. We reported the travesty to the marina manager, who talked to the yacht's skipper. It was agreed that the crew from the yacht would clean the oil off our boat. The motor yacht's skipper promised that he would make good on his promise before leaving.

When we awoke the next morning, the motor yacht was long gone. Apparently it absconded in the dark of night. The marina manager was furious because the yacht left without paying their dock fees. Not surprisingly all that oil stain on Laelia was still there.

I noticed that there was a paint spot on the concrete wall that matched Laelia's bottom color. By the position of the spot, Laelia's stern must have bumped into the wall during the night. It seemed strange for Laelia to be able to back into the wall at all.

Something must be wrong. Then I discovered that our 70-meter lines on the bow were limp. I could only surmise that the motor yacht must have loosened our lines by mistake when they untied theirs under the water in the dark. My complaint to the manager did little good except to have the lines tightened again by his divers at no additional fee.

The top of the wall, at ground level, was about five feet higher than Laelia's deck. To get ashore, there was a metal ladder against the wall. The ladder ended at the top of the wall evenly at ground level. There was no handhold for negotiating the last few steps of the ladder. It required prehensile knees, long arms, and the skill of spiderman to scrabble up to the ground.

The first time Judy encountered the ladder, she was standing on Laelia with her head at ground level. A Polynesian man came by and saw her dilemma. He took one of Judy's arms and gestured for me to take the other arm.

He said, "We got to get Momma onto the shore." Then he counted, "One, two, three!"

As he pulled, Judy just flew up in the air and landed on her feet. We thanked him as he left, but stood stunned. I was dumbfounded that Judy's arms were still attached to her shoulders. *These Polynesians are strong.*

We gave up climbing that ladder. Instead, we deployed our dinghy and went all the way inside the marina to land at a floating dock. That worked well except one time. On returning to the boat, Judy slipped as she climbed from the dinghy to Laelia's stern steps. As she fell, she grabbed one of the dock lines and was suspended on the line, upside down. Her back end was already touching the water, but she wouldn't let go. I told her to just drop into the water and climb back on Laelia. For some reason, she wasn't too good at taking suggestions at that moment. She hung there for quite some time complaining that I was in her way. Eventually she got back in the dinghy, but it felt like a life-and-death struggle.

One reason for stopping at a big port was to replenish provisions. We knew we were back in civilization when we discovered a Carrefour, a French version of Costco. It was a good place to shop for nonperishables and frozen foods. French cheeses were affordable, but alcoholic drinks were expensive. It was just as well that Judy didn't drink wine or beer, although she had trouble turning down a good margarita.

The best way to buy fresh food was at the big Central Market in downtown Papeete. The market opened at 0400 hours and started to close up by 0600 hours. There were many kinds of food stalls including a Chinese delicatessen. The locals did their weekly shopping at the market. There was plenty of fresh fish of all sizes and colors. Fish was also the cheapest food in Tahiti.

The best food for our money was at the Roulottes, restaurants on wheels, each specializing in seafood, Chinese, Italian, French, or Indian… Competition was keen at these minimal-rent establishments with low overhead. Consequently, they represented some of the best values in eating on the Island. We ate *al fresco* under an awning and chowed down some delectable concoctions. In contrast, at any restaurant with air conditioning, the prices were astronomical for very unremarkable cuisine. We tried these restaurants, but gave up on them. By not eating at expensive restaurants, we saved a lot of money for buying cultured pearls.

"Black pearls" sounded exotic, like the title of a mystery novel. The actual color could range from black to grey green, purple, and even dark shades of pink. They are a unique product in Tahiti. These pearls were produced in the mantle of oysters that required years of care and extremely high quality seawater to thrive.

We were ushered in an upstairs private room in Tahiti and could select from a vast collection of pearls all stored in wooden bins.

"Ohhh...these are beautiful." Judy stared at the hundreds of large black pearls.

The rule was that we could only select from one bin at a time. There were many hundreds of loose pearls in each bin, all preselected for about the same quality at the same price by weight. Each bin was weighed before we picked it up and again when we returned it to exchange for a different bin. It was overwhelming to be confronted with that many pearls worth hundreds of thousands of dollars in a single bin. It was hopeless trying to find the very best one. The biggest ones were not necessarily the best. The color and shape as well as possible defects were important. We got some help from a senior staff person who knew how to select them. She checked through them quickly with a jeweler's magnifier and narrowed the search for us. It was a most unusual experience in buying souvenirs.

Laelia is Leaking

A boater's ultimate nightmare was to have seawater gushing into the boat. We were already some distance out of the Papeete Pass away from Tahiti on a blustery day with whitecaps everywhere. As I stepped down into the port engine room to check on the engine, I noticed a stream of water flowing across the floor.

Yikes, it isn't just a trickle. It's a torrent. *Where is the water coming from? I need to plug the leak.*

It was coming from the stern under the steps behind the bulkhead. I got down on my hands and knees in the stream of seawater to look under the steps at the stern.

My gawd...I can see daylight...there are holes in the fiberglass.

Instantly, I recalled the paint spots on the concrete wall and the limp mooring lines from a few days ago. The stern must have been grinding against the rough concrete wall and gnawed away the thick fiberglass hull.

Laelia's hulls were shaped with a curve going up to the stern. In calm water, the tip of the stern, where the damage was confined, was just inches above the waterline. Underway in rough water, the stern was awash in waves. No wonder water was gushing in. I could see the holes, but I couldn't reach them to stem the incoming flood. If I could have access to the breach, I would have stuffed towels, a cushion, or my shirt...anything to stop the torrent coming through the gaping holes in the hull. By now I could hear the bilge pump humming. The rising water level in the bilge had triggered the float valve and activated the bilge pump. There was a second pump, but the water level hadn't reached above its float valve yet.

Got to keep the water level under control...

By this time I had calmed down a little. So far the water level in the bilge was still inching up slowly. As long as the first pump kept working, we were in no immediate danger until the second pump was activated...my second line of defense. Hopefully, that'll keep the water at a steady level.

What if that's not enough? Then what?

The third line of defense was a hand pump. It would not be as efficient as electric bilge pumps, but it would add to the pumping power and it would still work even if the electrical system somehow failed. A final desperate attempt, if it came to that, would be to use the engine cooling system's water pump. I mentally rehearsed how I could disconnect the engine's intake hose to suction the water in the bilge. The intake of the engine's water pump has the power to move a lot of water as long as the engine keeps running.

Without these pumps, a flood in the engine room could certainly do damage when the seawater reached a critical level. Engines and electrical components simply don't work well under water. On the other hand, catamarans will never sink to the bottom of the ocean, because they don't carry thousands of pounds of lead ballast.

I almost laughed out loud when I saw the bailing bucket I had brought to the engine room as a backup. Someone once told me, "There is no better water pump than a scared sailor with a bailing bucket." I was certainly scared enough!

For the moment, the water level in the engine room seemed to be holding steady. It was not possible to do any repairs while underway. The patching up would have to wait until Laelia was secured in a calm anchorage.

Our destination was Cook's Bay on the Island of Mo'orea, within sight of Tahiti. I could see the spires of the volcanic mountain thrusting straight up from the sea. We expected to arrive before dark. For the rest of the passage I kept a close watch on the port engine room, making sure the water level stayed where it was.

After we dropped anchor and secured the boat, the first order of business was to repair the leak. I had hoped that the water would be calm enough in the anchorage for the stern to be above water. To my dismay, the wind was blowing and the wave action in the anchorage kept the stern continuously wet. I was in the water with a tube of caulk. It was a good fast-curing marine caulk from 3M. On land it seemed to stick to anything. The label said the caulk is also good for below the waterline.

Damn...it's not sticking to the wet surface.

It floated away in ribbons as soon as it was squeezed out of the tube. The water was acting like a lubricant and the caulk just slipped off Laelia's wet surface. By then I was becoming desperate and resorted to desperate measures. I squeezed a large pool of caulk on a sheet of plastic and shoved it against the damaged surface. I held it for a long time and cajoled the caulk to set. As the minutes went by, my body was getting cold and couldn't stay in the water much longer. As I lifted my hands slowly, the sheet of plastic stayed with the breach. It worked! It was an ugly repair job, but it kept the water from flooding in.

Residents of the island touted Mo'orea as the "most beautiful island in the world." The dark green peaks shooting straight up from the turquois lagoon was breathtaking. The palms, the sand, and the corals were stunning. It was the travel-poster image of a tropical fantasy. Geologically, it was a volcanic island with soaring mountains and steep canyons. Cook's Bay situated on the north side of the island was an extension of one of those canyons. Often the wind would roar down the long steep canyon in a furious huff. The meteorologist called them "katabatic winds." Given the right conditions, the wind accelerated by the terrain could reach the hurricane strength of 74 miles per hour.

Picturesque huts intrude into the lagoon in Mo'orea

Having been warned by the guidebook about the sudden strong winds at Cook's Bay, we set Laelia's anchor with extra care and tested the holding by powering in reverse at high RPM. After repeated tries we finally anchored in the part of the Bay where the mud was thick and sticky. It was a little close to the shore, but the holding was good.

Soon after, several boats came into the anchorage for shelter during a storm. One boat anchored quickly and the crew went below. With the first gust of wind, that boat started backing away fast, dragging its anchor. It was almost aground on the far shore before its crew felt the motion and started up the engine preventing disaster in the nick of time.

Overnight, the wind speed had reached over 55 knots. Dinghies tied behind several other sailboats became airborne and flipped upside down in the water. We felt a little smug. Our dinghy was hoisted out of the water with its drain plug pulled. I didn't have to get up in the night to rescue it. Perhaps we were finally getting the hang of this cruising business. It was a lot like playing chess; it paid to think several steps ahead of the next disaster.

Mo'orea was enchanting and memorable. The Island residents fought to control its growth and had avoided the over-development that plagued Tahiti. Judy and I enjoyed Cook's Bay and toured the entire island. The Hotel Bali Hai on the waterfront was friendly to cruisers, providing the hotel dock as a secure place to leave our dinghy when going ashore. Of course we reciprocated by eating at the hotel. The restaurant was named after the best tasting pineapple I have ever encountered...the Blue Pineapple. It was a small variety with a dark color, but juicy and sweet. It was not exported and was grown and available only in Mo'orea.

We still had unfinished repairs. One day a Frenchman who had been referred to us by our Polynesian agent showed up next to Laelia in his dinghy. He offered to fabricate a hatch door on Laelia's stern to replace the one washed away during the stormy passage to Tahiti. He got the job, since he was the only person that offered to do the work. The finished product was terrific and at a decent price. It was a mutually satisfactory transaction. Now that Laelia was whole again, it was time to move on. Our visa was for ninety days and Laelia had to depart French Polynesia before 26 July 2005.

Taha'a

For us, Taha'a was the most memorable of all the islands in French Polynesia. The Society Islands, named by Captain Cook in honor of the Royal Society, are divided into Windward (Eastern group) and Leeward Islands. Taha'a is one of the smaller Leeward Islands. It has retained much of its lush unspoiled landscape and nicknamed the "Vanilla Island" because of the many vanilla plantations. Judy used to have an orchid greenhouse and had continued her interest in orchids, of which vanilla is a vined member. We anchored in one of the protected finger-like bays with the intention of touring a vanilla plantation.

Making phone calls in an unfamiliar foreign language was daunting under the best of circumstances. Each time we dialed the number to make a reservation for the tour, we got a recorded message in French. The French I knew from my elementary school days was not up to the task. We needed help. The phone booth was in front of a busy post office. I scanned the passers-by for a likely English speaker and approached one man who was heading into the post office with a purposeful manner. *Bingo!* He not only understood what I was asking, he answered me in perfect English.

He told me that he had something important to do in the post office, but would be happy to help when he came out.

We waited for him. When he finally listened to the recording on the phone, he shrugged his shoulders and said that the message was about the trunk line being busy.

"It's probably a permanent condition," he said.

We thanked him, but our disappointment probably showed.

"Whom are you trying to call? Is it something I can help with?" he asked.

"Oh, we were just trying to make a reservation to tour the vanilla plantation in the morning."

"I grow vanilla. I can show you how it's done. You have time now? Come with me, my car is across the road."

Judy and I looked at each other. It wasn't our habit to just jump in some stranger's car. The man was wearing blue jeans and a denim shirt. He was well tanned and his eyes had a hawk-like intensity. I supposed he could be a vanilla farmer. He seemed trustworthy. The fact that Taha'a was a small island with a friendly ambiance also provided us a sense of security.

"We would love to come with you." We chased after him on the way to his car.

We introduced ourselves in the car. Robert explained that he really was in a hurry earlier to pick up a package from the post office before it closed for the day.

He pointed at the package, "It's from Paris. I have waited several months for it. I think it's good news."

"I am glad it's good news," I replied, but both Judy and I were puzzled. We didn't know what was "good news" to him.

"The post is from the Tribunal in Paris. I'll explain more later." He turned to concentrate on driving the car on the narrow highway. I gathered that the Tribunal was something like our Federal Court in the US or even SCOTUS and decided to wait until he was ready to tell us more.

His house was big by island standards. As he drove up the path, he pointed to the vegetation on the hillside, "Those are all vanilla plants. They are grown without pesticides and can be certified as organic."

He introduced his wife, daughter, and a son to us. Another older daughter was away at school. We told them about our journey. He in turn told us about the mail he received from Paris. He had a dispute with the French Government regarding the land on this island he inherited from his mother. The government didn't recognize his inheritance and had made plans to develop much of his land.

The government based its case on laws generally applied to all of the Society Islands, both the Windward and the Leeward groups. Robert's position was that the French law was only valid on the five Windward Islands (including Tahiti and Mo'orea) because the chiefs had ceded those islands to France in June 1880. On the other hand, the nine Leeward Islands (including Huahine, Bora Bora, Raiatea, and Taha'a) had never agreed to give up their traditional law and authority. Robert was fortunate that he had in his possession the only written copy of the traditional law governing land ownership. He brought his case to the Tribunal in Paris against the French Government. The package he had just received in the mail was the official judgment of the Tribunal in his favor. He told us this as a matter of fact, but it was an important victory to savor.

It was a matter of historical record that France broke the Jarnc Convention of 1847 between Britain and France that guaranteed the independence of the Kingdoms on the Leeward Islands. It was also a known fact that the natives of the Leeward Islands never agreed to be annexed in 1888 by France. They fought for their rightful independence well into the late 1890's against the superior weapons of the French. According to the traditional law of the land that was never relinquished, Robert had a right to all property belonging to his mother's family. It seemed, after more than one hundred years, that Robert had finally won the battle on behalf of the natives.

The afternoon went by unnoticed while we talked. We suddenly realized that it was time for us to get back to the boat before dark. Robert and his wife invited us back to a lunch with them the next day. Of course we would love to come back.

The more I learned about Robert, the more I respected him. We had already heard how he went nose to nose against the French Government to win back his family heritage. Then we found out that, when he was a young man, he had protested against the testing of nuclear weapons by the French. At the time the French Government was using Atolls Mururoa and Fangataufa, southeast of the Tuamotu Archipelago, for testing thermonuclear weapons. Robert and others took their protest to Paris. For that he was imprisoned in France for several years without charge. Robert is certainly not a man afraid to stand up for his principles.

After lunch Robert took us all up to the hills behind his home to see the vanilla plants and demonstrated how he hand-pollinates the vanilla orchids. Then he showed us the fermentation process of the mature vanilla beans. These beans were the largest and most fragrant we have encountered. He gave each of us a supply of vanilla beans.

It was something that many cruisers discovered as they traveled. The most difficult part of cruising was not in fighting storms or tolerating hardships of frugal living. The hardest was to say farewell, when it was time for us to sail away, to good people we became fond of and admired.

Bora Bora
The Island of Bora Bora is an extinct volcano bathed in a turquoise

lagoon protected by a barrier reef. It's not far from the Island of Taha'a.

Laelia was tied to a mooring ball in front of the Bora Bora Yacht Club. That might sound pretty hoity-toity, but the Yacht Club was no more than a small restaurant with an open wooden deck connected to the dinghy dock. We could use the mooring ball for free provided we ate one meal a day at the restaurant. It didn't hurt our feelings to eat good food, but it did do some serious damage to the sailing kitty. As in all of French Polynesia, having a stomach was a financial liability.

From Laelia's cockpit we could see the boat traffic coming and going through the only pass into the Bora Bora Lagoon. It was also a strategic location to watch the sunset. We saw the "green flash" at sunset twice during our first week in the Lagoon. We can confirm that the green flash is a real phenomenon. Marcel Minnaert wrote in The Nature of Light & Color in the Open Air, "According to an old Scottish legend, anyone who has seen the green ray (flash) will never err again where matters of sentiment are concerned." Now that we had seen the phenomenon twice, we felt very wise.

It was July 14, Bastille Day. Early in the morning there was a group of Polynesian women making floral garlands with fresh flowers and Ti leaves (*Cordyline* or Hawaiian good-luck plant) for their families. As a special favor, they made one for me to give to Judy to wear and she was the envy of all the other women among the cruisers.

There were floats, parades, singing competitions, and a footrace. The runners carried breadfruit, pineapple, stalks of bananas, and other items on a pole during the race. We attended the evening singing and dancing competitions. Later, we went on a windy and wet ride in the dinghy in pitch darkness back to Laelia. It felt pretty crazy to zip around in a little dinghy in the dark under small-craft warning conditions. It was like being children again with not a care in the world.

Before we departed Bora Bora, Judy and I took a helicopter ride to see the lagoon from the air. It was a very windy day with plenty of whitecaps all across the lagoon. Our dinghy ride to and from the pickup point got us soaking wet. Even in the tropics, it was a chilling experience. When the water finally evaporated, the salt made the clothing heavier and stiffer. From the air, the lagoon was a vast expanse of turquoise dotted with sailboats between coral reefs. The pilot dropped down close to the water so I could take a photo of Laelia at anchor in a lagoon showing different shades of turquois and blue.

We checked the weather looking for a weather window for our passage to American Samoa, but the forecast was rotten. Fortunately, we still had a few days left on our visa.

Suwarrow Atoll

"I heard that Suwarrow Atoll has no access by commercial transport of any kind," Judy said while we were still in Bora Bora.

"Well, that is certainly different. Want to go there?" I added, "I know nothing about the place. Maybe I should check the chart to find out where it's located."

It turned out that Suwarrow is an uninhabited atoll in the middle of nowhere and the entire atoll is a National Park belonging to the Nation of Cook Islands. Furthermore, it was on our way from Bora Bora to American Samoa. It seemed reasonable to break up the passage by getting a few days rest during the long passage. The first leg of the passage, from Bora Bora to Suwarrow, would be about 700 miles and the remainder 450 miles. Except for the electronic chart, I didn't have detailed navigation charts or a guidebook for Suwarrow. Hopefully, if we arrived in daylight, perhaps we could navigate by eye.

It was only after our arrival near the atoll that we realized the full scope of our predicament. On the electronic chart, the atoll was about five to six miles in diameter, with coral reefs ringing the entire lagoon with an opening at the pass. Upon arrival, what we saw in front of us was entirely different. It was water, water everywhere with only a few scattered low islands miles apart. There were reefs no doubt, but submerged and not visible. Parts of the reef could be just below the water level depending on the tide. Without being able to see the reef, it was impossible to find the safe passage by sight.

I couldn't be absolutely sure that the electronic chart was accurate either. I had been reminded many times that some of the charting in the Pacific dated back to Captain Cook's era. He and other mariners did miracles with their sextants, but they were no match against the accuracy of today's GPS. In any event, the coral reefs could have grown in the ensuing centuries. It wouldn't have taken an error of four or five feet to put Laelia on a reef.

There were a few clues revealing the approximate location of the reefs. On the windward side of the atoll we could confirm the presence of a reef by the huge surf splashing up from the sea. There were also splashes of white water due to shallow patches of submerged rocks and coral heads farther inside the lagoon. The water was in various colors and we could tell some of the obvious hazards, but we couldn't tell for certain where the pass was. It would be foolhardy to guess. The price of an error would be high...our lives could be at stake. In any case, the wind was kicking up a fair amount of whitecaps making it even more difficult to detect coral heads or judge the depth by the color of the water.

When we were within VHF range, Judy went on the radio.

"This is sailing vessel Laelia, Laelia, Laelia. Calling any vessel in the Suwarrow anchorage...any vessel."

"Laelia! This is Ace. Go to Channel 17."

"Laelia switching to 17."

"Laelia, this is Ace. How are you guys? Over."

"We are so glad to hear from you. You have any advice on navigating the pass? Over." We met the family on s/v Ace in the Marquesas.

"I have a couple of waypoints from our log. That should do the trick. Over."

The radio transmission was continued by a series of numbers representing latitude and longitude coordinates.

The GPS technology is a fantastic development. Just a couple of waypoints were enough to guide us through the pass, although it was still necessary to keep a watchful eye for hazards. The narrow passage through the reef allowed very little margin of error and the shifting winds and currents added to the challenge. We had to be cautious not to get too close to light colored water where it was shallow.

We had missed the slack tide and had to buck a few knots of current. The wind continued to stiffen with whitecaps all across the atoll, putting up impressive looking wind swept surf. Judy was at the helm as we entered the pass. The beginning was wide and we were able to follow along the bank of a small island on our starboard, but then the pass narrowed. The point of the island became a rocky spit with a reef that extended into the pass.

Judy pointed ahead, "There, I can see the reef. It has the bright turquoise water on the fringe."

"Yeah, I see it too. It's colorful. The dark color in the center must be the coral head just under the surface...I wish I had my camera."

"Damn it, you don't have time for that. I am heading left to be on the safe side."

I checked the GPS waypoints we had gotten from Ace and compared them with our position. It was just following the waypoints one turn at a time. We were not at the waypoint for turning to starboard. That much was consistent with the chart that showed a dogleg to the right. Judy had to keep the boat moving at a reasonable speed to be able to maintain steering control.

"Hey, Howard, look at all that spray dead ahead!" Just then a gust of wind picked up the spume from the breaking surf, getting us all damp. "Are you sure this is the pass? I went left just a little. Now I see a reef dead ahead. We are boxed in."

"Yeah, we are in the right pass, I just checked the waypoint Ace gave us. There has got to be an opening between the reefs ahead of us. In a little bit... that's where we hang a right."

With all the irregular shapes of water and surf, it was hard to see where one reef ended and another began.

"Howard, are you sure? Are we there yet? We are getting very close to all that white water. I'm sure that's a reef under all that froth. I can't keep going or we'll run aground. Come on, I need to know now."

"Wait, I am checking our position...we are not there yet... just a little more. Just hold your course...ok? Over there on the right...you see the water? It looks darker," I said and pointed.

"I'm turning...you better be right or we're dead." As the boat turned to starboard, we both could see reefs on either side of Laelia. We continued on.

"Whew! I think we are in," I said. "Look to your left...there's a wreck."

No more than 15 feet away on the reef sat a sunken sailboat partially submerged, but appearing intact. "Wow, it looks like a ghost ship guarding the entrance. I wonder if they tried to come in during a storm."

We strained every nerve as Laelia negotiated the entrance to the atoll. It would have been impossible during a heavy storm. I had to pry Judy's hands off of the stainless steel steering wheel after we arrived. Despite the tension and stress, Judy always preferred to do the steering.

The anchorage was west of the low island near the entrance to the lagoon. The heavy grove of palm trees on the island provided shelter from the prevailing Southeast trades. Not surprisingly, there were boats already anchored in all the best spots. We ended up on a rather shallow patch of turquoise colored sea. The water was so sparkling clear, we could see big lumps of dead coral through the water, but couldn't be sure how deep the water was over them. The anchor was holding in shallow coral sand. It didn't feel terribly secure, but it was all that was available at the time. We decided that Suwarrow was a good place to hang out a long while for some rest.

Suwarrow was like no place we have ever experienced. It was a small atoll with only a few tiny islets no more than a foot or two above water; they were visible only because of the palm trees. The islets were literally in the middle of nowhere with no permanent resident. When a cyclone passes through, the sea surges over the entire place.

One could snorkel or scuba, divers were finding scallops in the deeper water. The fishing was terrific at the edge of the reef where the water depth drops off from fairly shallow to fifty or more feet. In the morning, one could walk along the fringe reef in about a foot of water and pick up lobsters. They call them "reef rabbits." Apparently, the lobsters came up to the reef to feed.

We checked in and paid our fifty dollars to John, the National Park Ranger. He and his wife, Veronica, lived on Suwarrow from June to October before returning to their home in Rarotonga. They hadn't brought their children because this was their first season on the job.

For several days, we had strong winds and heavy rain, interspersed with lightning and rumbling thunder. In the middle of all that we heard the VHF radio crackling and a disembodied voice. It was Harry, a single hander whom we had talked to on the radio. Again, s/v Ace gave him the GPS coordinates for navigating the pass. We could tell from Harry's voice that he was tired and a bit overwhelmed by the lightning storm. We talked to him to provide moral support while he navigated the passage.

I talked to Don (Summer Passage) in Oxnard, California by SSB radio that afternoon. He mentioned that there was a "mild" low at 1007 millibars moving just to the south of us. We would have winds in the range of 20 to 30 knots clocking around us as the low pressure passed. It was not a killer storm, but it was a large low system and would go on for several days.

We were warned not to drop any food or garbage in the water because the sharks were very hungry. One boat had cleaned fish on a filet table. They knew enough to take their fish guts far away from the anchorage for disposal, but after cleaning their filet table with paper, they rinsed it in seawater. Within minutes, they had three large sharks circling their boat for several hours. The sharks finally were chased away by running dinghy outboards around the boat.

Veronica and John led a guided tour of Bird Island, an islet full of bird life. Long before our arrival by dinghy at the beach, we could see birds by the thousands flying over the little islet. Booby and Frigate bird chicks were everywhere in the shrubs in nests. Tern eggs, on the other hand, were laid randomly all over the ground. We had to step carefully. We were allowed to touch and hold only one specific frigate-bird chick that was picked up previously and had not been rejected by the mother. None of us had seen so many birds at one place. They were noisy, but seemed unafraid of people.

We also learned about coconut crab (*Birgus latro*). It looked like a bluish lobster, although closer related to hermit crabs, but bigger and without a borrowed shell. These coconut crabs could climb up trees, build tunnels in the mud, and lived under roots of the mangrove.

John was very new at the job and had a very steep learning curve in figuring out the multiple roles for him and his wife as hosts at the atoll. Their original goal was to help cruisers have a good time, to teach Cook Island culture, and to protect the fragile atoll. He also learned about the different kinds of people. No doubt, he had to reset his priorities. John announced to everyone that he wanted cruisers to have a good time at Suwarrow, but it was not a place to replenish their food supply. No doubt he started to worry about what the heavy traffic would do to Suwarrow in the long term.

Before we left, John asked me to print out the new rules for the atoll as a favor to him. It was amazing to me to see the transformation that took place in him in such a short time. He went from a genial host to a Park Ranger concerned about the future of the atoll.

Judy and I invited John and Veronica on board at breakfast. It was a surprise to both of us that it was the first time they were invited on board a cruising boat.

They enjoyed meeting all the people from different countries, but missed their own children very much. They expected to be picked up by a boat from Rarotonga in October before the beginning of the hurricane season in the Southern Hemisphere. We discovered that they were running low on sugar, light bulbs, and fuel. The generator produced a fair amount of surge in the electricity causing the light bulbs to burn out prematurely. The sugar was used up making coconut pancakes. I could guess that a few trips to the bird island used more fuel than they expected. We gave them some of the excess fuel we carried on Laelia. Then we contacted our friends about to depart Bora Bora to bring extra sugar and light bulbs.

We were in touch with John and Veronica for a number of years via email. We learned that they were almost stranded on Suwarrow for the cyclone season after we left. Their pickup boat never arrived. They had to hitch a ride with one of the last vessels to visit the atoll in November. That did not deter them. They loved the island so much that they went back to Suwarrow the following year with their four children.

12. Tonga and the Two Samoas

Arriving American Samoa (14 16.39 S, 170.695 W), 12 August 2005. Arriving Apia, Samoa (13 49.696 S, 171 45.780 W), 26 August. Arriving Neiafu, Tonga (18 39.554 S, 173 58.892 W), 12 September 2005.

American Samoa

We discovered the stowaway at breakfast in the cockpit the morning after our departure from Suwarrow. We were having a little peanut butter and bread with some strawberry jam. Soon after the jam jar was opened, a little guy about one-inch long scampered across the floorboard, scaled up the table leg, and made a beeline for the jar.

"Look, it's a cheechuk...a baby," Judy said. A cheechuk lizard is also called a gecko. They are all over the warmer regions of the world, in and out of doors.

"Wow, it must have smelled the jam...it came straight for the jar," I said.

"Howard, don't move...don't scare him. He's cute." The little cheechuk settled for the smudges of jam on the spreading knife. We could see it eating. It didn't seem to be afraid.

At the time we were already at sea on our way to American Samoa. The cheechuk (probably *Hemidactylus frenatus*) must have hitchhiked under the laundry bucket Judy used to haul the wash back to the boat when we were at Suwarrow. There wasn't much we could do about the hitchhiker at sea. For the remainder of our passage, we had an extra mouth to feed at breakfast. It was well behaved and was a pleasant diversion for us.

The Pago Pago (pronounced Pango Pango) Harbor on the island of Tutuila in American Samoa was an impregnable harbor, a naturally well-protected deep-water haven with high, steep mountains on all sides. There were several reefs that provided protection at the entry. The port was an important coaling station for US naval vessels in the South Pacific. Early in the last century the harbor shores were piled high with coal ready to be loaded on passing vessels.

We were required to tie up at the custom's dock until the completion of the customs inspection before dropping anchor in the harbor. *What a sorry excuse for a dock!*

The once solid concrete dock was broken in several pieces with no cleats to secure the lines. Laelia was tied to a palm tree at the bow and to a derelict boat at the stern. The dock looked as if it had received a direct hit by a bomb. We were told that a hurricane demolished the dock some years earlier. There were funds allocated for repairs, but somehow the money disappeared.

This was the first US port we came to since departing San Diego Harbor. I had expected to see a modern naval fortress, not an ancient ruin. Embarrassment was mixed with disappointment at the sorry state of affairs. After all, this was the official customs dock of the US Government. The locals used it as their favorite fishing pier although they could get hurt, considering the broken concrete and rusty re-bars sticking out here and there.

We met a father and son fishing at the dock. Just to be friendly I introduced Judy and myself to them. I tried whenever possible to chat with the locals. The son, Jason, about eight years of age, seemed bright and curious.

Jason said, "I think your boat is the best one in the harbor."

I said, "Thank you, I think so too. Would you like to see the inside of the boat?"

"Yeah!" Jason turned to look at his father for approval. His father nodded.

"Please come aboard." I had to say it quickly as he already started to climb aboard.

"Wow, I like the inside too."

I turned on the GPS and the chart plotter to show the position of the boat. The father helped the son identify the different city landmarks on the chart. I was impressed to see that the GPS had placed Laelia not only at the dock, but oriented in the correct direction. I asked about the fishing. The father told me that a special fish was schooling in the Harbor only once a year. It was an old Polynesian tradition to fish on this particular night.

Before they left, the father said, "If I were you, I would pick up everything loose on the deck and lock it up for the night."

His advice reinforced what we had read about the high rate of petty crime, especially theft, in Pago Pago. We were already concerned that being at the dock overnight made Laelia a target of opportunity. When we went to sleep that night, not being sure what to expect, we locked the salon door from the inside. All night long we heard people coming and going at the dock and fishermen chatting.

The next morning when I went ashore, several strangers greeted me, "Good morning, Howard." They smiled and waved. I waved back and felt like part of the family.

How do they know my name?

The father and son no doubt had passed the word around. Any number of the people at the dock overnight had probably "looked out" for us. My courtesy to a curious boy was reciprocated with kindness and protection.

After completing the check-in formalities, we circled around in the harbor, despite a 25-knot wind, for a good spot to drop anchor. We ended up not far from the mouth of a small creek, but the holding was poor.

"We are dragging anchor...it's not holding. We are almost on top of the river bank." Judy at the helm was shouting above the wind and the hum of the engine.

"Well, don't back anymore then. I need time to strip off all the plastic bags caught on the anchor," I shouted back.

On deck at the bow, I had to winch the anchor back up and get down on my hands and knees to peel off the plastic bags from the anchor. Gobs of sticky mud and twisted plastic shopping bags had to be removed. I was up to my elbows in mud that smelled of decay and looked disgusting.

It seemed that the bottom of that part of the harbor was

plastered with many layers of plastic shopping bags that behaved like a lubricant, allowing the anchor to slip right through the mud. We kept Laelia at the same approximate position and repeatedly plowed the same strip of the bottom mud to clear it of plastic bags. After the fifth try and thirty shopping bags, the anchor finally dug in solidly.

To celebrate our arrival in American Samoa, Judy booked a dance performance and dinner at Sadie Thompson's, named for the feisty young woman in Somerset Maugham's short story "Rain." It was a story about a battle of will between a wily woman of dubious reputation and a self-righteous missionary. Not surprisingly, she won. Alas, Sadie was no longer there.

The story had some factual basis. Missionaries did have considerable sway across the Pacific. To this day, the islanders remained religious. All the Samoans we met were devout Christians.

We took a bus over the mountain to a village on the north side of the island where there was a US National Park. Not far from the Park was a little village. The first thing we saw was someone sweeping the path in the sparkling clean village that appeared neat and dazzling in the morning sunshine. I was astonished by the contrast between Pago Pago and this little village. We saw a gentleman about sixty sweeping the already neat path.

"Hello, good morning," I said, "How are you? I'm Howard and this is my wife, Judy."

"I'm Paul. I'm the chief of this village."

"Nice to meet you. It's a beautiful village." I said.

"Thank you. Are you saved?" Paul asked.

"I think I am ok. I have made it this far across the ocean." I really wanted to talk to someone local and he was the only one around.

"Where are you from? Japan?"

"No, we are from California, but I was born in China."

"I was in California too for many years. I drank too much, but I quit. I was born again. I don't drink anymore." He asked, "How did you get here?"

"We came by sailboat. Here is a picture of our boat." I showed him our boat card.

"Nice boat...just the two of you? Did you get in any storms?"

"Oh yeah, we had our ups and downs," I replied. "When you're out there long enough, you get to see a few storms."

"Were you ever afraid?"

"Well, no. Can't say that I was afraid, but mostly we tried to do what was required at the time." I tried to think back with each of our previous storms. It was always more about problem solving than fear. Fear tends to fixate on the negative and tends to paralyze the ability to act rationally. Keeping busy and doing things to forestall impending disaster tends to have the therapeutic effect of keeping the feeling of panic at bay.

"I wish you well on your journey. I'll pray for you both."

"Thanks, I appreciate you thinking of us." Indeed it was good to have someone praying for us since we didn't have that kind of connection with the higher ups ourselves. At least it would make Paul feel good. I certainly didn't mind someone putting in a good word for us. *It can't hurt...right?*

Pago Pago is a big city, but compared poorly with the little village we visited. The Pago Pago streets were dirty and people seemed listless. We also noticed that many of the school-age kids were overweight. No doubt all the fast food outlets had something to do with the obesity. Also, in part, I thought it was because the original village that occupied the shores of Pago Pago Harbor was no longer a functioning community. To see even a semblance of what the original Samoa was like it was necessary to get away from Pago Pago.

Western Samoa

Not more than sixty miles NW from American Samoa was the independent Nation of Samoa, formerly Western Samoa. Both these Samoan populations were the same people with the same culture. They were all Polynesians, descendants of the Lapita Culture. They had the same history at least until the1900s, when the chiefs ceded five islands that constituted American Samoa to the US.

Western Samoa was a German colony until 1914. It gained formal independence in 1962 from New Zealand and later changed its name to Samoa.

We anchored Laelia in Apia Harbor near the Fishing Club on the Island of Opolu. Both of us joined the club as members for the nominal sum of one dollar so we could use their dock to tie up our dinghy when we went ashore. It was always a pleasure when we could use a floating dock instead of climbing a ladder on a concrete seawall to get ashore.

There seemed to be a distinct difference in the spirit of the people in Apia, the only city in Samoa. The taxi drivers were eager for our business. Kids were seen hawking goods. There was an air of cheerfulness and hustle. Perhaps this was a result of being an independent nation? There was an enthusiastic and exuberant spirit. Perhaps it was from the excitement of the impending festival.

We discovered that we had fallen, by chance, into one of the biggest Polynesian festivals. The day after we arrived, there were drumbeats at six in the morning. I was sure someone was beating the monotonous rhythm just to wake me up. Laelia with its one-inch thick foam sandwich hull was normally well insulated against noise, but not this time. I turned over and covered my ears with the pillow, but the drumbeats continued relentlessly. Finally, admitting defeat, I got up and looked out the porthole.

"Wow, that's the biggest canoe I've ever seen. It must have forty or fifty big beefy guys paddling." I croaked as I became fully awake. "There! I see him...the drummer sitting on the stern... hammering.... my poor aching head."

We found out a little later that they were practicing for the longboat (Fautasi) race and would be doing this every morning right at six. The race was not until the end of the Teuila Festival on 8 September...I had a feeling that we would be early risers for the next eleven days.

A little later at 0750 hours we heard music. The police band was marching along Beach Road to raise the flag at 0800 sharp in front of the Government Building. This parade took place every weekday, stopping all traffic right on time. It seemed like a quaint tradition from the past. Samoa had no military force. There was little crime. The police maintained order, directed traffic, patrolled the fishing grounds, and performed rescues at sea as needed. They even participated in the UN Peace Keeping Force in East Timor. In more recent times, there had been an increase of drug related activities that could draw more attention from the Samoan Police.

The festival was a weeklong celebration involving floral

parades, choir competition, *umu* cooking (similar to how the Marquesans roast the pig), fire and knife dances, a beauty contest, a longboat race, and a tattoo demonstration. In Samoa, tattoo is not done frivolously for cosmetic purposes; the tattoo represented important acknowledgements of personal accomplishments. The process was apparently painful. We watched as several members of the family held the young recipient on a mat to keep him from moving while the tattoo was applied.

We rented a car together with friends from s/v Mystic Rhythms. Before renting a car, Judy had to pay a fee to get a local driver's license. The four of us toured all over the island. The roads were good and the only hazards were the many loose pigs. Samoans raised pigs on their property both for consumption and to display their wealth. The more pigs they owned, the more they were respected for their affluence. Unlike money locked up in a safe, pigs roamed freely on the highway. They had a habit of dashing across the road suddenly. Judy was driving and made every effort not to run over a pig. We didn't know what would happen if we carried a dead pig to its owner.

"Sir, we are sorry your precious pig had an unfortunate rendezvous with our automobile." I didn't think that would get us invited to a roast-pork dinner. It was just as well that while we saw many pigs, we left them all very much alive.

We came to one small village at the edge of a mangrove swamp. The villagers offered us a boat tour of the mangrove jungle. *How can we pass that up?* We would probably never again receive an offer to see mangroves so close up and personal. These were canoes with a single outrigger. The paddler sat at the stern.

The village children laughed and giggled and pointed at us. I took some photos of them and showed them their images on the camera screen. They were all excited. It was all I could do to keep their little fingers off the lens.

The children's voices receded as the canoe paddled away. It was nice and quiet for some minutes. The only sound was the paddle dipping into the water. As we rounded a point and headed in a different direction, all of a sudden there they were again. The children up to that moment had kept quiet in some kind of a conspiracy. Now they shouted all together to surprise us. They laughed as we waved at them. Then they took off again, taking a shortcut to the next place to surprise us.

We stopped at a turtle pond and swam with the big turtles. The owner came and shaved some papaya into the water to attract the turtles to the surface. I didn't think the water was too clean to begin with. Now it was less than appealing.

The home of Robert Louis Stevenson was in good restoration and housed a museum for the author best known for his books: *Treasure Island, Kidnapped, Dr. Jekyll and Mr. Hyde*, among many others. He too sailed the Pacific...but he stayed and never left.

He was admired and loved by the Samoans. When he died suddenly in 1894 at age 44, the Samoans carried him on their shoulders to be buried at a high spot on the island overlooking the sea. The last three lines on his tomb:

Here he lies where he longed to be;
Home is the sailor, home from the sea,
And the hunter home from the hill.

Near the end of the festival, all the boats in the harbor were told to tie up at the container shipping dock to make room for the Longboat Race. It was a big deal with drums beating and music blaring. More crowds arrived from other islands to cheer their favorite team. We thought we would depart after the race. We would sail to Tonga before making preparation for the long passage to New Zealand.

New Zealand had very strict rules against importing animal species of any kind. We thought it would be best if we disembarked our little stowaway before New Zealand. We had seen plenty of similar cheechuks in Samoa and hoped our stowaway wouldn't create an ecological disaster if we let it loose there. Trapping it with a bottle baited with jam was no problem, but saying goodbye was never easy. It scampered into a shrub in a residential area and probably would never taste strawberry jam again.

The Kingdom of Tonga

Water was running down our yellow rain slickers. What we could see of the land, through the mist and fog, was lush and green. It was not our best moment as we arrived at Koko Bay not far from the town of Neiafu on Vava'u Island in the Kingdom of Tonga. Both Judy and I were sick with some sort of respiratory infection, but we had to navigate through the twists and turns of the waterway in the heavy rain.

We had been sailing all night and I was craving a little sleep. As we approached the anchorage, our spirits were lifted when we spotted Bill and Joan, our friends from s/v Sage, and Perry from s/v Corona, waiting for us in the pouring rain at the dock to catch Laelia's lines. Joan even had some cinnamon rolls ready for us. It is good to have friends.

A strange bureaucratic twist required port fees to be paid only in Pa'anga, the local Tongan money. It was also in their rules that we couldn't set foot ashore until we were checked in. Since we arrived without any Tongan money, we were caught in a "catch-22." Bill handed me a wad of Pa'anga before he left. We waited on Laelia for the check-in.

Three large athletic-looking officials representing the Customs, Immigration, and the Port Captain boarded Laelia. Tongans are known for their large physiques. These three were certainly impressive specimens. They had to bend over in order to enter the salon. Laelia was designed to accommodate persons up to 6 foot 2 inches. These gentlemen were unable to stand up straight in the salon and had to sit down to be comfortable. They had bronze colored skin and full heads of curly hair.

They were formal, but friendly. One was perspiring profusely, despite the fact that it was not an exceptionally warm day. I offered him the remainder of a roll of paper towels. Judy offered sodas that they declined.

As was the usual procedure, I produced copies of our passports, crew list, USCG vessel documentation, and clearance papers from the previous port. They gave me forms to fill out. When each was completed, I paid the amount in Pa'anga. Their hands appeared too big for the official seals as they slammed them down to stamp the papers and receipts with vigor and authority.

"There is an inspection fee," the leader of the group said. "That'll be twenty Pa'anga."

I said, "Uh, twenty Pa'anga? I don't have any more Tongan money. My friend gave me just what I needed." I was wondering if

Bill had given me the wrong amount.

"Ok, ok...don't worry, ten US dollars is good."

Hmmm...now I understand...I better not accuse him of anything...or embarrass him.

"I can pay you in dollars, but I will need a receipt," I replied respectfully. There was a pause and he gave me a look of displeasure. At that moment, I wasn't sure what kind of trouble I had incurred.

"Ah, forget it." He waved his hand dismissively.

He stood up bent over so he wouldn't bump his head on the salon roof and left without any pleasantries. The other two followed him out and cordially bid Judy and me good-bye.

With the formalities completed, we left the dock to find a buoy to tie up. We got buoy #19, not far from the Mermaid Bar, the local watering hole for cruisers, where we ate frequently during our stay.

I tried sausage and mash for the first time at the Mermaid. It was a New Zealand or Australian concoction of sausages mingled with a generous portion of mashed potatoes drowned in brown gravy. It wasn't too bad...if I was hungry enough. We enjoyed the camaraderie of the cruisers at the bar and tried a variety of ethnic foods. Judy's favorite was the "impossible coconut pie."

The Mermaid also had thrilling performances of a fire dance. The wild drum beat and the glistening bronze muscles evoked a primitive battle scene. The flames lashing out at the dry thatch roof threatened a conflagration in the crowded bar. I quietly looked around for a bayside window over deep water for a quick escape route.

We were not terribly active, probably because of our illness. While most cruisers sailed to different anchorages and other Tongan islands, we just stayed close to the Mermaid. Our spirit of discovery was at low ebb because we were still recuperating. We did go on a whale watching tour.

We even went to church on a Sunday morning. It wasn't because we wanted to pray for better health. I had heard that Tongans were good vocalists. They didn't disappoint. The ladies in particular could belt out Christian hymns in angelic timbre with gusto. I regretted not having a voice recorder to preserve the powerful singing voices.

148

We went to a big hotel by the waterfront to hear a lecture on environmental issues about whales by an Australian. The hotel was an enormous old structure, but poorly maintained and seemed to have a very low occupancy rate.

"How could any business survive with such poor management?" I wondered aloud while waiting for the lecture to begin.

The gentleman sitting next to me gave me a conspiratorial look and whispered, "Don't you know? The Royal Family owns this establishment. It's actually a real business for a change."

I had read about the king's many business schemes that ended in shambles. When he did make millions by selling passports to the Chinese, he couldn't hold onto the profit; an American banker allegedly swindled most of his ill-gotten gain.

As a result of the passport sales, some Chinese actually settled in Tonga and became Tongan citizens. I met the owner of the *Auspicious Market*, a small grocery store. The man, in his 50's, spoke mostly a regional dialect and not a word of English or Tongan. We managed a conversation in Mandarin Chinese. He was thrilled to have someone to talk to and I became his fast friend forever. He seemed isolated and disoriented. He was confused on how he ended up at a market in Tonga, but he thought it involved investment either by the government or encouraged by the government.

Tonga was a bit of an enigma. It was never fully conquered or colonized by a foreign power. It became a constitutional monarchy as early as 1875 and a British Protectorate until 1970. The kingdom was nominally a democracy with an elected parliament, but the common people had no voice in the affairs of the state. Surprisingly, Tongans I talked to preferred keeping the monarchy, but they were dissatisfied with the ineptness of the government. I followed news of sporadic riots and jailing of the opposition long after we left Tonga. It was not until 2010, five years after we left, that a reformed constitution was installed with the king relinquishing his power voluntarily.

The days went by for us rapidly in Tonga. Between "sausages and mash" and the "impossible coconut pie" for dessert, washed down with Tongan beer, I recovered my strength and shook off the feeling of malaise. It was important to be ready physically and mentally for the long haul to New Zealand in early October.

Before we left, we went to a deserted patch of water, not far from the anchorage, to clean the boat bottom to make Laelia glide swifter. It was also important to have a clean bottom so as not to transmit undesirable organisms to New Zealand. After most of the chores were finished, we rewarded ourselves with a dinghy tour of the nearby caves. These caves were only accessible by kayaks or by dinghy. Caves seemed to have a strange attraction for people. The various colors of the water and the exposed rock formation in the flickering light conjured a dark mystery inside the earth.

On the way back, I ran the dinghy over a shallow reef. The outboard motor protested by making grinding noises and shaking the dinghy, then promptly quit running. I tilted the outboard up and used the oar to pole the dinghy off the reef. Other than some dings on the propeller, there were no serious damages, but it was not an auspicious sign for our forthcoming passage.

13. Destination New Zealand

Departing Tonga (18 41.983 S, 174 01.799 W), 07 October 2005. Arriving quarantine dock, Opua, New Zealand (35 18.800 S, 174 07.346 E), 18 October 2005. Arriving Gulf Harbour Marina, Whangaparoa, New Zealand (36 37.263 S, 174 47.418 E), 31 October 2005. Departing Opua, New Zealand, 03 May 2006.

Passage to New Zealand

In early June 1994, long before we set sail from California, a sudden storm developed between New Zealand and Tonga and deteriorated to ferocious winds of hurricane strength with 35-foot seas. It was near the British Queen's Birthday when seven boats were abandoned and one boat, with three persons on board, was never found, except for its empty life raft. Ever after, the incident was called the "Queen's Birthday Disaster," the mention of which struck fear in the hearts of sailors.

Fast forward to October 2005: we were preparing to sail the same patch of the South Pacific Ocean, from Tonga to New Zealand, to duck the approaching cyclone season in the tropics. The South Pacific cyclone season is officially from November to May, but that doesn't mean it is safe during the rest of the year.

A few of the cruisers were having a beer during happy hour at the Mermaid Bar in Tonga.

A first-time cruiser named Joe said, "Did you know that there had been three boats lost this season already and it's not even the cyclone season yet?"

An old Kiwi replied, "Oh yeah, nasty storms could blow any time of the year. I've sailed round here almost twenty years. A low pressure can just suddenly dip into a depression. It's the Antarctic you know. Meteorologists call it a "bomb." That's why you've got to look for a weather window."

Joe said, "I've been listening to McDavitt's forecast on the radio, but he doesn't go more than five days."

The old Kiwi said, "That's because his weather model is only accurate for about five days. After that it's not much better than guesswork. Sometimes the forecast is only good for two or three days."

Joe's wife who had been listening quietly, said "But, but...the passage is more than a thousand nautical miles! It could take as much as ten days to get to New Zealand. What happens if we get caught?"

"Well, that's what happened to those poor buggers earlier this year. If you can get a good five-day window, then run like hell at your top boat speed. Just hope you don't get caught or..."

An American cruiser perked up, "What do you do if you get caught?"

Someone who had just arrived said, "I heard you could just let the boat lie ahull."

The old Kiwi shook his head. "Well, people have done that before by shutting the boat up and letting it drift...be at the sea's mercy...that can work. But, lying ahull is not the best strategy in a storm with big waves. Sooner or later the boat will get rolled, causing damage to both the crew and the boat. I favor some kind of drogue or sea anchor."

The American said, "I like the sea anchor idea. The sea anchor will keep the boat pointing into the wind and keep it steady in the water. What does the drogue do?"

The old Kiwi explained. "In the old days, people used old tires or just long coils of rope dragging behind the boat. It keeps the boat from lying abeam, sideways, in the waves...and it slows down the boat so it won't trip and pitch pole (flipping end to end) from surfing too fast down a big wave."

The American said, "I heard a talk by the Pardeys in San Francisco on heaving-to. They are big on heave-to in a storm."

"Yeah that works too, but not every boat can heave-to the same.

The skipper needs to have a plan on what to do when all hell breaks loose. He needs a plan for abandon-boat too...what to put in the ditch bag...even what to do in case of a helicopter or ship rescue."

Everyone was quiet for a moment and guzzling more beer... probably to avoid thinking of howling winds and crashing waves...and drowning.

The Kiwi continued, "I always have my sea anchor set up and ready to deploy...that way I don't ever need to be rescued."

I had mixed feelings. The passage to New Zealand sounded extra risky because of the fast changing weather pattern. On the other hand, we were pretty well prepared. Judy had already packed our ditch bag. It had our passports, some small money, flares, snack food in sealed bags, lots of sun protection, a portable water maker, fishing supplies, a deck of playing cards. We also had a sea anchor on board, but it had never been deployed, not even in practice. The sea anchor looked like a parachute, except it was made of heavy canvas and very cumbersome to work with. Once wet it would take forever to dry and be impossible to repack. There were also two hundred feet of one-inch nylon line and heavy-duty swivels to attach the sea anchor.

Laelia did have a weakness that worried me. I was hoping to get the starboard transmission repaired in New Zealand. It kept slipping when shifting into gear. There was no hope of having it repaired in Tonga. A failed transmission could be our Achilles heel on this passage. The only consolation was that Laelia, being a catamaran, had dual engines and powertrains. If one side failed, we could still manage except for intricate maneuvers or powering through a rough storm.

We planned to stay in New Zealand quite a long while, pending the approval of our long-stay visa application. It was filed while we were still in Samoa, but somehow we never received a response from the New Zealand High Commission. We would deal with the visa snafu after our arrival in the country. Our landfall was Opua near the northern tip of the North Island in New Zealand, in the Bay of Islands...a sailing haven.

The wind was light as predicted. We were doing a lot of wallowing at two knots and flat seas. The wind indicator was showing zero true wind while the GPS showed 1.5 knots for the boat speed. Perhaps there was a current, but that seemed too good to be true. More than likely something was wrong with the anemometer. On a boat there was always something that needed to be repaired. We were beginning our New Zealand passage. It was hot and the motion of the boat made us queasy. Judy had to go to sleep to ward off seasickness. I furled the sail, turned on one engine, and kept the boat moving at low speed to conserve fuel.

Map of South Pacific Countries

It was a trade-off. If we used too much fuel now, we might not have enough when the weather turned ugly, but if we motored too slowly, we increased the chance of getting caught in a bad storm.

It was just as well that Laelia was moving along slowly at that moment. Suddenly, I felt a bump. At first I thought it was a wave sloshing against the boat, but then I realized the ocean was glassy smooth. I looked around and saw a whale very close by our port beam as Laelia was moseying past.

The big guy gave me a reproachful look, as if saying, "What are you guys doing disturbing my afternoon nap?" It then blew a spout of water and went on its way.

My gawd...we hit a whale!

It was probably a humpback returning to the Antarctic to feed. I scurried around checking Laelia to make sure there were no damages. We had heard reports of boats that sank within minutes of colliding with whales.

It was ironic that most of my preparations for the passage to New Zealand had been geared for surviving catastrophic storms, such as getting the sea anchor ready for deployment. At that moment, the last thing I needed was a sea anchor. The ditch bag with survival supplies at the ready seemed out of place in the salon while we were wallowing in light wind and flat seas.

One forecast we got that day from the "Rag of the Air," an SSB radio net, was for five more days of this light variable wind. Well, we shouldn't complain too much. Variable wind at five or six knots was a lot better than fifty or sixty knots. Even Judy acclimatized to the slow boat motion after a couple of days. With the extra time at sea, we could do a little reading and eat without worrying about losing it. One bit of sage advice from our reading on cooking at sea was that "the food should taste good not only on the way down, but also acceptable on the way up."

The toughest part of cruising was dealing with weather. Where was our trusty weather person when we needed him? I had talked to Don (Summer Passage) on the SSB a couple of times the week before, but all he was willing to conjure up was: "Ugh, it's going to be pretty light." I couldn't get him to say, "North 15 to 20 all the way to New Zealand." On the other hand, I was happy not to have to huddle in the cockpit in my foul weather gear, wishing for calmer seas.

After very little wind for the first several days and then a couple of days of strong wind on the nose, we had a number of really good sailing days, when we made almost 200 nautical miles. We had to reef to prevent the strong winds from damaging the rigging. It took us 11 days to sail from Neiafu, Tonga, to Opua, New Zealand.

As we moved south, the air temperature dropped gradually. We finally had to dig out our cold-weather clothes. First the long sleeve shirts, then the sweaters and jackets, and finally long pants. We knew for sure we were back in the temperate zone when we had to put on socks.

In the tropics, shorts and tee shirts were all that was needed. Some people even sailed naked. Someone once asked Judy, "Do you ever sail naked?"

"Oh, no. That would take way too much sun block," she replied.

As we headed to higher latitudes, foul weather gear was required. No longer could we just let ourselves air dry naturally. Here getting wet meant hypothermia.

When we were a couple of hundred miles from New Zealand, an Air Force plane overflew Laelia. It was a Lockheed P-3 Orion, painted in green camouflage colors. The plane was distinctive with its four props and the tail stinger. It flew low, right over our mast. Then the pilot hailed us on the VHF radio

"Vessel heading south...your boat name?"

"This is Laelia, Lima Alpha Echo, Lima India Alpha," replied Judy on the VHF.

Then the pilot wanted to know our radio call sign, homeport, documentation number, and our ETA in New Zealand. Such contacts were comforting because these would also be planes to drop rescue equipment for boats in distress. Not having seen anything except water and waves for days and days, a big airplane buzzing over the boat was a major event. These planes were originally built for anti-submarine warfare, but for us it felt like an official welcome to New Zealand as it roared low overhead.

New Zealand was most cautious about arriving boats and took the quarantine process seriously. No one could step ashore before the Quarantine Officer had inspected the boat thoroughly. They had problems with introduced species that became pests. Many of New Zealand's endangered bird species now existed only on a few of the offshore islands. Just one pregnant rat could erase those endangered birds for all eternity in a short amount of time. The quarantine also restricted any sort of seeds and unprocessed foods, especially chicken. Other items they worried about were diseases of cattle and sheep, of which they had a lot to lose. Any sort of soil on boots and camping equipment was a concern to them.

We understood these concerns and wanted to cooperate. We had cleaned the bottom of the boat while in Tongan waters to get rid of as much growth as we were able. The Port of Entry at Opua, New Zealand had a curved floating dock completely isolated from land to accommodate arriving vessels. We arrived late in the day and stayed overnight at the dock until Customs and the Quarantine Officers inspected our boat and contents.

Upon arrival we wanted to celebrate. We cooked a big dinner using up the remaining fresh foods before the quarantine inspection and opened a bottle of California Champagne. Although each passage was an important component of the journey, this one held more emotional value. It was not only because of the added risk; it could have been the final segment of our trip. We could conclude our journey here and ship Laelia back to North America on Dockwise Yacht Transport.

The inspection went well. They took all of our ship's accumulated garbage as well as what was left of the frozen chicken meat. The big surprise was that they also took our New Zealand honey. We knew New Zealand had a honey industry that they wanted to protect against diseases affecting bees. We thought we were so cleaver for having bought New Zealand honey when we re-provisioned previously. It turned out that we had opened the honey jar and the contents could have been contaminated. We thought that was a little far-fetched, but didn't argue the point. (I just rolled my eyeballs.) After all, the Customs and the Quarantine Officers were most professional and cordial. I didn't want to spoil things over a small jar of half-eaten honey.

There were other boats still en route from Tonga to New Zealand. One of them was crewed by a father and son team. They departed only two days after us, but were caught in an unpleasant cold front with strong winds on the nose. They were unable to make much headway for several days. Bill and Joan, on s/v Sage still in Tonga, and Judy and I, already in New Zealand, kept in touch with them by SSB radio. Bill recorded their positions when there were radio contacts at pre-arranged times. The records showed that they had been blown by the storm more than a hundred miles off course during one particular night. If we hadn't known they were heading for New Zealand, we would have thought they were on a course for South America. I didn't understand why Perry, the father, didn't turn on his engine.

Auxiliary diesel engines were intended precisely for situations like what he was encountering.

On the morning just after their worst night at sea, Perry was reporting his position and local conditions to the radio net, the Rag-of-the-Air.

Perry said, "The situation is sheer hell most of the night... (crackling static)... two reefs... main... jib...thirty-knot wind from SSW...six- to......foot waves... seven to eight seconds... we're getting nowhere fast. Over."

Rag controller: "Man, if you don't like this weather, just wait a couple of hours."

Perry, alarmed, said, "What...What do you mean? How much worse is it gonna be?"

The Rag controller on the radio was only being flippant, but Perry, in his exhausted state, took it to heart and was on the verge of despair.

Rag controller said, "No, no, don't panic...it's going to be ok. Motor south...there is a north wind farther south of your present position. Over."

Perry: "Uh, I can only run the engine fifteen minutes at a time. It's overheating. I think the water pump is bad...it's not pumping enough."

There really wasn't much any of us could do, but having some contact on the radio, even with all that static electricity in the atmosphere, was a morale booster. Humans need social contact to know they are not alone in the struggle. As we talked, Perry became resigned to the fact that they would have to face the storm for several more days and became surprisingly upbeat, resolving to make the best of the situation.

At one point, Judy tried to encourage them by promising them cold beers at the dock. Then she realized how frigid it must be at sea in the wind-whipped rain and salt spray. She added hot croissants to the cold beer. Having been in similar situations before, she could empathize. When Perry and his son finally arrived at the dock in Opua, Judy made good her promise by greeting them with two bottles of cold New Zealand beer and some hot croissants.

The emotional tension was especially evident in the account* of our friends, Bill and Joan on s/v Sage, who arrived about two weeks after us. We knew from their reports over the radio that they made every effort to move the boat as fast as they were able to minimize their exposure at sea. They motored hard when the wind was light and kept the sail full when they generally would have reefed. No one would blame them for not wanting to get caught in bad weather on this passage. They actually had an excellent passage by their own account, but they were very tense throughout the entire voyage. On the first night after their arrival, Joan fell asleep while reading in bed although her husband stayed awake and continued with his reading.

She sat up all of a sudden and said, "The boat is not moving right." Bill looked at her and said, "Joan, are you alright?" She, increasing her voice by several decibels, "The boat is moving, but it's just not moving fast enough!"

Bill looked at her and said, "Joan, are you awake? The boat is tied to the dock."

It took her quite some moments before she relaxed her shoulders and said, "Oh...we made it." Indeed her ordeal was over.

* This account was related to me by Bill and Joan McKnight on s/v Sage and is presented here with their permission.

Thanksgiving in Kiwi Land

How hard would it be for a cruiser to readjust to living on land again? By the time we arrived at Opua, New Zealand it had been one whole year since our departure from California. During that time we had been boat people almost every day. We wanted to try land living again, even if it was just for a few days.

It was time to take a break and recharge. Judy and I rented a car to spend a few days away from the water and boats. We stayed at a B&B in a private home owned by the nicest couple and their two children. It was refreshing to indulge ourselves in normal land living, away from the frugality and the constant vigilance of cruising. The bed was so plush it was like sleeping on a cloud. We didn't have to get up early to prepare breakfast...it just appeared on the table. The bath and shower looked dazzlingly new and pristine. There were various sized towels, all so soft and jet white. It was quite a contrast from the quick drying backpacking chamois towel I used on the boat.

"I think I'm going to take a shower with real hot water and

plenty of it," I said, remembering how I washed and rinsed with less than one or two gallons of water on Laelia where fresh water was precious and there was no hot water unless we happened to have been running the starboard engine.

"How's the shower?" Judy asked.

"It's great. I scrubbed with lots of soap. Would you scrub my back for me please?" I handed the soapy towel to Judy.

"Yuck, how come the towel is so dirty?" Judy just couldn't do anything without a critical eye.

"I don't know. I don't think I'm that dirty... Ooh... that feels good," I said as she started scrubbing my back.

"Oh no... more brown color is coming off. It's your skin! You're peeling like a snake." Judy exclaimed while examining the towel.

"You are not scrubbing off all my suntan are you?" I said.

"I just hope you can wash all that off the towel. Our hosts will wonder what kind of people they let in their home," Judy said.

Apparently, the chamois on the boat was not rough enough to abrade the skin. Now my tan was coming off on the towel with tiny bits of my skin.

Maybe I should molt before I take a shower.

There was Chinese food just about anywhere in the world and I had sampled quite a bit of it. In Opua there was a Chinese takeout with outdoor tables for those who were hungry and couldn't wait. We took our orders to the table at lunch.

"This broccoli beef tastes awful," said Judy. "How could they mess up something so simple?"

"The beef is tough too. What did they do to make it so tough?" I said as I continued to chew, but my jaw muscles were getting tired.

Judy and I both admitted defeat and dropped most of our food in the trash bin behind us. .

Then we went across the street back to our rental car, but I couldn't unlock the car door. I struggled with the key and tried the other keys on the ring.

"Don't you know how to use a key anymore?" Judy was getting impatient.

"Well, you can try it with your magic touch," I said calmly.

No dice...she couldn't get the key to work either. We both fiddled with the car door some more with no success. This went on for over five or ten minutes. We didn't know what else we could do. We couldn't just abandon the car.

"Well, I could break a window to get in the car," I said without much conviction.

"What good is that if the key doesn't work anymore? Besides, it's a rental car," said Judy.

Perhaps we had been on the boat so long and were no longer suited for the complications of land living. Still, it was probably not a good idea to break a window or to abandon the car. I looked around to see if we could get someone to help. Just then, I spotted another white car parked twenty feet away...it was the same brand and model.

Eureka!

I wouldn't rate our first foray on land as a great success, but it wasn't a total failure. We didn't get arrested for stealing an automobile...or for breaking the window of someone else's car. We eventually found our way back with no mishaps.

We departed the dock at Opua for a short passage south to a marina with haul-out facilities for servicing Laelia. Our destination was Gulf Harbor Marina in a small resort suburb on the Whangaparaoa Peninsula, about half an hour by car north of Auckland. In Maori, Whangaparaoa meant "the Bay of Whales."

We did an overnight sail heading south along the East Coast of New Zealand from Opua in the Bay of Islands to the Gulf Harbour Marina. During the change of shift at night, Judy alerted me to the scattered islands along the Coast.

"There are lights all around. It's scary," she said.

The Polynesians ancestors of the Maoris called New Zealand Aotearoa, meaning "the land of the long white clouds." With heavy cloud cover, the night sky looked as dark as the water. The shore lights stood out looking menacingly close. At night on a passage, any light means danger. It was not obvious how far away the lights were, so it was much more wearisome doing the night watch along the coast than on the high seas.

We arrived at the Gulf Harbour Marina in daylight with no problems. It was a large, magnificent modern marina.

I came across a pamphlet in the laundry room left there by a car dealership about a "buyback plan for yachties." We went to the car dealer on a Tuesday afternoon to take a look...just to look of course. We were there about thirty minutes and drove out with a very clean, ten-year old Nissan Pulsar.

"Oh, just drive it around until Thursday to see how you like it," the dealer said as he handed me the keys.

"Don't you want to see our driver licenses?" I was surprised that he didn't even ask for our last names.

"Oh, no worries, you folks will be fine. Besides, where can you run with a fire-engine red car like that?" He said that with a big smile. He knew he had us already.

The price seemed a little high, but it had a fixed buyback price in six months. I had already calculated that it would be much cheaper than renting a car at the long-term rental rate. We found out later that these cars were from Japan where people didn't drive much, but they wouldn't be caught dead owning a car more than a few years old.

Judy's requirements for a car, which consisted of automatic transmission, four doors, and a large boot, were all met. So we bought the car and went to the AA (Auto Association) to activate our membership on reciprocity with AAA in California.

Thanksgiving was approaching; there were enough American cruisers around interested in organizing a holiday dinner. The Yacht Club was willing to let us use their dining room, although their contracted caterer would do the food preparation. The caterer would be in charge of everything except the pies. That was all the excuse the American ladies needed to take over the Yacht Club kitchen for a few days before the big dinner...to make pies.

Judy got the job of securing pie tins and getting uncooked piecrust from the market. That was when it dawned on us why the caterer didn't want to deal with making pies. She knew how to make savory pies like pork and kidney pies, but knew absolutely nothing about fruit pies or pumpkin pies. There were no pie tins or frozen piecrusts available in the market. I could see this was going to become a crisis.

Where is Marie Callender when we need her?

Judy and I went on the Internet and the telephone searching for pie tins. We finally located an outfit on the North Island that made aluminum plates.

"Yes, we make pie tins that are 23 centimeters in diameter," said the gentleman in the sales department.

"Perfect, that's about nine inches." I was delighted.

"We sell wholesale overseas, but we can ship anywhere in the world. Minimum order is two thousand."

"Uh...two thousand?" I was flabbergasted, "We only need two dozen."

I sensed that he was about to apologize and hang up the phone. I tried to keep him on the phone...perhaps I could talk him into selling just few.

"We need the tins for an American Thanksgiving dinner. You don't need to ship them anywhere. I'm happy to pick up the order at your location," I said.

"I'm sorry, we don't sell in small quantities." He added, "Well, tell you what, why don't I send a complimentary sample box of one hundred? That should take care of what you need. Will that do for you?"

"Uh...Sure, thank you. That's very kind of you." I made sure he got the shipping address at the Marina. The box of pie tins arrived promptly in the mail a few days later.

Judy then went to the local bakery ordering custom-prepared piecrusts. She gave the baker a pie tin as a sample and explained to them what she needed. On the appointed day, she picked up a stack of pie dough for the party at the Yacht Club kitchen. The ladies made pumpkin pies, Grandma Grace's Apple Pie, Judy's Pumpkin Pecan Pie, and many more.

The Thanksgiving dinner went off without a hitch!

Our car gave us more freedom to explore. We discovered dim sum in Auckland and Mexican food in Orewa as well as an Indian restaurant in Manly Village near the Marina.

My brother and his wife came to New Zealand to go on a car trip with us, a grand tour of the North Island, over the New Year Holidays. We toured the Hobbit Village where the movie was filmed and visited an ostrich farm. The wild Gannet rookery provided stunning photos.

Beginning with the New Year, we had to start being serious about our boat preparation. We rented a small house close to the boatyard and hauled Laelia out of the water for engine work and painting at the boatyard. A pleasant turn of events was that the cone-drive in Laelia's diesel engine was replaced under warranty. The original cones were too small for the size and power of the engine. We were most grateful to the mechanics at Gulf Harbour for doing an outstanding job. We also had the dinghy davits reinforced because the original hardware was almost torn loose during one of the storms at sea. To make doubly sure the davits would be adequate, we replaced the heavy dinghy with a lighter and smaller aluminum-bottom inflatable. We also bought a 5-horse outboard so Judy could start it by herself.

We did have problems with the paint shop at Gulf Harbour, and had to personally supervise much of the painting. As a result we couldn't get away for an extended period to explore more of New Zealand. Although the owner and manager of the paint shop were knowledgeable marine painters, the people they hired to do the actual work were unskilled day laborers. In order for marine bottom paints to set properly, there had to be sufficient drying time between each coat. The workers didn't bother to read the instructions and were putting the paint on too soon. The manager was nowhere to be found. I had to stay and make sure the drying time was respected.

When I went away for a few hours, one worker even painted over the zinc on Laelia's sail drives. Anyone who knew anything about boats would have known that the zinc was never painted over. It needed to be in contact with seawater to protect other metal parts against electrolysis. Workmanship generally was good in New Zealand, but good supervision was still required.

It was the middle of April when the New Zealand autumn was starting to feel a bit chilly. In the sun it was comfortable, but it cooled off dramatically after sunset. As the crew was putting on the last few coats of paint, it rained often. Even in the paint shed, the increase in humidity and the drop in temperature caused the paint's drying time to increase further.

A Kiwi cruiser had told me back in January: "summer is right around the corner."

I saw him again at the dock and asked, "Hey, the wind is having kind of a bite to it now. What happened to the summer you promised?"

"Well, it happened already. Remember, I told you not to blink."

I said, "Yeah, I guess there was a stretch of about ten days in February when it didn't rain. That was when everybody was worried about a drought."

He kind of sniffed, "Mmmm...you're right. You know... we don't have any oil in the ground and we voted out nuclear energy. No rain, no hydro...we may have to turn out the light."

While we were working on Laelia in the boatyard, a couple living nearby was taking a stroll and we talked. They were interested in our journey and invited us to dinner at their home two days later. In New Zealand, a meal at someone's home is usually lamb roast with all the trimmings. The roast went exceedingly well with the mint sauce which was somewhat like a pickle relish and not so minty. Needless to say, it was quite a treat.

The Great Barrier Island

After almost six months of comfortable living at Gulf Harbour, returning to the harsh and frugal life at sea was not so enchanting anymore. Winter was approaching in the Southern Hemisphere and the weather had been ominous, with a new storm every few days. Strong winds and pelting rain made going to sea forbidding. We knew what it felt like to be at the mercy of the ocean swells and gale-force winds. At sea we would be on our own again, with nothing within hundreds of miles except the wind and the waves.

There were so many ways to put off departure. Even on a sunny day, I could feel the malefic winds lurking behind the horizon. Sunny days were becoming less frequent. The low-pressure systems that swooped across the Tasman Sea from the west brought dark clouds and angry seas. With our six-month visas about to expire, we had to move on.

On one sunny Thursday morning, we decided to depart Gulf Harbour on a slim weather window. The forecast was for increasing wind strength the next day and ferocious winds the day after. A deep low was approaching. We picked Port Fitzroy at the Great Barrier Island near the east coast of New Zealand as our first haven. (The Great Barrier Island, about 15 miles long and 5 miles wide, has nothing to do with the Great Barrier Reef of Australia, despite the similarity in the name.) It was described in the guidebook as a secure harbor, although the navigation can be tricky spanning several rocky areas and a narrow pass. But, with the harbor situated only about 40 nautical miles from Gulf Harbour, I figured we could make it in one day while the weather was still holding. Assuming of course that the storm would arrive no sooner than in the forecast.

Unfortunately, we were delayed and did not depart Gulf Harbour until one o'clock in the afternoon. Even as we left the Marina, it seemed unlikely that we would make Port Fitzroy by nightfall.

It was already autumn and the sunset was earlier, at about 5:45 PM. I had both engines blasting at full throttle propelling Laelia through the water at eight knots, despite the 15-knot true wind from dead ahead. The mechanic had said that we should run the engines at cruising RPM for a few hours. This was our first chance to give the engines and the new transmissions a serious test. If we should run into any snags with the engine or the transmission, we could be in trouble. Even at the speed we were pushing, Laelia had a good chance of arriving at Port Fitzroy after dark, assuming we dared power at full throttle through those rocky passages. Perhaps the original plan was not the most sensible.

We did have a Plan B to arrive at an alternate harbor called Whangaparapara, just south of Port Fiztroy. It is a wide-open harbor where we could zoom in at eight knots and drop anchor at the first sign of shallow water. If the storm arrived early, we could sit tight in that harbor until the bad weather passed.

Laelia continued on the frenetic pace heading for Whangaparapara as the sun sank ever lower towards the western horizon.

"The harbor is only about ten minutes away," I said as Laelia approached the Great Barrier Island.

"The sun is already below the horizon. The twilight won't last much longer," observed Judy at the wheel.

"I'll get the anchor ready," I said as Laelia entered the Whangaparapara Harbor in the last ray of daylight.

"It's too dark...I can't see your hand signal anymore." Judy shouted from the helm while I was on the foredeck managing the anchor.

By that time, I could hardly see my own hand in front of me. It was an inky, moonless night.

We resorted to using flashlights to signal each other. Despite not being able to use our visual signals, we managed to drop the anchor and tested the holding.

Wow, it has to be the easiest harbor for a quick refuge.

Ironically, later that night long after we had dropped anchor, we saw one of the rare star-lit nights in New Zealand. There was no moon and the stars were out in force. Orion was half set over the mountains of New Zealand mainland and the Southern Cross (Crux) was high in the sky brighter than usual with the Milky Way flowing across the sky.

We raised anchor the next morning and continued for Port Fitzroy. The wind strength had increased noticeably, but still manageable. The forecast was for very strong winds for several days following. Port Fitzroy is an all-direction, well-protected anchorage and, more importantly, there was a pub at the waterfront.

It turned out to be a very good decision that we didn't try to enter Port Fitzroy at night. As we approached the coast around the Man-Of-War Pass to enter Port Fitzroy, we skirted around big lumps of rocks lurking in the vicinity of the narrow pass. I checked the chart plotter to make sure the boat was pointing at the pass on the chart screen. There is always a risk in relying on the chart screen. The position of the boat as determined by the GPS was accurate to better than 10 feet, but if the chart (on a memory chip copied from nautical charts) was not sufficiently accurate, the boat could run onto rocks and cliffs. We had previously discovered charts that were off by as much as half a mile. I figured that our electronic chip updated three years ago from a New Zealand chart had to be pretty good.

Just the same, we kept watch for the rocks. As Judy was steering, she kept pointing the boat somewhere different from what was indicated on the chart screen. Neither of us could be sure of the exact location of the entrance. All we could see were cliffs and tree-covered slopes dipping all the way to the water's edge, although Judy had the additional benefit of having the binoculars in her hands.

"From past experience, you're not gonna see the entrance until we are right on top of it," I said.

"You get that close, you'll be on top of those rocks." Judy is usually more circumspect with her navigation.

As Judy and I were still snarling at each other, a big powerboat zoomed out from the rocky cliff, generating big wakes all around. It gave us a clue where we should be going. As we got closer, another powerboat came out of the pass. We had to stop Laelia to let the powerboat cross Laelia's bow. Having seen where the powerboats came out, we were able to keep going. As we transited

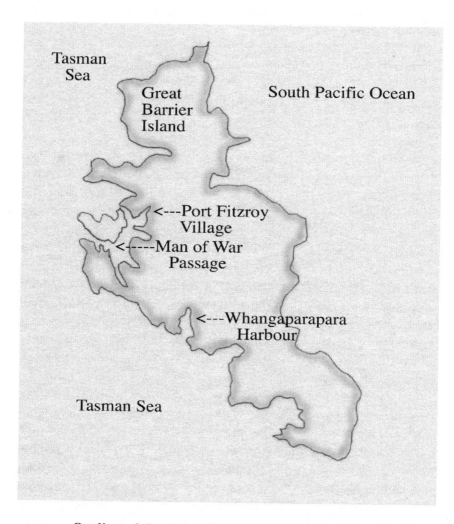

Tasman Sea

Great Barrier Island

South Pacific Ocean

<---Port Fitzroy Village

<-----Man of War Passage

<---Whangaparapara Harbour

Tasman Sea

Outline of the Great Barrier Island, New Zealand

the pass, I took another look at the chart plotter...it had put our boat, at that exact moment, on dry land about 200 feet from the water. Two hundred feet may not sound like much, but the Man-of-War Passage was less than 200 feet wide altogether. Well, with that kind of accuracy, we gave up on the chart plotter and chalked up another one for Judy! The lesson here was that even the best electronic navigation could not replace a good helmsperson.

Port Fitzroy is a tiny hamlet with a fuel dock and a bunch of coves where boats can anchor. The Port is protected by a little island (Kaikoura) on its coast, but the little island is so close that the water at Port Fitzroy is like a lake with two narrow passages, one north, and one south, connecting to the ocean. We planned to hang out there until the bad weather passed over New Zealand. We expected the NE wind to veer to SW in two or three days. Depending on what came after, we could possibly ride that SW wind all the way north to Opua, Bay of Islands.

The Village of Port Fitzroy

After we anchored and secured the boat, we went ashore to explore. We took the dinghy to a little floating pontoon not far from the fuel dock. We came across a pretty yellow house that the locals called the Boat Club. Inside it had a nice kauri wood bar and other fine woodwork. We bought drinks and waited for six o'clock to order dinner. More and more people showed up. We had forgotten that it was Friday and apparently the locals gather here for drinks at the pub and visit with each other. We met a family with two young kids, Sam, 6, and Mike, 4. Sam conversed more like an adult.

The entire Island had a population of around 900, decreasing every year. There were few jobs remaining here to sustain a large number of people. All the kauri pines (*Agathis australis*) had been logged and there were only two farms still productive to provide for the island population. Most of the yachts and fishing boats that came here were seasonal. Much of the land and many homes at Great Barrier Island had been purchased by wealthy people from Auckland as vacation homes, but the owners were mostly absent and contributed minimally to the local economy.

Sam and Mike went to an elementary school with twenty other students at different levels. Even this little school would close, by government policy, if the total number of students dropped below twelve. Sam and Mike's father, Bob, was on the school board and worked as a general contractor doing building and renovations work as available on the Island. The children's mum, Jane, worked for the Department of Conservation to restore the Island to its native state.

Earlier, Judy had observed a small grove of young kauri trees. It turned out they were planted by the Department of Conservation some years ago. Those trees were the only kauris remaining on an island previously well known for its old-growth kauri forest. The kauri wood was famous for its resistance to rot as well as marine worms. Its straight, tall, knot-free wood was also excellent for ships' masts. There was only 2% of the old-growth forest remaining in isolated reserves in New Zealand at the time. Other conservation efforts were being made to rid the Island of introduced animal species that hampered the return of the native birds.

We invited Sam to see Laelia the next day, but it turned out to be a day of blinding rain and howling winds, gusting to 47 knots, even in the well-protected harbor. We did fine. Laelia's anchor was holding in the thick muddy substrate and our wind generator was producing a prodigious amount of electricity for the boat. Of course, Sam was unable to visit.

We were planning to leave to sail north after the storm blew past two days later. Just as we were making preparations to depart, Sam and his father came by and had a lovely tour on board Laelia. Sam's father invited us to their home for dinner that night. It only took a few milliseconds for us to decide that an invitation from a local family was not to be passed up.

They lived in a comfortable wood-framed house surrounded by a small vegetable garden on the northern tip of the Island with a view of the ocean and the surf. Sam was quite excited about the whale he had seen that day on the beach. He made a picture in crayon of himself and his brother as a present to us. He also gave Judy a package of chocolates. Mike wrapped half a dozen pistachio nuts as a present upon our arrival at their home. We gave them a couple of plastic animals we had brought with us from Mexico.

Jane helped us identify the pretty brown "duck" that we had seen near Laelia that morning. It turned out to be the primary subject in her research. The brown teal (*Anas chlorotis*) with the common name of pateke was an endangered species existing on only two of the offshore islands of New Zealand. The department was working to reestablish the species on mainland New Zealand. In their quiet ways, all of these people were making long strides in improving our world. We continued correspondence with the family for many years afterwards. It always touched us when their letter would bid us in Maori: "Kia tau te rangimarie," meaning peace to be with you.

We went back to Laelia in the dark, but by now we knew our way around the harbor. Besides, we had the forethought of turning on the LED anchor light before leaving the boat.

Another boat arrived while we were on shore and anchored not far from Laelia. Although it didn't seem to be a problem when the wind strength was moderately strong from the NE, now with the wind direction changing, I was not so sure about the anchoring arrangement. It was enough of a worry that I didn't go to sleep, but stayed up to keep an "anchor watch." During the night the wind kept changing directions and the wind strength was becoming erratic. At one point the other boat was drifting towards Laelia, getting closer and closer. Finally, I put on my foul-weather gear and went out on the stern step to push the other boat away. The skipper of the other boat was awakened when I called out to him. He was shocked by how close the two boats were from each other. It was a little after midnight with a long night still ahead.

It was clear that neither of us would get any sleep that night. He muttered, "I was the last one to anchor, so I will have to move."

I felt bad to see him pull up anchor and look for another spot in the darkness and pouring rain, but I was certainly not going to dissuade him from leaving. As it turned out he was familiar with the area and had no problem finding another spot to drop anchor for the night.

The next day, we raised anchor and sailed away from the Great Barrier Island and headed north to Cape Brett and Opua, Bay of Islands.

Kauri-Wood Classic

After we arrived back at Opua, we were assigned a dock on the main wharf, next to a large wooden yacht about sixty feet in length. The boat had considerable weathered wood exposed. A man was painting the boat, splattering paint in a careless manner. He was about fifty-five with reddish brown hair and very fair complexion with a liberal sprinkling of freckles.

As I walked by his boat, I greeted him, "Good afternoon, it's a lot of work with all that painting."

He looked hard at me and said with considerable emphasis, "This is a classic yacht."

"Oh...yes, of course, the classic lines are obvious. I should have recognized it right away. My apologies," I said.

Classic or not, the boat has not been well maintained if not downright neglected. The weathered wood appeared to be kauri, one of the most worm- and rot-resistant woods for shipbuilding.

The man continued with my education, "It's an all-kauri classic, built with timber from the Great Barrier Island."

I thought that, if he had taken care of the wood sooner, the kauri would have shined with gratefulness. I read about the kauri later in an issue of the Wooden Boat Magazine: "It (kauri wood) has a silky-smooth, almost sensual quality. Good medium-heart kauri is an absolute joy. It has an aura about it. It's gold and it glows. Put a coat of oil on it, and you see this glorious golden sheen."

I didn't think the man ever noticed that I was silent. Perhaps he thought I was stunned by his revelations. Having traveled in New Zealand, Judy and I had come across plenty of kauri wood handcraft made from discarded stumps recovered from lake bottoms. The wood does have an aura, and it gleams with warmth. It was no longer legal to cut down kauri pine trees *(Agathis australis)* in New Zealand. The bulk of the original kauri was shipped overseas and much was wasted in the early days. It was not until 1960's there was a wave of conservation effort to save the remaining kauri trees. By then it was too late for many of the original old-growth kauri forests.

"There were only two of these yachts built in 1937. One is now in North America and the remaining one has been in my family from the beginning," he said proudly.

I could see now that the owner was from one of the well-to-do, established families in New Zealand. Up to this point the people we had met in New Zealand had been either new immigrants or had managed to find their own place in the sun by hard work. For the first time in six months, I was meeting a member of an "established family" with inherited wealth.

"It must be fun sailing in the Bay of Islands with a beautiful classic," I said, trying to change the subject to sailing.

"I bring the yacht from Auckland each year after Christmas and take it home at the end of summer in late April." He said all that as if sailing the yacht was a familial duty devoid of any sense of joy. He then turned around to yell at his two kids of about ten or eleven to clean the dinghy that was turned upside down on the dock.

The dinghy's bottom was completely covered with a mature growth of oysters or something like it. It had to have taken more than one season for that much growth to accumulate. I hoped he was doing better with the bottom of his yacht or it wouldn't stay classic or afloat for much longer. Even the durable, worm-resisting kauri wood must have its limits.

A little later a Maori lady showed up and gathered the kids to go somewhere. She was quite striking with a bronze complexion and elegant manners. I thought she would have been a lot more interesting to talk to, but the man was now yelling at his kids. Perhaps I was not being charitable. I didn't like the way he was treating his boat, classic or not, and he seemed to have a chip on his shoulder. Perhaps billionaire Warren Buffet got it right when he said that he would leave his kids "enough money so they would feel they could do anything, but not so much that they could do nothing."

Waiting for Weather in Opua

In 1789 Captain Bligh of the Royal Navy and his crew refused to set foot ashore despite having been cast adrift in a dangerously overloaded small vessel by mutineers on the HMS Bounty. They feared the ferocious cannibals inhabiting these lush green islands in the South Pacific. In 2006, our destination was these same Islands of Fiji as we awaited a weather window for departing Opua, New Zealand.

We did boat chores and had provisioned Laelia for the passage. All we needed was a favorable weather window. That was the only thing anyone talked about at the dock in Opua...weather, weather, and more weather. This year there had been several very late-season cyclones. They often start in Far-North Queensland of Australia and swoop across the tropical Pacific to cause havoc. The latest one was Cyclone Monica that hit the Cape York region of Australia in late April. Many people were laying bets on whether there would be one more cyclone this season.

We heard that there was a talk by the weather guru, Bob McDavitt, the weather ambassador of New Zealand. He would talk at the Yacht Club in Russell, a little historic town across the Bay north of Opua, on Friday night. We took the ferry out to Russell and got directions to the Yacht Club from the ferry attendant. The edge of town in Russell was not hard to find; the town proper was not much more than 150 yards. We saw a little house at the edge of the water or perhaps floating on the water. There were a lot of empty beer bottles stacked outside. Inside were crowds of people buzzing with conversation. A projection of a weather synopsis was on the screen with isobars, arrows, and other squiggles.

Bare feet and sandals passed for foot wear. And the best dressed wore tee shirts not yet faded completely. Of course shorts for all the males, although it was getting quite chilly this time of the year, especially at night.

Bob McDavitt talked and talked. Much of it was theory that we already knew from our Ventura Power Squadron weather class. Part of the lecture covered the meteorological details of the Queen's Birthday Disaster. He was quite entertaining, but most of the people there came only to hear him say, "Perhaps the following Wednesday is a possible weather window."

There was a Cruising Club in Opua that served BBQ meals three nights a week and many of the local boaties hung out there. The price and food quality were both superior to the tourist fare in the nearby town of Pahia. This night they had a special guest as opposed to the rest of us not very special guests.

The commodore introduced the guest by saying, "Because many foreign boats make landfall and depart New Zealand from Opua, club members are accustomed to meeting many odd people either coming or going, but occasionally they get to meet some very odd people..." The more I learned about this special guest, the more I agreed with the commodore's introduction.

It turned out that this very odd person was a lady named Donna Lange, a 44-year old single hander originally from upper New York State. She was on a one-stop circumnavigation and had chosen Opua as her stop. She had traveled from Rhode Island by herself on a 27-footer for 167 days. She sailed from the east coast of North America, across the South Atlantic, rounding South

Africa, crossing the Indian Ocean, and bypassing Australia, non-stop to New Zealand. Believe me, 167 days are a lot of days at sea and a 27-footer is not a very large boat in the ocean. The rule of thumb was that the length of the boat should be at least double the height of the waves to be safe.

The Indian Ocean was known for some of the larger waves on earth, some of which could be as much as 60 feet high. According to Lange, she had made a mistake about the prevailing wind direction and the expected wave height because she had read the pilot charts for the wrong month. Not surprisingly, she had encountered some bad weather and rough seas.

Donna Lange avoided making landfall by choice because she thought of this voyage as a "Pilgrimage." She wanted to stay as long as possible at sea seeking "something" in the solitude of the ocean. Her boat's name was "Inspired Insanity." I suppose the boat name kind of told the whole story, although she seemed perfectly normal, considering she had only made landfall that morning. She had a very good voice and was singing to entertain the club members. She played a penny whistle, a harmonica, and a guitar, it seemed, all at the same time. As the special guest, she got to eat for free. Perhaps I was a little jealous of the latter.

We knew her boat had some problems because we had followed a VHF radio transmission late the night before. We couldn't hear her, but we could hear the Whangarei Radio Station, which had sent out an alert to vessels at sea. We gathered that a boat named "Inspired Insanity" had hove-to (sailing in place) with no navigation lights. Other vessels were warned to keep a look out when navigating in that area.

After the dinner, I asked her about her boat. It appeared that she had dirty fuel and was running out of replacement fuel filters, and dared not run her engine any longer that night. She needed to save the engine power for entering difficult harbors or for emergencies. She was also running out of power from her house battery because her alternator had not been working. She used the wind generator to recharge her engine battery so she could re-start her engine when needed. She was planning in the immediate future to take her boat to Auckland to do some repairs while she returned by air to the States to see her new granddaughter.

We saw Donna the next morning. I was amazed that she could

walk normally. I remembered how Judy and I were unable, for almost two weeks, to walk a straight line after only twenty-two days at sea. She seemed to be doing exceptionally well after almost half a year at sea.

14 Michener's Islands

Arriving at the Copra Shed Marina, Savusavu Bay, Fiji (16 46.640 S, 179 19.964 E), 12 May 2006. Arriving Makogai, Fiji (17 25.910 S, 178 58.030 E), 18 June. Travel to California. Arriving Port Vila, Vanuatu (17 44.317 S, 168 18.579 E), 23 September 2006. Arriving Port Moselle, Noumea, New Caledonia (22 16.688 S, 166 26.269 E), 16 October 2006.

This chapter is about Laelia's tracks in island nations of Fiji, Vanuatu, and New Caledonia. James Michener was a Lieutenant Commander in the US Navy during the Second World War and had traveled in the region extensively on assignment. His *Tales of the South Pacific* was loosely based on these islands.

Arriving at the Cannibal Isle

With Cyclone Monica still swirling around Cape York, Australia, it seemed there was still a chance for us to encounter rough weather. Of course we were not going to Cape York, but these cyclones had a habit of swooping down across the Coral Sea to Vanuatu and Fiji. Despite all the discussion going on at Opua about a favorable weather window, it was still not absolutely clear when would be the best time to set sail for Fiji.

We contacted a weather router in Perth who gave us two options. One, we could leave on Wednesday at the tail end of the first of two low-pressure systems, but be prepared for some strong

NW and NE winds and four-meter waves initially. This option required Laelia to make 300 miles to the north before Friday to avoid the second system with gale-force winds. If we could get that far north, as the second system passed through south of us, it would catapult Laelia for a flying ride to Fiji with several days of 15 to 20 knots of SSW winds. The alternative option was to wait and set sail on the tail of the second system with milder SSW and SE winds.

Laelia departed on Wednesday as soon as we received clearance from Customs and Immigration. As part of the checkout procedure, all non-New Zealand skippers had to sign an agreement that they would not return to New Zealand within six months. They really didn't want boat people to hang around forever.

Notes from four days later:

It is the middle of the night, but quite a bright night with a half moon low on the western horizon. The reflection of the moon is shimmering across the dark water. Orion has already set. A few clouds are obscuring the Southern Cross. The air is balmy, almost like that of a summer night minus the tropical fragrance.

This is the first night that we can even appreciate anything. We left Opua last Wednesday on the trailing half of a low-pressure system moving across New Zealand. It gave us the southwest winds we needed for sailing and a wild, wet rollicking ride we didn't need. We raced north past latitude 30 S in mostly 25 knot winds to avoid being hit by the core of the second low where the winds were up to 35 knots and gusting to 45 plus according to reports. We learned first-hand that the fringe of a deep low was quite enough to slingshot Laelia along.

Howard and Judy, Laelia at sea (26 57 S, 175 55 E).

We were having a sunny day with little wind and very calm seas. Not willing to let the boat drift, I turned on the engine and a little later went to check on the fuel filters to make sure they were clean. To my shock, the starboard engine room was full of smoke.

Holy cow! All that smoke is not a good sign. A fire could

certainly reduce the hull of a fiberglass boat to the waterline in minutes. I was about to grab a fire extinguisher, but wait...the engine room didn't feel extra hot. I looked around and saw no flickering flame. I checked the fuel hoses and found no fuel leaking anywhere. I rushed to shut off the engine. By now most of the smoke had dissipated. I looked for the source, but all I found was a very hot alternator belt hanging limply on the pulley. The belt must have become loose and was slipping, then melted in a puff of smoke. So that was another unplanned boat project that I needed to do before we could turn on the engine again.

It was a good thing that the sea was calm. In an automobile parked on a driveway on land, it would take no more than fifteen minutes to change an alternator belt. On Laelia it took hours.

Even with the alternator bolts loosened, the new belt still wouldn't slip on the pulley without a struggle. Then it took two hands to tighten the alternator bolts and, simultaneously, a third hand on the pry bar to tension the belt. The trouble was that I didn't have a third hand. Neither was there space for another person in the engine room. In any event, Judy made sure she had no part of the engine rooms.

"If I climbed down into that engine room, I probably could never climb out again," she said.

I was told in school to always use my head. So I used my head to push the pry bar while I tightened the nut and bolt with my hands. For my troubles, I heard a loud clunk as the pry bar fell in the bilge water beyond my reach. To reach the bilge, I had to slither through a maze of cables, wires, and hoses. It was important to do no harm to these battery cables, fuel tubing, and holding tank hoses for obvious reasons. It only took me half an hour to retrieve the pry bar from the bilge. With perseverance the job got done, but it was an exercise in patience, doggedness, and strong anger management skills rolled into one.

Boat builders and engineers should be required to do these maintenance jobs before they are allowed to design anything. They need to understand that people have wrists and elbows, not universal joints, and most of them have only two hands.

We arrived at the entrance to Savusavu Bay several hours before dawn. I was reluctant to navigate the shallow water of the bay in the dark. Fiji was well known for coral reefs. The guidebook recommended sailing in Fiji waters only when the sun is high to avoid glare. One person needed to be a dedicated spotter from the highest point on the vessel, wearing Polaroid sunglasses to look for obstructions below the water surface. Considering the risks of such unfamiliar water, I kept Laelia circling over deep water near the bay entrance until daybreak.

The Copra Shed Marina was located in a narrow finger of water between the Nawi Island and the shores of Savusavu. We were tied to a mooring ball to await quarantine clearance. All around us was lush vegetation and the renovated Copra Shed on the shore. It was warm, but tolerable. We had to adapt our New Zealand-acclimatized bodies to the tropics.

Edwina, the Health Officer, inspected Laelia to make sure we were not ill or otherwise suffering from some serious communicable disease. She gave us permission to lower the yellow quarantine flag (Q-flag) so the Custom and Immigration Officials could come aboard. She was young with a chocolate-brown complexion, big dark eyes, very pretty, and when she smiled it involved her whole face. She had features suggesting both Indian and indigenous Fijian heritage. It was her first month on the job as Health Inspector. She hadn't gotten her sea legs yet and was having a bit of problem getting on and off the boat from the dinghy. Both Judy and I thought she was delightful.

The Immigration and Customs officials came aboard with multiple official forms. They did their work with good humor, laughing at some of their own bureaucratic forms. The Agricultural Inspector was a big man and had to stoop to get inside the salon of our boat. He was perspiring big droplets of sweat and feeling the warmth of the day worse than us. He used up the last few sheets of our paper towels wiping his brow but left our foods in the refrigerator alone, with instructions not to dispose of the fresh foods on shore.

Before our arrival, we had misgivings about the Fiji officials because former British colonies in general had the reputation of being overly bureaucratic. The check-in at Savusavu turned out to be a very pleasant surprise. The officials were among the most professional and personable people we have met anywhere.

So these are the people Captain Bligh was too fearful to meet at the Cannibal Isle?

The Curse of History

For some groups of people, knowing their own history seems more like a curse. Instead of learning from history to avoid repeating their mistakes, the past brews hatred that divides people and blights their future. Fiji is an example of such a tragedy.

We arrived on the week of the big national election in 2006. During this period few seemed to want to talk politics, certainly not with *palangies* (foreigners). I could sense an undercurrent of nervousness among the locals about the outcome of the election. Cab drivers out of earshot of others often provided us with interesting views although their political sophistication varied.

One of the drivers said, "I couldn't believe it...a high-level former general was arrested right after the election."

"Why was he arrested? Did he try to cheat?" I asked.

"No... he was arrested for what he did five years ago... he tried to start a coup. This is not good news. Maybe there will be another coup."

The election received considerable play from the international news media because there had been several coups in previous years. In one of those conflicts, it came to light later that some thirty Methodist leaders had participated in fire-bombings of Hindu temples. The violence was disastrous for the economy driving away much of what had been a thriving tourist trade. The resulting emigration of Indo-Fijians meant the country lost many of its best professional people in technology, medicine, teaching, and others with transferable skills. We had met many of these emigrant Fijians in New Zealand and even a few in Mexico.

The indigenous Fijians owned more than 80% of the land, with another 10% under the control of the government. Only 10% of the land was available as freehold. However, Indo-Fijians controlled the economy and owned almost all of the businesses. They were brought here by the British to work the cane fields and had increased their population faster than the indigenous Fijians. Before the exodus, the Indo-Fijians had better than a 50% majority, but powerless to do much because the military was in the hands of the indigenous generals.

I chatted with a teacher who was waiting to pick up his son after school. I said, "Fiji has good sunshine and plenty of rain."

"That we have...and a lot of prime land too. This country can easily be self-sufficient, but instead, we receive handouts from Australia and New Zealand."

"I notice at the market all the variety of produce and fruits and the shops are busy," I said, trying to remain upbeat.

"Unfortunately, some of our best people are gone," the teacher replied. "They don't feel their families are safe anymore. The political leaders deliberately stir up racial conflict just to get elected."

"I noticed a lot of the plantations seem uncared for...they look kind of like the jungle," I said.

"That is another bit of sad news. A lot of the leases were not renewed even though the Indo-Fijian families had worked the land for more than a hundred years. If there is not enough sugar cane harvested for the press, the mill will have to lay off workers. Sugar is one of our biggest exports...it has been for many decades."

Most of the land was in the name of the villages controlled by the Council of Chiefs in a land trust. As a result of the unrest in previous years, many of the land parcels leased to Indo-Fijians were not renewed. The indigenous Fijians were not willing to do the backbreaking job in the cane fields, so the cane fields were now lying fallow and the land being reclaimed by the jungle.

In Savusavu, shops were arranged in no particular order. Banks and bakeries, a few hardware stores, and restaurants were crowded one against the next in between other stores. We loved the bakeries and got up very early to buy fresh cinnamon rolls. Some of these shops had upstairs balconies providing patches of much needed shade. Signs were old, faded, and not replaced as businesses changed hands. The only bookstore was the Post that had schoolbooks, stationery, and miscellaneous school items. There was a large farmers' market where fish, meats, and fresh vegetables were sold. We could buy kava roots used for making a drink formerly reserved only for ceremonial rituals and sacred rites. Although it was still treated by many as a respected tradition, we noticed workers used kava after work and others abuse kava and alcohol after dark.

For a dollar or two one could buy quite a lot of vegetables and fruits. For ten dollars one could buy a kilo of meat, fish, or shrimp. Fijian beef was excellent. There were also two supermarket-type stores crammed full of variety of staples, canned goods, and a limited supply of fresh foods. Food was not expensive here.

People were very friendly to foreigners. If I said "bula" to even total strangers, I would hear replies of "bula" or sometimes even "bula, bula" which meant hello or literally good health. We noticed that the Indo-Fijians were less enthusiastic about the "bula" and more receptive to "hello."

We went to visit one village just on the outskirts of the town of Labasa (pronounced Lanbasa), the largest town on Vanua Levu Island. As our tour group arrived, a representative of the village came to greet us and led us to the chief's house, where we took off our shoes or sandals. All of us were already dressed appropriately with men in full-length shorts and women had their legs and shoulders covered.

We sat cross-legged at one end of the large room. The chief sat in the middle with half a dozen of the villagers scattered at various parts of the room sitting cross-legged. This was painful for some of us, but sit we did. Our representative introduced us in Fijian. We had no idea what he said, but it seemed formal and respectful. We passed the kava root to the representative, who then forwarded it to the chief, who talked for a few minutes and apparently accepted our offer. He clapped his hands a few times. We all followed, trying to clap in a rather incoherent way, which seemed comical to the villagers. After that we left the chief's house to tour the village under the representative's guidance and watchful eyes.

The gift of kava was a way of asking permission to enter the village and to show our respect. Had we arrived much later and participated in drinking the kava, it would have meant that we were pledging allegiance to the chief and asking for his protection in his village.

The reason we wanted to visit this particular village was because of the monolith, a tall rock stuck straight out of the ground. It was a sacred rock not to be offended despite the fact that most indigenous Fijians were now either Methodists or Catholics.

There were also shorter rocks about two or three feet from the ground among a rectangular border of smaller rocks, which were apparently burial sites. The villagers said that the shorter rocks were where heads of captured enemies were cut off. The brains were scooped out and placed in front of the chief to be consumed in order for him to gain in power. Not too many yards down the way, the gravesites changed drastically in style, reflecting the beginning of the Christian era. There was one fresh burial site all covered with mounds of fresh flowers.

We had become the center of attraction for a few dozen children who were too young to be in school. They laughed and ran around in circles. I showed them their images on my camera screen at which they pointed and laughed with excitement.

We went by the communal eating area in the village where many women were working to prepare food with huge stacks of plates on the table. An important villager had died and it was the feast day with many relatives attending from a long distance away.

As we got ready to leave, we heard a great commotion and loud squeals. Kids were running and shouting. A very large hog with its legs tied was being dragged to some central place in the village. No doubt the hog would be part of the feast and it was protesting. Our guide told us that a smaller hog was becoming mature and would replace the large hog that was getting big enough for a very nice feast. I thought the slaughter would make a fabulous photo, but our guide would not allow a photo of the bloody scene.

Later, we visited a Hindu shrine called Cobra Rock, a large rock with fractures resembling the hood of a cobra snake. This was a sacred icon worshipped by the Hindu faithful. It was festooned with flowers and in front of the rock were offerings of incense and candles. We took off our shoes as we entered the building and walked counterclockwise around the rock. With each circle we could ring the bell and put some money in the box. The donor could at that moment make a wish. *Such a deal!*

Then we all walked up the hillside on exactly 297 steps to a meditation gazebo. After that many steps up, a little quiet meditating felt very appropriate. Each step was supposed to represent a good luck omen of some sort. Unfortunately for me, I took two or three steps at a time, thus missing many of the good fortunes in between. Judy and the others in our group walked carefully and ever so slowly to secure for themselves all 297 good fortunes.

We visited the Labasa Market. It was huge, selling all sorts of vegetables, fruits, nuts, eggs, baskets, kava, and many things we didn't even recognize.

A friend of ours wanted to buy a pair of gold earrings she had found at a nice jewelry shop. She hadn't brought enough cash and asked Judy for a loan to make up the difference.

"Sure, you are good for a loan," Judy said, "but let Howard go with you to complete the purchase." I asked the salesclerk to show us the merchandise. All three clerks were telling us how beautiful it was. "It is our very best...one of a kind...hand made."

"Yes, it does look very pretty," I said. "What kind of a discount can you give me today?"

"No, no discount, that's not possible...sorry. It's already at the rock bottom price. The lady should try it on and see how she likes it," said the woman salesclerk as she handed the precious earrings across the counter.

"Well, there is no point in wasting time if there is no discount," I said as I turned and headed for the door. "Let's go."

"Wait...wait, we'll get the manager." Within seconds, a well-dressed Indo-Fijian gentleman, in a three-piece suit appeared. I pegged him as the owner. Having the owner there was a good sign. He would have the freedom to negotiate.

To my surprise, he cut to the chase right away. "I'll give you 30% discount, all cash, no credit card." He almost spoiled the fun by being so abrupt. I probably could have pushed him another ten percent, but that would make him look bad in front of his staff.

"OK, that's a deal," I said.

Our friend was delighted and told me after we left the store, "Thanks, Howard, for saving all that money for me. I could never have bargained like that."

Actually, I did very little, but it was a good transaction because all parties ended up happy. I was sure the owner still had plenty of profit margins to keep him wealthy.

The boat was tied to a mooring ball at the Copra Shed Marina where copra was processed during a time when coconut oil was the only export from this town. It was a credit to the new owners to have renovated it with such care that it now housed elegant waterfront shops, restaurants, Marina office, and several service rooms (lodging) upstairs. It also served as the Savusavu Yacht Club that sponsored an under-14 kids' dinghy sailing program. These kids had often been champions in Fiji and went on to international competition among the Pacific Island nations.

I went ashore to take a shower at the Marina facility. On my way back, I heard someone calling, "Hey, Joe, can you help us?"

It was pitch dark. "Hey, can you give us a tow? Our outboard quit."

It dawned on me that I was probably the "Joe" he was calling for help. As a cruiser going back and forth between boat and shore by dinghy, it was not a request I could in good conscience turn down.

I ran my dinghy to where they were in the middle of the harbor. When they saw me, they both said, "Hey, you are wearing our shirt."

What are they talking about? "No, it's not...It's a kava juice-dyed tee I just bought at the gift shop a few days ago," I said.

"We know...we made the tee shirt. Our shop is next door to the Methodist Church. You have to come and see the rest of them...you just have to," said the woman.

"Well, I have a lot of chores to do before we sail to Fawn Harbor. I'll come if I get my chores done." That was about as polite as I could manage. It was getting late.

I side-tied their dinghy to mine and went slowly to their sailboat. I couldn't go any faster without swamping their dinghy. The towing took quite some time and we had a chance to chat.

Both of them were about my age, and were returning to their boat after having dinner ashore, but somehow they both ended up on the same side of their little home-built dinghy and flipped it over. Although they got the water bailed out and were able to start their outboard again, it was not running reliably. They thought they had water in their fuel tank. Anyway, they needed a tow back to their boat. They wanted to pay me for the fuel, but of course I couldn't accept.

When I told Judy the story on my return, she seemed interested in this tee-shirt shop, and she went there the next day. Not surprisingly, we became proud owners of many more tee shirts.

During the visit, according to Judy, our planned trip was discussed. The couple at the tee shirt shop had sailed all over the Fiji waters for years and gave Judy a ton of information about what they had learned. One important gem was that, although our electronic chip was off by three-quarters of a mile in the southeast side of Vanua Levu Island, it was "spot-on" at Nemanalala and at Makogai Islands. This was important local information and made it possible for us to enter barrier reefs through passes at those islands with only electronic guidance later in our journey.

Bommies at Namenalala

In Fiji most cruising sailboats would travel between ten and two o'clock if possible. It was safer to have the sun up high and, if possible, shine from the stern to minimize reflection. I had a pair of prescription Polaroid lenses to help cut through the surface glare. It was important to see under the water.

When traveling in high-risk, reef-infested waters Judy would be at the helm and I would climb on the salon roof to watch for reefs. Depending on the direction of the light, these shallow obstructions usually come in pale aqua to green and occasionally light brownish colors from the seaweed. Underneath these varied colors were coral heads and other sea life. Cruisers called these isolated coral heads "bommies."

Often the shallow areas were in the form of long continuous coral reefs that could stretch many miles, enclosing a lagoon with islands in the middle. Or they could be atolls of various sizes with nothing but seawater in the lagoon. Any ordinary looking patch of seawater could have a reef not many feet below the surface even when we were cruising along in deep water. So we tended to travel in areas where the charts did not show reefs and in waters frequented by other boats.

By now coral heads and reef passages were no longer novelties to us, but in Fiji the numbers of these reefs strewn across the sea were extraordinary. To make matters worse, there were warnings on official charts that there were "uncharted reefs." Also, there were a fair number of large patches of "un-surveyed" blank areas scattered across the nautical charts.

We untied our mooring line in Savusavu Harbor early at 0830 hours because we knew the surrounding area well already for the first part of the trip. What worried us was the destination where we knew nothing except what was in the guidebook and the charts.

Our destination was Namenalala, a designated bird sanctuary with a very exclusive resort on the island. Boats were allowed to anchor only out of sight of the resort, and no crew was allowed to go ashore beyond the high tide mark. The little island was enclosed within a reef that stretched hundreds of miles with only two narrow passages marked on the chart.

When we approached Namenalala, we couldn't find the beacon marking the north passage. The chart designated two beacons marking either side of the passage.

"Around here the beacons are probably just a couple of sticks protruding out of the water," I said.

Judy scanned the sea surface with binoculars. "I don't see a thing...not even a stick."

"Well, the beacons could have been washed away in the last storm."

There were no surf activities to provide some clues on where the reef was lurking just below the surface. If we hit the reef or a coral head, we could put a hole in Laelia's fiberglass hull. We could also end up high and dry on the reef waiting to be pulled off at high tide...or abandoned on the reef as a monument to navigational errors.

"Hey, the depth meter just jumped from 250 to 45 feet," Judy shouted at me from the helm.

I was on top of the salon roof as a spotter. "I can see 'bommies' in front of us," I cried loud enough for Judy to hear me. "Go to port," I shouted as I pointed to the left.

Judy was frantically trying to steer the boat, but at slow speed the rudder was not very responsive. I could see her steering by adjusting the two engines to avoid the "bommies."

The shallowest reading was 25 feet as we went through the pass. We never had a chance to find out how much water was over the bommies. As Laelia continued, the water depth went back to about 120 feet and stayed at that depth until we came near the shore of the little island.

We searched for a patch of water suitable to drop the anchor. We preferred a depth somewhere around 30 to 40 feet, with sand or mud at the bottom, and enough swinging room for the boat in case the wind shifted. We soon discovered that there were reefs extending outward from the beach. We could see sand at the bottom and with dark rocks and corals forming ridges as we cross them. Mostly the water was sixty feet according to the depth sounder, a little too deep to drop the anchor.

All of a sudden Judy reported, "16 feet!" *Good grief!*

We needed to turn away from the shore since we didn't know

what the water in front of us was like. Just then a gust of wind made it hard for the boat to turn and pushed Laelia even closer to the shallow water and submerged rocks near the shore.

"Reverse!" I shouted.

I saw shallow corals and even pretty anemones not far from the surface. These were fine places to snorkel, but treacherous places for Laelia to scrape across. We moved away from the shallows and finally settled on a spot in 50 feet of water where the anchor seemed to have set securely in sand.

We could see birds nesting at the top and outer branches of trees covering the entire steep slope of the small island. All the branches stopped at the water's edge so evenly that it seemed manicured. From time to time birds would catch an updraft and circle around. We noted boobies, tropicbirds (*Phaethon*) with their long graceful tail feathers, Frigate birds (*Fregata*), a few gulls, and some bats. Only the boobies were unkind enough to try to rain their welcoming messages on us. While we examined the birds with our binoculars, we also spotted one remaining beacon marking the southern passage out of the atoll. It was about two miles away at a bearing of 225 degrees magnetic from the anchorage. At least one beacon out of the four indicated on the chart was still there.

We spotted the resort at some distance and took pictures with the telephoto lens. These were fair sized houses, painted green and red, scattered among the trees on the hillside and thatch structures closer to the beach. We looked up the resort in the *Lonely Planet Guide*; it cost at the time, US$375 per day with a minimum stay of five days. The one advantage at this place was the isolation.

We stayed overnight at the quiet little anchorage, all to ourselves. Before we went to sleep we watched the distant lightning flashes, but heard no thunder. It felt like the weather was about to change. Indeed, it was raining by morning.

The one remaining beacon was enough to speed us along without having to search for the pass and worry over shallow reefs. However, the weather was bad. The squalls came with rain and wind. When it rained hard enough, it was even difficult to see the beacon...a little stick standing on the reef. We waited for a respite in between two squalls and exited the southern pass of the atoll without any complications or dramatics.

Giant Clams of Makogai

It was only a fifteen-mile passage to arrive at the little island where untold stories of perseverance, romance, lust, disease, as well as acceptance and love were long buried. Laelia had a pleasant sail to Makogai (pronounced Ma-kon'-gai). After entering an unmarked pass, we anchored at a little cove in about 40 feet of water over sand. We felt secure despite the strong wind that blew for several nights.

We explored the tide pools and discovered many eels slithering between small bunches of exposed corals, rocks, and algae. We saw a medium sized wild juvenile clam about 8 inches across (most likely *Tridacna maxima*) in the tide pool taking full advantage of the sunlight photosynthesizing while exposed at low tide. We took pictures of a blue sea star that looked more like a blue rubber glove than an animal. Hermit crabs and crabs abound, but were either too fast or not very photogenic.

Judy was studying the animals in the tide pool on a long stretch of deserted beach while I was checking out an old campfire behind a cluster of small trees farther ashore. When I returned, she said, "I was looking at the brittle stars...all their black tentacles were beating slowly in the shallow water... thousands of them in every direction. I had this eerie Alfred-Hitchcock moment." She continued, "It was like in a science fiction movie. All these thousands of tentacles were becoming a hostile creature...I was surrounded."

"Well, the hairy tentacles do seem to beat synchronously. Maybe they are a giant colony working together. You just happened to be a tasty morsel in their midst," I said.

"Ooh... you are no help!"

We had read in the guidebook that there was an abandoned leper colony here as well as an experimental rookery for turtles. We drove our dinghy over to the beach at the main anchorage. There we met Meli who was the manager of the Fishery Station.

Meli told us where there were large clams growing in the water. It was not too deep and I was able to free dive to see them growing at the bottom of the small bay. These were the largest clams I had ever seen, about two feet across (*Tridacna gigas*) planted some years ago. There were others in the outer reef some miles away.

Meli began the tour at the turtle rookery and the clam culturing facilities. With the decline of the Fijian economy, support from the government had been poor. The turtle program was pretty much at low ebb. He still had quite a few tanks full of two-year-old giant clams that were almost ready to be released into the ocean in protective wire nets.

The program was started by an Australian initiative 21 years earlier to prevent the giant clams from becoming extinct. Of the nine known species of giant clams, seven of them grew in Fijian waters. The largest of these clams were often shown in movies where the shells were fluted and were large enough to fit a small adult human. They don't eat people; they are filter feeders and photosynthetic symbionts.

These giant clams had in the mantle millions of photosynthetic algae. The algae produce nutrients from sunlight and release some of the nutrients into the clam's "blood stream." The benefit to the clam was substantial because they could live through an entire life cycle with only clean seawater and sunshine. As a result they were fast growers and could reach adult size in 20 years. Their exposed mantles were green to almost bluish in color, so vivid and bright, the lips of these clams appeared luminous.

We saw many two year-old clams about one to two inches in size in seawater tanks ready to be transplanted. They started as fertilized eggs and were cultured in seawater for about two years, then glued to rock slabs and released with wire cages for protection from predators. Unfortunately, the worst predators were humans. I found, in an old campfire pit just behind a deserted beach, two halves of a large clamshell partially charred. Someone had found a clam and cooked it for food.

"Oh yes, we have problem with poachers. They come by boat to harvest clams," Meli said, "For a long time we didn't have a way to stop them, but now we have an outboard and we can go and catch them with the clams still in their boat." No doubt poaching and pollution were the two biggest threats to these beautiful creatures.

There were concrete power poles from the original Leper Colony still standing. Meli showed us the diesel generator that produced electricity for pumping fresh seawater to keep the young clams and turtles alive.

"We will be releasing all these young clams soon," Meli said.

"Oh, are they ready to be released?" I asked.

"No, usually they are released after they are attached to rocks and put in cages. It takes a long time to release all of them," Meli said.

"Then what happens when you release them before they are attached to rocks?" I said.

"Some will be ok, the rest will get washed away by the current," Meli said.

"Then why are you releasing them so soon?" I was puzzled.

"Our supply ship is late because of the storm. We have two days of diesel left for the generator. When it stops, there will be no seawater for the clams. It is better to release them than letting them all die."

"That will be terrible, after raising them for almost two years," Judy said.

"I still have hope that the ship will arrive in time," Meli said as he spread his hands in a gesture of resignation.

While we walked along, Meli told us about the history of the Leper Colony. The French Catholic missionaries founded the Colony in 1911. At the peak, the colony had 2000 patients from all over the Pacific Islands including Samoa, Tonga, and the Cook Islands as well as Fiji.

Now the fishery station was using many of the surviving buildings of the colony. The physical remains told a story of a highly organized community. Not only were there stores, men and women's isolation dormitories, clinics, and quarters for the medical personnel, but a courthouse, jail, school, and a large cinema. Only the foundation of the cinema auditorium remained. The projection booth and the support for the screen were both still standing.

Men would sit on one side and women on the other side with doctors and nurses in the middle during shows," said Meli.

"There were schools so there must have been kids on this island," said Judy, "Were they born here?"

"There were a few young children who came with their mothers, but most of the men and women were alone when they came and married here on the island," said Meli.

"These people found acceptance here...and a new life," I said.

"I don't imagine life was easy on the island."

"I'm sure they had to struggle to survive...but they had movies even if they had to sit separately," Judy said.

"Well, no matter how hard the life, humans will find love. It's biology. The need for a courthouse and a jail tells plenty about conflicts too...greed, lust, jealousy."

We walked up the hill. On both sides of the path to the cemetery, there were rows of colorful foliage commonly used for decorative purposes in the Pacific Islands. The grounds were knee deep in weeds.

"The villagers keep the weeds cut, but it's hard fighting the jungle," Meli said, "The French still send money to keep the place nice."

The grave markers were generally in good condition with no sign of vandalism. We could read one of the more prominent headstones, that of Mother Mary Agnes, 1870-1955. There were a number of graves belonging to missionaries and many concrete crosses in the background belonging to patients. It was haunting and melancholy. Away from the trees, the scorching sun was bright and pitiless. I tried to imagine the residents' valiant struggle to survive. There must have been powerful stories of joy and sorrow untold buried here...forever.

Not far away, nailed to a tree, was a sign declaring that the "funds for maintenance of the cemetery are provided by the French Government." Below on the same sign it read: "Greater love hath no man than this, that a man lays down his life for his friends...John 15:13." As much as I believed that institutional religions are corrupt and unworthy of our trust, I couldn't help but admire and respect individuals who forsook family and friends as well as the comforts of home to devote their lives in service to the sick on this little island.

Makogai was a beautiful island with sparkling clear water and bountiful banana, papaya, and coconut trees. It would appear to be the fabled paradise on earth, and for certain it was the kind of picture-perfect display in travel posters. The beauty was real, but reality went deeper. The practical tasks of day-to-day survival during hot, humid, and rainy summers must have been daunting and required perseverance. Then they had to endure mosquitos and diseases like malaria and tropical fevers. Life was not easy.

We were pleasantly surprised to hear that, when the colony was disbanded in 1955, a number of patients, although cured, refused to leave the island. By that time leprosy was no longer incurable and was called Hansen's disease. For these patients, having spent most of their lives here, it was home. The last two former lepers to die on the island were an Indian (Fulsi Naran, 7 September 1969) and, two weeks later, a Chinese man (Lee Hop, 21 September1969).

After returning to our boat, I checked the fuel gauge and calculated the mileage and decided that we could donate ten gallons of diesel fuel to the fishery station. It was gratifying to see how happy they were for the fuel to keep their clams from perishing. Before I took my empty jerry cans back to our boat, I was told that the village would have a dance performance for a live-abroad dive boat in two days and we were invited.

The arrangement was complicated, but I gathered that we were the guests of Meli while the tourists on the dive boat were guests of the village. The tourists were going through a *sevusevu*, a formal ceremony for the participants to make an offering of kava to show allegiance to the Village Chief, and in return they were to receive the chief's protection and blessing. We were not doing the *sevusevu*, but the villagers treated us very well because they were using electric lights from the same generator that powered the seawater pump. Without the electric lights, the dance performance would not have been possible. I didn't know that the diesel fuel benefited anyone other than the clams. Judy and I would have been pleased simply to make a bunch of very nice people so happy.

We went to shore a little early to see more of the clams in the tank and to bring Meli and his family some brownies that Judy had just baked. The chief and several of the men prepared the *lovo*, which was an in-ground oven for cooking and roasting. (In Samoa, it was called the umu.) The fire had been heating the rocks for several hours to make them red-hot.

Soon the tourists and their dive-boat crew arrived by dinghy while the villagers sang their welcoming songs at the waters edge.

Now banana leaves were layered over the hot rocks followed by food wrapped in leaves including several large food bundles from the dive boat were added to the *lovo*. More leaves were layered before the whole pit was buried in sand.

We joined about thirty villagers in the small hall sitting cross-legged on the mat. The men sat in a group and some of the village women behind them. Judy and I sat on the side of the room. The men prepared the kava in a traditional kava bowl. They put the hand-ground kava powder in a cloth sack in the water bowl for a few minutes before wringing the last drop of liquid out of the sack. The turbid liquid was then served in half coconut shells with everyone drinking in turns. The men in the village each had some before we were offered the honor. Poor Judy, who never ever intended to imbibe kava, could not diplomatically turn it down. It would have been a terrible insult. She followed the *Lonely Planet Guide* instructions and glugged it down fast without making a face.

Lonely Planet described the drink as "looks like muddy water and tastes like muddy water." It numbed only the throat if it was swallowed quickly and not kept in the mouth too long. I had to drink about half a dozen that night. Kava was supposed to relax the muscles, but somehow my poor legs not only didn't seem to relax, they were complaining with stabbing pains as we sat cross-legged on the floor.

Finally, the four tourists from the dive boat came in the hall and took their places in front of the room. They introduced themselves. The chief and another village leader then spoke, followed by the big Fijian chef from the dive-boat who spoke on behalf of the tourists. It was all in Fijian. The dry kava roots were presented to the chief before several rounds of kava drinking took place again.

The dance was first performed by six girls ranging from about ten to perhaps fifteen all in their fine costumes. The tops of the costume appeared to be made of tapa with beautiful, complicated traditional designs wrapped tightly around their chests. A cloth skirt showing rows of geometric designs of flowers, waves, and triangles reached to just below the knees. Shoulders and backs were bare except for green leaves around their wrists and flower leis around their necks, and each had a single-cowry choker around the throat. They also each had an intricate fan of dried palm leaves. The girls were very striking and attractive with wide beautiful smiles and bright dark eyes that look straight at us.

Judy took a picture of one of the little girls in the audience sitting not far from us...her big watchful eyes were stunning. The boys wearing *Pandanus* skirts danced with their stick weapons and war paint on their faces, their threatening yells and attacking postures were at times intimidating. The men also performed sitting with very energetic movements for a suitable finale of the performance.

At the end of the performance the dancers invited all the guests to join them in their dance. Then it was time to open the *lovo* and get the food out of the pit oven. We were a little astonished that the dive-boat tourists took all their food back to their boat and didn't share any with the villagers.

Meli gave us some cooked cassava, a starchy root that they use as their primary carbohydrate, flavored with coconut cream and pork wrapped in taro leaves. He also included a big bag of papayas, bananas, and coconuts. With all that, we got into our little dinghy and rode the two miles back to our boat in pitch darkness. We had our search light in the dinghy and a VHF radio. We also had the foresight of turning on Laelia's anchor light to guide us back to our home. All we had to do was avoid the reef that extended a long distance from the point of land that separated the two coves, but by this time, we knew the way home.

The Village on Naigani Island
It took two tries for us to sail away from Makogai.

"Laelia, Laelia, this is Mystic Rhythms." It was our friend, Richard, on the radio.

"Laelia here. Going to 17," Judy answered on the radio.

"We are heading out of the pass...you guys want to follow us out? That pass is pretty narrow...we are heading out backtracking on our chart plotter. You didn't come through that way, it would save you a lot of navigating." We decided quickly that we would follow them out, "Ok we'll take just a few minutes...as soon as we pull our anchor."

We saw their catamaran motoring past and followed behind them with the engine at low speed. As we cleared the point of land sheltering the anchorage, Laelia was hit by a big gust of wind. Most of the bay was full of whitecaps. The crosswind was forcing Laelia off course because at this slow speed the rudder was not responsive. The water was so turbulent we couldn't see the reef even if we were on top of one. There was no chance we could navigate the pass by ourselves. We could only get through it safely if we were immediately behind the lead boat. Even at thirty yards, we couldn't follow with any precision.

"This is beginning to look like a very bad idea," I said.

One of the most important traits in a cruiser was self-reliance. I disliked the thought of not doing my own navigation. Trying to follow someone else under these conditions was downright dangerous.

"The weather is pretty nasty. It's not a good day to risk going through the pass," I said.

"That's what I was thinking exactly," Judy replied. It was not unusual for her to read my mind like that.

"Maybe you should give Richard a call. We better head back," I said.

Judy picked up the mic by the radio, "Mystic Rhythms, Mystic Rhythms, we are turning back. Over."

"Ok, we'll cross paths later. Mystic Rhythms out."

"Laelia, out."

There was sunshine and calm seas a couple of days later. We even took some photos of the breaking surf as we went through the pass at the reef. We sailed to Naigani (pronounced Ny-ee-ng-ahni) in about three hours and anchored in 35 feet of water over sand.

At the cove where we anchored, there was a very nice sandy beach. There were more neighboring coves all separated by coral-reef fingers extending out from shore. Just as at Makogai, many of the beaches were also fringed by coral reefs that were exposed at low tide.

Getting to shore was easy at high tide by beaching the dinghy on the sand, but at low tide we had to leave the dinghy in the water and wade through rocks and razor sharp dead corals. Woe is the skipper who left the dinghy on the beach at high tide only to discover later that the dinghy would now need to be carried back to the water over the reef. We often anchored the dinghy in hip-deep water and tied a long line to the nearest shrub.

The water was sparkling clear and the snorkeling here was a short swim off the boat. Lots of multicolored fish and brightly colored corals were just 30 yards away. The chart plotter put the boat high and dry on the reef, but we could see about 30 feet of water under the boat. It was just another reminder that the charts for this area were not reliable even if our GPS was highly accurate. Considering that some of the fixes on the chart were by Captains Cook, Bligh, and others using their sextant sightings, we were very impressed by their navigation skills.

Ken and Jean from s/v Renaissance 2000 went with Judy and me to the village by following a trail starting from the beach at the next cove. There was a grove of palms laden with an abundance of coconuts.

"Did you know that more people were killed by coconuts falling on their heads every year than people killed by sharks?" Ken asked.

"Whoa, this is not the time to bring that up. I don't have my pith helmet on my head," I said.

"You don't have a pith helmet," Judy said.

"I did when I was nine…it was in Hong Kong. The sun was fierce there."

As it turned out, on that day we saw no falling coconuts.

A little closer to the village we met some village ladies washing their laundry in a pool fed by a small creek. One of them sat in a small tub with her laundry as she washed the clothes. Throughout the Pacific Islands we saw a lot of laundry drying on the lines. Fiji was no exception. Their clothing might be worn and threadbare, but the women kept it clean. The women wore Mother Hubbards, loosely fitting long dresses. Apparently, the missionaries considered that was appropriate for women to cover their bodies. Men generally wore shorts that covered to below the knee and shirts of one sort or another. To be properly respectful, I would have to wear long pants or at least keep my knees covered.

We found the chief and presented him with the bundle of kava. He sat us down under a mango tree.

He asked us where we were from and what we would like to do. He gave us permission to take photos and walk around anywhere in the village.

"I thank you for being respectful to the tradition. We don't use kava on this island anymore, but thank you anyway."

This was just about the most informal meeting we had with a village chief. I got the feeling that this particular village followed Christianity more closely than some of the other villages. The revelation that they didn't use kava anymore said as much.

The village life was quite simple. There was no Internet or telephone, but there was a diesel generator that turned on for a few hours each night. They fished; the man alone, the husband and wife together, or sometimes older children would go fishing on pangas with outboards or on the more traditional bilibilis. The bilibilis are made of bamboo poles lashed together. About fifteen or twenty bamboo poles, each about four or five inches in diameter and fifteen to twenty feet long, lashed together would set out to sea. They propelled such a watercraft using small tree branches as paddles. They would fish all night even when it rained.

The villagers planted cassava, taro, and harvested bananas and paw paws (papaya). Of course there were the ever-present coconuts. Breadfruit and mango trees were common. We saw pigs and chickens running loose.

This village had about eighty people composed of three extended families, which were all related some generations back. We saw only the older folks and very young children. Because they didn't have a sufficient population on the island, they couldn't have a school. Most of the school-age kids were away on the bigger islands living with relatives. Many of the young people were working in Nadi or Suva. They would come back to the village for holidays and perhaps send money home too.

Navigating the Lagoon

Disaster can crop up unexpectedly at any time. The best defense was to plan ahead and be prepared.

Our destination was Musket Cove off the West Coast of Viti Levu, the most populous island in Fiji. Laelia was anchored at Naigani, a small island on the opposite (east) coast of Viti Levu. The simplest way was to sail an arc to the north through Bligh Waters to arrive at Musket Cove. That route would bring Laelia through open seas with heavy swells and a large patch of water "not well surveyed."

There was a much shorter route on the north side of Viti Levu Island inside the lagoon. The barrier reef forming the lagoon provided protection from heavy swells for the entire north coast of Viti Levu. It would mean a more comfortable and a shorter passage. There was no reliable chart for this route, but we had bought for $20 a set of GPS waypoints from Curley's Dive Shop in

Savusavu. The waypoints, if accurate, were our best chance for a safe passage through the lagoon riddled with coral reefs.

In the lagoon, Laelia was traveling from east to west, so it was safe to start early in the day and anchor well before sunset to keep the sun behind us and the reflected sunlight to a minimum.

"A storm is approaching according to this morning's forecast," I said.

"Maybe we better hole up somewhere for a few days until it blows over," Judy replied.

"Yeah, that's a good idea...we won't be able to see the submerged reefs with the water all churned up in a storm."

"Well, you'll get to practice making bread if we stay...we will be out of bread in a day or two." Judy had checked our food supplies earlier.

Light rain was already beginning as we anchored. We were the only vessel in a large, shallow bay. Before long the sky opened up and poured in torrents. The wind blasted across the water unabated. Laelia was swinging 180 degrees on the anchor chain. I had a one-to-six scope on the chain in twenty-four feet of water. We were secure.

We could hear the surf crashing. Certainly we were thankful for being inside the lagoon. When it was raining, we stayed warm and dry and enjoyed the aroma of freshly baked bread, then feasted our eyes on a spectacular sunset before nightfall. We stayed several days until the storm eased and the sky cleared.

The lagoon looked like any large expanse of water, but the safe channels were often narrow and required Laelia to twist and turn. We used Curley's waypoints as well as the chart and looked for beacons that were often missing because they were only sticks protruding from the reef. Spotting a beacon helped to reassure our collective faith in Curley's waypoints, especially when the chart showed Laelia to be in the middle of a large patch of reef already. Often the chart was off by as much as a quarter of a mile.

On long straight stretches between waypoints, there was deep water and we dared to make up time by cranking up the diesel engines. As a precaution, I would stand on the salon roof to keep a look out while Judy would stay at the helm.

"Wow, we are flying...what's our speed?" I asked Judy.

"Eight knots," she said from the helm station.

This went on for some time and the water depth remained fairly constant.

Soon, I saw that the water ahead of us appeared to be a shade more greenish. *Wait, why is there a long transition line of color change?* It was a very faint fuzzy line, but there definitely was a difference in color of the water.

"Slow down...Judy, slow the boat down," I shouted. It dawned on me slowly that the line must be the beginning of a reef. The reef could be any colors depending on what was growing on it. Laelia slowed, but was still gliding at a pretty good clip and we were getting closer to the line where the color shifted.

"Reverse...reverse," I yelled.

Judy threw the throttles hard into reverse. The boat started moving backwards. It was not designed to move back at such speed and threw up seawater all the way to the helm station and drenched Judy. When the boat stopped, Laelia was forty or fifty feet from the reef. Crashing on the coral reef at eight knots would probably have thrown me into the water and Laelia would have suffered serious damage to the bottom of the hull. It would have been a major journey-ending disaster.

It was not clear what had brought us off course. Certainly Curley's waypoints had been extremely reliable. It was possible that I had transposed the digits or missed one of the waypoints. The obstruction in front of us appeared to be part of the main barrier reef. To continue, we needed to find the pass to get through the reef.

As luck would have it, there was a fishing boat that overtook us earlier and it was going through the pass ahead of us. We could see it in the distance. That gave us a rough idea where the pass began. We continued, but slower and with more restraint. We also found a prominent stick marking the entrance to the pass. Seeing the beacon and having the fishing boat ahead of us boosted our confidence. We were no longer lost and not knowing where to turn. We were able to exit the lagoon and headed for our destination.

At Musket Cove, Fiji we enjoyed picnics on the Malolo Lailai Island where the marina provided the firewood for the BBQ pit. All I had to do was start the fire with my propane blowtorch. At the time, Musket Cove and the islands to the north were popular destinations for snorkeling and scuba diving. The water was pristine and corals were thriving.

Vanuatu, the Happiest Island in the World

"Olsem wanem? Mi glad tumas. Tangkyu tumas." In Bislama it means, "How are things? I am very happy. Thank you very much."

The Tusker Beer motto, "Bia blong yumi," translates to "Our beer." By the way, the Tusker Beer was inexpensive although the taste varied from bottle to bottle. Nothing bad, but I wondered about their quality control.

Violin is translated as "Smol sista blong bigfala Bokis sipos yu skrasem bel blong em i kraes." Or, "Little sister to the big box (piano), if you scratch its belly, it cries."

The best one was, "basket blong titi" or "bra." (Quotes are lifted from the book *Evri samting yu wantem save long Bislama be yu fraet tumas blong askem* by Darell Tryon.)

Bislama was a standardized version of the common tongue used across much of Oceania since the whaling days. Workers from different islands shipped to Australia to work in the cane fields reinforced its usage. With the archipelago's independence from both France and UK, the common tongue was adopted as the official language of the Nation of Vanuatu (formerly New Hebrides).

Scholars considered it a legitimate language with grammar that paralleled that of the indigenous Melanesian languages, but using a modified English vocabulary. One of the locals we got to know could speak Bislama, English, French, and his mother's Melanesian island language. (There are 105 indigenous island languages in the Vanuatu Archipelago.) Certainly he could speak English sufficiently well to communicate with us, although not with precise grammar.

Most of the islanders who went to school would have learned either English or French and, depending on which island they were from, they would speak one of the native island languages. The maternal uncle generally had the greatest influence on the development of the youngster; thus it was usually the mother's island tongue that was learned. One of the two newspapers, *The Daily Post*, had sections in English, French, and Bislama.

Before independence, the British and the French jointly

governed New Hebrides. This was often referred to as the "Condominium" government. Unkind critics called it "Pandemonium" government because there were French laws, British laws, and joint laws as well as traditional local Kastom laws. Depending on the nature of the crime and the background of the criminal, there were different courts and different jails awaiting the culprit. Even now the islanders in Vanuatu were still trying to untangle the land ownership problems resulting from those bygone days although all land was supposed to have been returned to local traditional ownership upon independence.

Vanuatu is a country with a total population of about 200,000, struggling between development, foreign influence, and the traditional ways of the village. Much had changed with the influx of Christianity. Under Christian influence, they no longer practice cannibalism. For that we were grateful. Yes, religion has had a strong influence here as it has all over the Pacific islands. At least here the restaurants and supermarkets stayed open on Sundays, but nothing else. God was frequently invoked in the news, the editorials, and letters to the editor. The island nation's motto: "Long God Yumi Stanap" meant "With God We Stand." There was quite a strong presence of Seventh Day Adventists here, but many other Christian faiths were also in evidence.

We arrived at Port Vila on the island of Efate in Vanuatu under an overcast sky with a light misty rain after a three-and-a-half day passage from Musket Cove, Fiji. This was the land where "bungee jumping" was invented. Only it was called "Land Diving" here. They built tall towers of sticks and branches on an incline and jumpers had vines tied to their ankles. Unlike bungee jumping, these Vanuatu jumpers hit the ground with a loud thud. We didn't get to see an actual ceremony because it was out of season and the vines did not have the proper elasticity to keep the jumpers from getting hurt. There was a death last season because the boy jumped out of season for a show to entertain tourists. According to the locals, there had been only two other accidents in recent years both of those were due to vines separating during a jump.

The history of land diving had a twist involving domestic dispute according to the story: A woman was desperately running away from her husband. After a long chase, she was treed with no escape while her husband was climbing up the tree. In desperation, she tied some vines to her legs jumped off the tree and got away. Her husband, too fearful to jump and unable to get down from the tree quickly, was left far behind. Ever since that time, young men approaching adulthood were required by tradition to learn how to jump off a high structure in that fashion. There was no mention why the woman was so afraid of her husband that she would risk her life to jump off a tall tree. I am sure some might also ask, "Why not teach boys and girls negotiation skills to forestall domestic disputes that end in wild chases through tall trees?"

On first sight, Port Vila appeared quite modern. From the bay, we saw multistoried buildings and minivans and small trucks. At the real estate office, there were many modern-looking homes selling for US $200,000 to $300,000. They had two Au Bon Marche supermarkets in town. These were Costco-like supermarkets that sold just about any food that one could wish to eat. The restaurants were also excellent with some of the best beef we tasted across the Pacific. The French influence seems to have distinct advantages when it came to culinary skills. The food was also incredibly cheap. I bought a bundle of bok choy about 16 inches in diameter for the equivalent of US fifty cents. A good grade of beef sold for about US$2.5 a pound. For a dollar one could buy a whole stalk of green bananas.

Away from Port Vila, the capital, there was much less development. In fact, cannibalism was practiced as late as 1968 on one of the outer islands. Some islands didn't have much contact with the outside world. One of the cruisers actually met a villager in one of the northerly islands who had never heard of Coca-Cola. *Not knowing Coca Cola? That really isn't such a tragedy...they should count their blessings.*

The islanders were not shy about their cannibalistic past. We saw a vendor selling aprons depicting a large stew pot over a wood fire with a white leg still sticking out of the water in the pot. It was irresistible and we bought a bunch of aprons.

The Efate islanders thought of themselves as the happiest people in the world. They were not wealthy by any measure, but they had their families and plenty of food, and as a result there was not much else to desire.

Judy and I flew to Tanna, an island southeast of Efate. Michener, who spent considerable time there, wrote about the island in his *Tales of the South Pacific*. There is an active volcano, Mount Yasur, on Tanna Island. We took a four-wheel drive to the volcano and walked up to the rim to watch fountains of molten lava spewing out like fireworks. The Yasur Volcano was one of the most accessible active volcanoes in the world.

The eruptions were quiet for a moment; then it made sounds like the surf at the beach. Steam was discharged. Suddenly there was an explosion with a loud boom followed by rumbles and roar. Everyone jumped...some ran. Not that there was any shelter they could run for protection. Dark smoke billowed trailed by white smoke creating a thick mushroom cloud. It blocked off the sun.

We were up wind in the consistent trades, but when the wind slowed even for a few seconds, we smelled sulfur and acid. Occasionally we saw spurts of red-hot lava shooting up. Most pieces of lava ended up inside the caldera near the rim, but still molten, red, and threatening. When it cooled down, it became one of the many black, crusty volcanic rocks that were scattered all around us. While we were there, none of the red-hot lumps of lava ever came near us to have been dangerous.

Among the many villages on Tanna, the Yakel Village was one that had maintained the traditional "Kastom." We arrived at a forest clearing surrounding by several large ancient Banyan trees (*Ficus prolixa*). There were treehouses sixty feet high off the ground. We saw two little boys climbing a narrow, shaky ladder up into the tree house. Others beat the Tam-tam to announce our presence. The Tam-tam is a vertical log about eight feet in height with a figure carved at the top and a hollowed out slit in the trunk to serve as the drum chamber. Before long a young man who appeared to be wearing not a stitch came up the path, but he did wear a penis sheath. The sheath is called *namba* in Bislama.

"It looks like a whiskbroom with a long handle." Judy whispered to me.

Actually, the handle was a sheath that covered the organ and the part that looked like a broom or brush served to protect the crown jewels from evil eyes. Other than that there was only a belt around his waist that had a string to help lift the sheath to keep it in an upright position. He also had a pair of curved pig tusks hanging around his neck for good fortune.

The naked young man spoke excellent English and introduced

himself as our guide. We followed him to the village, which consisted of a group of fifteen to twenty thatch huts. The grounds were very neat and clean. He took us to the chief's hut. The chief appeared very lean, had white hair and a full beard, no teeth, and was bent at the waist. He seemed healthy and mentally very alert. Sartorially, he was the same as our guide...not a stitch except for the sheath. He spoke in his native language. The chief told us he was 108 years old and that he had worked with Americans in Port Vila building the airfield during the war. We thanked him for allowing us to visit his village.

At the clearing a dance was performed to welcome us and to seek fertility for their crops. There were about a dozen male dancers all wearing the *namba*. They carried spears, chanted, and stomped their feet with considerable vigor. The women danced around the outer circle, but mainly hopped with both feet. They wore skirts of Pandanus leaves. Most of them had to put their arms around their chest to help support their breasts. The children, all boys, followed along and imitated the men.

Our guide looked at my digital watch and mentioned that he had owned one some years ago. It was a watch that I had bought in Port Vila for about ten dollars. I could see that he admired it greatly. Unthinkingly, I slipped the watch off my wrist and gave it to him as a gift. He obviously liked it. I thought that was the end of it.

He quickly asked one of the boys to run back to the hut. I didn't know what that was all about until the boy returned with a pig's tusk necklace. I had to wear it around my neck immediately.

It then dawned on me that I should have been more careful and not gift something that the recipient might have difficulty reciprocating as an equal. These traditional islanders would not just accept a gift...they only exchanged gifts. It would be unthinkable for him to take something from me without providing something equivalent in return. It is something about self-respect. Of course in this case, pigs were valued and the tusks had special manna. I accepted the gift graciously in return. My thoughtlessness had almost led me to commit a cultural *faux pas*. Despite his attire or the lack there of, our guide was more civilized than many people I had encountered.

We learned from our guide that the village was self-sufficient.

They grew all their own food. The money they earned from performing for the tourists went to pay for items they could not produce, such as metal tools. Only two children among his generation were allowed to go to school, one boy, and one girl. He, the boy, was allowed to learn English and the girl French so they could serve as guides.

We flew back on a small plane with a lot of boxes in the cabin. About half way back to Port Vila, the plane seemed to descend steeply.

"Look, we have a little island below us," I said to Judy.

"The island is very green…full of vegetation. Why are we flying so low?" Judy asked.

"Good question… hey, I think we are going to land…but I don't see any airport or landing strip." I said as I tried to peek out of the small window.

"There better be a landing strip…or else it's going to crash…" Judy said, as the plane was not much higher than the low trees at that moment. Before she could finish, we both felt a clunk as the wheels touched something. We saw people standing on the grass ahead on either side of a dirt track.

"I guess we have landed on a dirt runway. Look at all the people…probably the whole village is out here…it's an event," I said. There were kids running around as well as men and women of all ages.

One of the pilots came back to the cabin and unloaded the boxes off the plane. I surmised that it was a cargo delivery.

"Where are we?" I asked him as he climbed back in the plane.

"Oh, this is Eromango Island. It's an unscheduled stop to drop off medical supplies," he replied as he went back to the cockpit.

There were many things that were unexpected by us, but as usual we were "not in Kansas anymore." *Things are different here.*

The paperboy knew that he could always sell an over-priced newspaper to me at the dock near Laelia. On the English section of the Daily Post there was news of a former champion boxer, a Mr. Kating nicknamed the Tiger Shark of the South Pacific. He wanted to devote his time to protecting young women. So far so good until I read about his plan of "not allowing women to wear trousers because that is too provocative." He went on blaming women, saying they were the cause of rape.

I wrote a letter to the editor strongly protesting this view that the women were responsible in rape cases. I was particularly disappointed that religious leaders seemed to condone his viewpoint. I closed the letter, "I am a visitor who enjoyed my stay in Vanuatu. You have been good to me and I am writing all this because I care."

We departed Port Vila, Vanuatu on 14 October 2006 for Port Moselle, New Caledonia. Vanuatu was probably the most exotic country among the South Pacific islands we visited. We would have liked to stay longer, but the impending South Pacific cyclone season was a good reason for Laelia to keep moving. We bid farewell to new friends and cruisers we left behind.

Weather in New Caledonia

It was a short passage of about 300 nautical miles to the southwest of Vanuatu. Port Moselle is in Noumea, the capital of New Caledonia, on the southern end of the Island of Grande Terre. During World War II, Noumea served as the headquarters of the US Army and Navy in the South Pacific and played an important role in the defense of Guadacanal. It was in Noumea that USS Enterprise (CV-6), the only remaining carrier in the US Pacific fleet, was patched up and returned to battle. We visited a prominent memorial, not far from the Marina, honoring US military personnel involved in the Pacific War. In French and English on the bronze plaque:

IN HONOR OF THE U.S. FORCES WHO BY THEIR PRESENCE DURING THE PACIFIC WAR FROM MARCH 1942 TO FEBRUARY 1946 INSURED THE FREEDOM OF NEW CALEDONIA HER PEOPLE ARE DEEPLY GRATEFUL

Inside the museum were various memorabilia of a fierce war from more than half a century ago. We learned that the US soldiers were well liked by the local people because of their friendliness. The soldiers behaved distinctly differently from the European colonists in their attitude towards the locals. One of the displays also described that the local Melanesians were amazed to see black US soldiers treated as equals by the US military.

There had been aspirations for independence by local Kanaks.

Unfortunately, an ultranationalist assassin killed, in 1989, the only credible leader for independence. The Kanak killer thought the leader was too moderate. The French Government expended considerable funds building a memorial, the Jean Marie Tjibaou Cultural Center, dedicated to the deceased leader.

It was one of the fervent desires of Tjibaou to blend the cultures of the Kanak people. The elaborate sculpted architecture and the blending of nature succeeded in recognizing the linguistic and artistic achievements of the Kanak culture. It gave identity to the native people and the respect they desired.

Referendums for independence had failed in the past and success in another referendum was doubtful. The French Parliament had accepted all New Caledonians as French citizens decades ago. Over time, with immigration, the combined population of Europeans and Polynesians had overtaken the Kanaks in numbers. Furthermore, life on the island had been agreeable, perhaps even affluent. Not surprisingly, the prosperity, weighed against the uncertainty of independence, had blunted the justification for a separate nation.

Most of New Caledonia is surrounded by the world's "second-longest barrier reef" which enclosed the world's largest lagoon. It is an UNESCO World Heritage Site. We took a commercial boat tour to the Amadee Lighthouse on the island by the same name. The lighthouse was constructed in 1865 to guide ships entering the Boulari Passage, one of only three natural passages through the reef.

The lighthouse, in the Lagoon, is twenty-four kilometers from Noumea and sixty-five meters tall. Its pristine water harbored the endangered Dugongs (*Dugong dugon)*, the nesting green turtles (*Chelonia mydas*), and sea kraits (*Laticauda colubrina* or tricot raye). We saw only the sea snakes on land when they were returning after feeding in the sea. They were known to be deadly poisonous, but rarely bite people. As good tourists, we climbed the 247 steps of the lighthouse and took photos of the spiraling staircase.

We were concerned with the potential of cyclones as well as rough seas caused by tropical depressions between Vanuatu and the Gulf of Carpentaria, Australia. It seemed the cyclone season was starting earlier than usual so we had our minds set for an early departure from the tropics. We intended to sail directly from Noumea, New Caledonia, to Sydney, Australia. It would have been a passage of about 1,100 nautical miles.

Our Perth-based weather router advised us otherwise.

Hi Howard and Judy:

I am pleased you made it through safely. Unfortunately there will be more southerly swells getting over to Australia ... I would strongly recommend going across to Bundaberg then taking smaller legs down the coast, possibly to Southport on the Gold Coast, then to Coffs Harbour, and then to Sydney. It will make for a safer and more comfortable trip.

While we were in Noumea, a good part of the conversation at the dock was about the impending cyclone season.

"Did you hear the weather report this morning? The tropical depression was gaining strength. It may turn into a cyclone," said someone in the crowd in front of the bulletin board where the new weather synopsis was posted. A few days later, the situation had not improved. "Do you think the cyclone will hit Noumea? It seems to be heading this way."

"Who knows, forecasting the path of a cyclone is not yet an exact science. There seems to be a difference of opinion on where the cyclone will end up," said another in the crowd.

I was glad that Judy and I both had taken the weather course from the Ventura Power Squadron while we were still in California. We could understand the weather synopsis on the bulletin board. Indeed the depression had deepened and was moving away from the far north of Australia towards Vanuatu and New Caledonia. To forecast the speed and path of a cyclone was beyond our skills. Much depended on the various computer models that meteorologists argued about among themselves. We had especial confidence in the forecast from the group in Monterey, California. Our confidence was based on the fact that their model had called correctly the killer storm during the Sydney-to-Hobart Yacht Race in 1998.

The marina was preparing for the cyclone. Steel cables had been laid down in the marina long ago for boats to be attached. We received instructions to strip every bit of canvas and remove all loose parts from the deck. Diagrams were given to us on how to secure the vessel. All we were waiting was for the cyclone to be within a few days before putting all that into action. It would have been a huge amount of work just to take the mainsail off the track. We noted that the Monterey group had forecast that the cyclone would turn away from New Caledonia. We didn't pray, but we did cross our fingers.

Instead of heading for Sydney harbor, we decided to make landfall in Bundaberg, Queensland, as recommend by our weather router. The weather along the Australian East Coast changes quickly. By cutting the duration of the passage, we would limit our exposure to potential bad weather at sea. We received the following message that the weather window we were counting on was about to close on the Australian Coast.

Hi Howard and Judy

I have been looking at the weather for you. The best weather window is right now, as it turns out, or within the next day or two.

If you can get away on, say, Monday morning, you should have around 20 knots of ESE breeze to start you on your way. On Tuesday the wind speed looks like going through large oscillations as strong as 20 knots then dying back to around 12 knots with the direction swinging between ESE and SE. Overall, it is not too bad at all.

We received that message about the weather window in late afternoon and we managed to set sail within two hours. That meant we had to navigate the pass out of the barrier reef in the dark. We didn't mind that too much because in New Caledonia the passes through the reef were clearly marked and the beacons well maintained.

Once we exited the barrier reef, we were in the open ocean heading WSW. We had good wind for several days and no wind for some time as well as head wind for most of the last two days. The swells had been on the high side as was common throughout this region between Fiji and Australia. Overall it was a good passage with no suffering and we ate well.

15. The Continent Down Under

Arriving Port Bundaberg, Queensland, Australia (24 45.636 S, 152 23.242 E), 07 November 2006. Arriving Cammeray Marina, Sydney Harbour, Australia (33 49.056 S, 151 13.458 E), 21 November 2006.

Arriving at Port Bundaberg

In darkness, we rounded the Sandy Cape Light at the northern-most point of Fraser Island on the Queensland Coast of Australia. It was a single white flash at ten second intervals. Laelia was on course.

Laelia continued westward through the night until a few hours before sunrise...the sky and the sea were still pitch black and indistinguishable. We were not far from the mouth of the Burnett River. A few miles up the river was Port Bundaberg. We were tired and needed sleep, but it was time to be extra vigilant as Laelia approached the coast.

"It's like Christmas with all those red and green flashing lights," Judy said. "This must be the best-marked channel anywhere in the world."

The rows of red and green navigation lights marked the deep-water channel to the River. The lighthouse ashore flashed four times every twenty seconds. This was a feast for salt-encrusted eyes after looking at nothing but water for the last six days.

The existence of navigation buoys extended some distance into the shallow waters along the coast was also noted on the chart to further confirm Laelia's position. What was alarming on the chart was that there were many sand bars scattered along the shallow coastal water. Perhaps that was the reason for all the extra navigation buoys with the flashing lights off shore.

The entire coast was shallow and the water was black as ink with no moonlight. I couldn't see the sandbars. There was also a stiff current pushing Laelia to the south. It was not our usual habit to attempt an unknown harbor in the dark.

"Hey, we are getting pushed around by the current. What's the chance of running aground hanging around here?" I asked. "It's not easy keeping the boat under control in this current."

"Maybe it's safer if we go up the river," Judy said.

"I think you are right. The channel is well marked...these navigation lights are amazing."

We tried to motor along between the red and green buoys although the strong cross current made staying in the channel not so easy.

"You know the boat is pointing to the side of the channel...it's heading straight at that buoy," Judy said.

"Yeah, it's unnerving, but it's the only way to keep the boat in the channel," I replied.

It was an awkward way to pilot a boat, but Laelia had to point into the cross current at a 45-degree angle from the direction of travel to avoid getting washed out of the channel by the coastal current.

We motored up the Burnett River to the quarantine anchorage across the river from the marina. After dropping the anchor, we dozed and waited for the Quarantine Inspection. We understood that they would confiscate meats raw, cooked, or canned. Of course all fresh vegetables and fruits would also be taken and destroyed.

The inspection at Bundaberg Port was uneventful. All our papers were in order and our boat bottom was clean. There was a new Australian law requiring arriving vessels to report their ETA 96 hours in advance to avoid an A$2000 fine. We had reported our estimated arrival time by email en route.

During our inspection, the Quarantine Officer would not allow a pair of tooth hammers made of animal bones. The hammers were actually made in the Solomon Islands, but I bought them in Vanuatu. The hammers were used to chip the teeth of young boys to make their teeth look jagged and sharp. Tools like that in California could really boost business for dental clinics. Alas, they were confiscated. The other item not allowed was a necklace made from pig tusks. It was a gift from a native islander on Tanna Island, Vanuatu.

After Laelia was secured at the dock, torrential rain started pouring in buckets accompanied with thunder and lightning. It was the storm warned by our weather router. We let out a sigh of relief for missing the rough condition at sea.

There was a dinner organized by the VMR (Volunteer Marine Rescue) of Bundaberg celebrating their 34th anniversary. Of course we wouldn't miss a party with food prepared by someone else. After the dinner there was an auction. Most of the participants were mariners with great respect for volunteers who would go out to sea in bad weather to rescue fellow boaters. The auction was lively and made a bundle of money to support VMR activities. We worked hard to outbid a persistent competitor and ended up with some very expensive VMR hats, but it was for a good cause.

We were close to tropical Australia. Long days were warm and evenings comfortable. We explored the parks and sights like any other tourist. There were birds we had never seen before.

Our friend, June, needed a hernia operation. While driving to various clinics with her, we managed to learn about the Australian Health Service. As foreigners, any surgical operation at a "private" hospital could be scheduled quickly and the cost was not exorbitant.

There was a breeding ground of the endangered green turtle (*Chelonia mydas*) on the beach in one of the National Parks. Due to the tour's popularity we had to reserve in advance. Judy and June worked hard over the phone to score us four tickets. We had seen turtles hatching at the beach in Mexico, but had never seen turtles laying eggs.

We waited until it was dark, then waited... and waited for turtles to appear on the beach. I was beginning to think there were no turtles at all...perhaps it was like a snipe hunt.

"One turtle just landed in the surf zone!" someone shouted.

We all kept very quiet in order not to frighten the turtle away as it was making painfully slow progress up the sandy beach. The turtle had to travel quite some distance to move up to dry sand. It must lay its eggs in dry sand to avoid the danger of having the eggs washed away by the next tide.

Before long, I was beginning to think that a turtle could never beat a hare in a race. *The story lied.* Why would a turtle race a hare anyway? Only intelligent humans race around in the hot sun for a piece of shiny metal.

We waited for the turtle to move. It moved its appendages only intermittently and only one or two at a time, and would stop to rest between movements. All this time, we couldn't see anything. The ranger would occasionally take a peek and give us a progress report in a hushed voice.

After an eternity, he said, "The turtle is starting to lay eggs."

Hallelujah!

It was a big animal, about three hundred plus pounds and just under four feet long. Apparently, once it started the egg-laying process it was unable to escape. We all surrounded the poor thing as the eggs dropped one at a time into the pit dug by the turtle. When this was completed, the turtle buried the eggs in sand and went back to sea...slowly.

The ranger thought the location where the eggs were buried was not optimal. He dug up the eggs about the size of ping-pong balls, but not hard or brittle like hen eggshells. They were soft to the touch and felt like they were made of inflated sailcloth material.

We also visited the Botanic Garden in Bundaberg and discovered a flock of wild ibises. Our Queenslander friend fell off the chair laughing when he heard how we went gah gah over ibises. To the locals, ibises were pests. Those birds ate cattle feed, get in the garbage, and loiter around restaurants. We were rather pleased with all the pictures of "wild" ibises.

Bundaberg is in the middle of the sugar cane growing area in the state of Queensland. The climate is favorable enough for several harvests a year. Driving along country roads, all we could see was tall sugar cane on either side. When we happened to be up on high ground, we could see the green tops of sugar cane all the way to the foothills.

We visited the Bundaberg Brewery where the famous Bundaberg Rum was made. There was also ginger beer and a variety of liqueurs. Judy, who does not drink beer or wine, brought on board a bottle of chocolate liqueur. Now she would have something for celebratory occasions other than chocolate truffles.

The Great Sandy Strait

Some choices we make in life, large and small, have serious consequences. Upon departure from Port Bundaberg, we made a decision to take the shortcut between Fraser Island and the mainland coast of Queensland. It was a perfectly reasonable choice at the time.

The northern cape of Fraser Island projects way out into the Coral Sea, where Laelia had rounded the Sandy Cape Light a few nights earlier on our way west to Bundaberg. Now as we were heading south, backtracking around Sandy Cape again would have taken us sixty nautical miles out of our way. Another reason for taking the shortcut was because Hervey Bay, the large expanse of water between Fraser Island and the mainland, was somewhat sheltered from rough seas. It made sense to keep Laelia in the protected Bay instead of the 30-knot wind and 7-foot waves reported in the Coral Sea. The problem was that I didn't know how difficult it would be navigating the Great Sandy Strait

Fraser Island is closely associated to the Queensland coast, separated only by a shallow sandy estuary called the Great Sandy Strait. It was also the Great Sandy National Park and a World Heritage Area. Fraser Island, about seventy-five miles in length, is an enormous pile of sand on top of old volcanic substrates. The sand deposited by the Pacific Ocean has been collecting there for 750,000 years.

The Great Sandy Strait is forty miles of shallow water crisscrossed with sand bars and shallow pockets of water. The shallowest spot in the navigable channel, at Sheridan Flats, was only five feet deep at high tide. Laelia drew just about five feet of water. I expected Laelia's stubby keels to just touch bottom there. For us this was a very different kind of environment from that of our experience in open oceans. We were accustomed to depths of at least several hundred feet if not thousands.

We were both on deck in the bright sun looking out for sand bars. The navigable channels were well marked and corresponded exactly as enumerated in the guidebook, Beacon to Beacon, produced by the Queensland Maritime Safety Office.

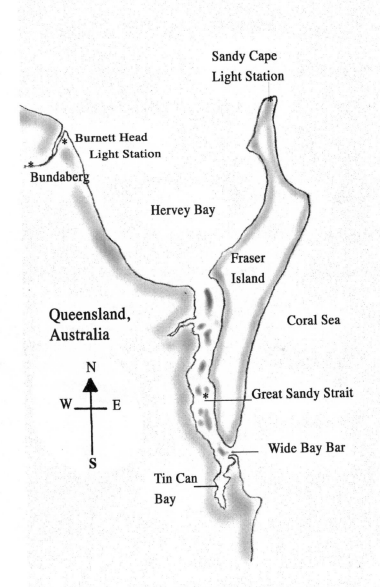

Great Sandy Strait and Fraser Island, Queensland, Australia

I had never mucked around in sandy waterways like this, although our experience in Fiji did come in handy. The difference was that, instead of coral reefs, we now had sand bars. Also, the water was murky and we couldn't see what was below the surface.

We had to hurry so we wouldn't miss high tide at Sheridan Flats. The forecast was for a gale storm with increasing wind to 45 knots and 12-foot seas in the open ocean by evening. I wasn't sure what that would portend for conditions in the Strait. We wanted to get past all the sandbars and have some safe place to spend the night. It would be wonderful to drop anchor in a quiet patch of water before dark.

By afternoon Laelia arrived at the general area of Sheridan Flats. The water depth was now shallow, but there was no sign suggesting where exactly the shallowest spot was. Laelia was slowed to a crawl. How could we extricate ourselves if we got stuck here? There was not a soul around. No help. We were on our own. This was no place to get stranded aground.

"How deep?" I called out to Judy, who was at the helm, to read from the depth meter…an electronic echo sounder.

"Three point five," she replied.

The depth sounder was mounted at the bottom of the hull, so that meant there was one foot of water below the stubby keels that extended about 2.5 feet below the hull. We kept checking the depth. The sounder read between three to four feet for what felt like an eternity as Laelia navigated through the sandy estuary slowly. *How do we know when we are out of danger?*

"We must have passed Sheridan Flats, it's been hours," I said as I took a deep breath. "We didn't run aground."

"That's good news… we made it," Judy said.

Soon we arrived at a bay with several anchorages not far from the exit, the Wide Bay Bar, to the open ocean. One anchorage was fairly shallow even before low tide. A second anchorage was too windy with white caps all over. Finally, we came to a quiet little anchorage called Kauri Creek where Laelia anchored behind five unoccupied houseboats. It was a well-protected patch of water surrounded by mangrove.

Just as we finished anchoring, a ray jumped five feet out of the water and made a big splash.

"Well, thank you for the enthusiastic welcome," I said to the ray as it disappeared under the ripples.

By early morning, the rain intensified and thunder continued rumbling from heavy dark clouds. The latest weather report from VMR 417 based at Tin Can Bay made me realize that we wouldn't be departing any time soon. We had planned a 90-mile run to Scarbrough Harbour south of us, but that would have been a miserable bash with an adverse harsh SE wind.

Laelia anchored at Kauri Creek for several days, much longer than planned, but we still had plenty of provisions and there was no need to hurry. We had no fixed schedule. By staying longer we were eating well, getting a few more books read, and avoiding seasickness.

On what seemed like a quiet day, we pulled anchor early in the morning and headed for the exit only to find a stiff wind blowing against the ebbing tidal current at the bar. The contrary wind created a ferocious surf condition. The monstrous breaking waves in the surf zone were churning savagely. Even large fishing trawlers plying this part of the sea for a living were waiting for a respite. Laelia would have been thrashed into little pieces by the surf. We turned Laelia around and went back to the same anchorage.

By now we had learned to listen in on the exchanges between fishing boats and the VMR duty officer on the VHF radio. We discovered from their bantering that, apparently, it was necessary to get the tide, the wind direction, and the surf height all correct for crossing the Wide Bay Bar. At high tide there was more water under the keel for clearing the sand bars. That seemed obvious enough. To exit from the strait to the ocean, it was desirable to have slack water or an out-going current with the wind in the same direction. I was skeptical that there would ever be a confluence of all these conditions during daylight hours when we dared to "run" the bar.

We are trapped...it may be weeks before we can cross the sandbar and escape.

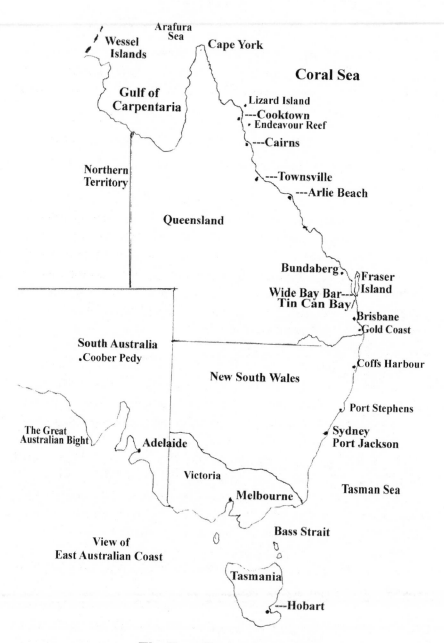

The East Coast of Australia

While we waited, we read more books and sent email to our cruising friends:

Ken and Jean:
We are pinned down by bad weather here in a secure little anchorage near the southern tip of Fraser Island. We had hoped to make a stop at Scarbrough, but we may head straight for Sydney. A weather window may open up for southbound sailing...if we take off soon, we could arrive in Sydney before Thanksgiving. Where are you? We hope to see you soon.
Howard and Judy

On the fourth morning, the weather forecast sounded promising. As we approached the Wide Bay Bar, we saw several fishing trawlers in the process of crossing the bar one after another. Laelia queued up a short distance behind the last trawler. Soon it was our turn. We cranked up the RPM on Laelia's diesel engines and followed the last fishing boat in exactly the same course.
We are free! We ran the Wide Bay Bar.

Coffs Harbour

As soon as we were in the open ocean, we felt at home. The wind direction became favorable for heading south along the coast as we rounded the nearby landmass. Laelia was able to sail at a fast clip.

"Well...the GPS is showing Laelia moving right along at eight knots," Judy observed. The GPS reading gave the boat speed relative to the ground (speed over ground). I then checked Laelia's speed relative to the water (speed over water) on the paddle wheel meter. It showed only six knots. That meant there was a two-knot current in our favor.

"Wow, we must be in the famous East Australian Current mentioned in the guidebook," I said. The favorable sailing conditions continued into the night, but there was a forecast of an impending storm. Our intended destination was Sydney Harbour. We had already bypassed many well-known sailing destinations along the Australian coast. Shipping traffic was on the increase. We had to dodge tankers, cargo ships, and fishing vessels.

With the weather becoming stormy, we thought it would be a good idea to take shelter in the marina at Coffs Harbour. We pulled into the marina at 1030 hours in the morning and tied up at the fuel dock. Just about every other vessel and what seemed like the entire fishing fleet had taken shelter there. No doubt, they all had heard the same weather forecast.

"Sorry, we don't have a slip for your boat…you can tie up at the fuel dock, but only for an hour," the marina manager said. "I have a fishing boat coming for that spot."

There wasn't much I could do. I could see for myself that the marina was packed full. While I was taking up fuel, Judy went to get us some lunch. She came back with two hamburgers with "the lot"…an Australian hamburger with everything on it. Besides the meat patty, it had butter, lettuce, tomato, pickled beets, bacon, and a fried egg. It was a thick, joyous, slippery, and mouth-watering creation.

"Well, I guess we'll have to take our chances at sea," I said in between bites.

We untied from the dock and headed towards the opening in the breakwater. As Laelia was motoring out of the marina, we could hear the VMR weather forecast on the VHF radio.

"A gale warning is in effect in the Coffs Harbour waters…the wind strength is expected to be 30 to 40 knots and wave height…" The radio crackled from a lightning discharge not far away.

I had a feeling that the VMR Duty Officer could see Laelia heading out to sea and that the weather report was specifically directed at us without saying so. It would be very unlike an Australian for him to tell us not to go. I wasn't thrilled to go headlong into the storm either. It could be risky out there in the menacing weather condition. The fact that the entire fishing fleet came for shelter said as much.

The sky was gray and foreboding. The air was frigid and laden with moisture. The American flag on the stern was whipping hard in the wind and crackling loudly in protest. The sea was boiling with white caps everywhere.

"I think we'll be OK. We have been in worse storms before," I said. "It's gonna be uncomfortable though."

"I am going to sleep. I don't want to get sick after eating all that lunch," Judy said.

After motoring out to the open ocean and setting a course for Sydney, I decided to unfurl the jib. It was a harsh wind, but favorable to sail with only the jib. I unfurled it only part way. The jib was an easy sail to control and I could always furl the jib back by winching in the control line without waking Judy for help. I silently thanked whoever invented the furling drum for controlling the jib.

The wind was strong, but consistent. Laelia dashed south at better than nine knots powered by a minimum amount of sailcloth. Judy took over after a few hours. The log showed that she had to dodge numerous freighters. That same evening, we had a very red sunset. Later, in the darkness, there were more ships, but all we could see were their navigation lights. We were now in coastal waters and had to contend with the heavy shipping traffic. As we discovered again, coastal sailing is much more dangerous than navigating the open ocean.

The Sugar Point Light just south of Seal Rock was sighted around midnight. It was a white light flashing every 7.5 seconds. A rough measure of the chart showed that the light is 170 miles from Sydney Harbour. At our present speed, we expected to reach Sydney in about 20 hours. It would be in the evening, but this was late November in the Southern Hemisphere. The day lengths were longer with approaching summer solstice. The strong following wind and the current were working to our advantage.

Laelia arrived at Port Jackson, the official name for the waterways around Sydney, late in the day. We didn't take time to sightsee. We made a quick right turn and headed north directly towards the Middle Harbour in time for the drawbridge opening. By the time we approached the dock at the Cammeray Marina, dusk was falling rapidly. Through the dim light, we could barely see our friends on the dock waiting to catch our dock lines.

Life in Sydney

Laelia was berthed at a mooring buoy within sight of the marina dock. From the dock, it was 104 steps up the hill to the street level. It was good exercise to get our hearts racing rapidly every morning on our way to explore Sydney. Near the top of the stairs, we met a retired Australian who lived near the Marina.

"Did you know that they add one more step at the top each

night?" he asked.

"I believe it. It gets harder up this hill every morning," Judy agreed with him while still trying to catch her breath.

The parking in the Central Business District of Sydney started at Australian $20 per hour so it was just as well that the city had an outstanding system of rapid transit including the metro, buses, and ferries. We each bought an unlimited pass good for all these transports. With the pass, we wouldn't go broke when we got lost and rode buses and trains back and forth trying to find our way. We were doing pretty well and had not gotten very lost for any length of time.

Thanksgiving was upon us again; it had been two years since we had celebrated with friends in New Zealand. We called every American hotel in Sydney including the Radisson, Marriot, Hilton, Travel Lodge, Holiday Inn, and Crown Plaza. It seemed nobody even knew it was Thanksgiving in America. Well, why should they? In Australia, if they have turkey at dinner, it would only be during Christmas.

We had almost given up the idea of a Thanksgiving dinner, but we still had to eat.

We were wandering in Sydney and ended up at the Ferry Terminal called the Circular Quay. It was a very busy transportation hub for tourists and locals especially during commute hours.

"Judy, what do you think of that place just ahead...it's called Rossini's." I pointed at one of the eateries at the Terminal.

"What kind of food do they have?" Judy asked cautiously.

"Rossini sounds Italian," I replied.

"Italians wouldn't have anything for Thanksgiving." Judy sounded skeptical.

"Well, wasn't there someone named Rossini among the Pilgrims?" I was getting quite hungry and was not obsessed about historical accuracy. "Let's just take a look at the food."

A lot of food items were in trays behind a glassed barrier, and they looked scrumptious. Once we ordered our food and paid, we were escorted to our table and were treated like royalty. I think it had something to do with the amount of food I ordered. Most people, many were tourists, ordered miniscule amounts...we were ordering a feast. Well, Thanksgiving dinner is always a feast.

Our table was within sight of the Opera House and we could watch all the ferries coming and going and people bustling to catch them. I had a starter of yummy roasted vegetables consisting of tomatoes, red, green, and yellow peppers, purple eggplants, and onions, pine nuts all drowned and simmered in olive oil. It was worth the money just for the color, but it was delicious. Then, for the main, I had a roasted chicken breast stuffed with spinach and ricotta cheese in a cream sauce. The accompaniment was oven-roasted new potatoes and spring cut beans cooked in garlic and olive oil. I washed all that down with some very nice Merlot to make up for the lack of cranberry sauce.

Oh, yes, Judy ate too. She had a salad that I helped her finish. She also traded some of her crepe in a creamy meat sauce for some slices of my chicken. She has a weakness for desserts and ordered a panna cotta...a sticky, creamy cheesecake-like dessert with a big round of chocolate imbedded in the center...it was huge. Of course being ever so helpful I came to her rescue by finishing the dessert for her.

Food is too precious to waste...right?

The Italian waiters became quite enthusiastic when they saw us wolfing down a proper Sicilian dinner. Unlike many of the tourists who could hardly finish a bowl of soup, we showed them that we appreciated good food. They came and talked to us wanting to know where these big eaters were from and where we planned to go. One even offered to crew for us when he heard that we had sailed to Australia. He probably figured, judging by the way we ate, that we would have an outstanding galley on our yacht and a couple of chefs on board.

Life is not without discouraging words on cruising boats. A California cruising boat we knew from previous ports also arrived in Cammeray Marina. The big guy was at the wheel and his wife was on the bow trying to catch the mooring line using a boat hook. Each time as he drove the boat at the mooring buoy while his wife pulled up the mooring line attached to the buoy, the boat would overshoot the buoy before she could drape the line on the bow cleat. As the boat sped past the buoy, she could no longer hold on to the mooring line and had to let it drop back into the water.

"God dam'it, hook it on the cleat," he would yell at his wife in his booming voice.

His wife said nothing. The process would repeat with the language becoming louder, coarser, and less gracious. I felt bad for her and got in the dinghy to help them picking up the mooring line. Unfortunately, it was high tide and there was very little slack in the line. Consequently, there was only a small window of opportunity to hook the line on the bow cleat. He was also driving the boat too fast and not close enough to the buoy. It took several more tries before we were successful. By that time everyone in the marina was listening in on the melodrama.

An Australian on the dock said, "I don't know how they could have made it this far. I could have done all that when I was ten."

We explored Sydney during the months Laelia was moored in Cammeray. Before Christmas we booked a concert at the Opera House to hear the Messiah. It was a stirring performance that put me in the holiday mood. I am not religious, but I love religious music including the Messiah and the Hallelujah Chorus.

While at the Opera House, we learned about the long and short of the iconic architecture on a guided tour. The landmark building certainly achieved the goal of providing a focus to the city and put Sydney on the world map. The structure blended so well with its environment we could imagine the curved roofs of the Opera House leading the billowing sails of boats tacking in the harbor on a sunny afternoon.

It was summer at Christmas in Australia. Many Australians would put their Esky (cooler) in the boot (trunk) and head to the beach with the family. At the Cammeray Marina, we were invited to a barbie (BBQ) and to eat Moreton Bay Bugs (a kind of lobster, *Thenus orientalis*). As part of our indoctrination, we learned to sing the Australian version of Jingle Bells.

The big event was the start of the Sydney to Hobart Race on Boxing Day. We saw the race from the deck of a ferry without having to maneuver for viewing position and dodge the mad crowd of vessels. It was a pandemonium of small crafts among the spectators. Motorboats and sailboats, some of them had not been on the water for months, were maneuvering against each other. There were vessels out of fuel being towed by the Harbour Police.

The Sydney New Year's Eve firework extravaganza was world famous. The best place to watch the pyrotechnics was on the water across from the Opera House in a bay below the Botanic Garden.

SAILING AROUND THE WORLD

As luck would have it, our friends, Janet and Henry were taking their boat for that event.

We arrived with a big bucket of KFC Chicken at the dock and took a water taxi to our host's sailboat. Getting through the huge crowd was not easy. The policemen were inspecting and confiscating alcoholic beverages at the dock. Fortunately, fried chicken was not considered to be contraband.

We heard American voices on the VHF radio. The voice was from the cruiser we knew. Only this time, the big guy was not yelling at his wife. He was protesting loudly that another boat was anchoring too close to them. Then he was yelling for the police. We were embarrassed to hear such indecorous spouting off by a fellow countryman…it was definitely not cool. Our hostess got so mortified she went and took down the American ensign from the stern of their boat.

The fireworks started promptly and were all around us. White flares went up and red rockets exploded right over our heads. The bright lights came first followed by the sound of the explosion. Before the image of the first volley faded, more crackling sounds and flashing sparkles lit up the entire sky from horizon to horizon. The bursts came up in twos or threes. One burst went off on the far side of the bay backlighting a giant metal coat hanger, officially called the Harbour Bridge. Another shot seemed to have come from the rooftop of a tall office building. We looked this way then that way straining our neck muscles.

That night going back to our own boat in the Cammeray anchorage was a challenge. The huge crowd was everywhere. Every train was full. We squeezed ourselves into one of the compartments before the door shut. We finally rode the dinghy back to Laelia at three in the morning. It was certainly a most unusual and exciting New Year's Eve for us.

End of Volume One

ABOUT THE AUTHORS

Howard and Judy were born in 1942. Howard immigrated to the US from Hong Kong, in 1957, and settled in Seattle, Washington where he went to Cleveland High School. Judy is a native Californian growing up in Long Beach and went to Long Beach Poly High School. They met on the Caltech campus in Pasadena,

California where Howard was an undergraduate and Judy was a student nurse at the Los Angeles County Hospital School of Nursing. After their marriage, Judy worked as a Registered Nurse while Howard studied neurobiology as a graduate student at UCLA. Howard was also a Postdoctoral Research Fellow at UCB and MIT. For thirty-three years they lived in Santa Cruz, California, where Howard taught and did research at UCSC and Judy continued working as a nurse. Howard learned how to sail on small boats at the University of Washington Sailing Club in Seattle when he had a summer job on campus, and had continued to sail as a member of the UCSC Sailing Club. Judy is not fond of small sailboats; she didn't learn how to sail until after her fiftieth birthday. Both Howard and Judy are members of the Ventura Sail and Power Squadron. They now live in Santa Barbara, California...boatless.

Show Me the Way to Go Home

We are now in Australia. The shortest way home is to sail through Southeast Asia and the Indian Ocean to reach the Gulf of Aden, a strip of water sandwiched between Yemen and Somalia. Some call the Gulf the pirate alley, but it is the gateway to the Red Sea and the Suez Canal, a shortcut to the Mediterranean Sea and the Atlantic.

The pirates are active. Cruisers talk about buying weapons for self-defense. The pirate alley is only the beginning; there are other hazards along the way home. The journey, fraught with difficulties, seems impossible. Yet, we are home. Find out how the daunting tasks and impossible hurdles just melt away. We invite you to share this journey with us in comfort and safety.

Read the rest of the story, *Sailing Around the World: Volume 2, finding our way home.*

Howard & Judy Wang

Sailing Around the World:
Volume 2, finding our way home

Contents

Howard & Judy Wang

57273292R00146

Made in the USA
San Bernardino, CA
19 November 2017